THE BLUE GUIDES

Austria
Belgium and Luxembourg
China
Cyprus
Czechoslovakia
Denmark
Egypt

FRANCE
France
Paris and Versailles
Burgundy
Normandy
Corsica

GREECE
Greece
Athens
Crete

HOLLAND
Holland
Amsterdam

Hungary

ITALY
Northern Italy
Southern Italy
Florence
Rome and environs
Venice
Tuscany
Umbria
Sicily

Jerusalem
Malta and Gozo

Morocco
Moscow and Leningrad
Portugal

SPAIN
Spain
Barcelona

Switzerland

TURKEY
Turkey: the Aegean
  and Mediterranean Coasts
Istanbul

UK
England
Ireland
Scotland
Wales
London
Museums and Galleries
  of London
Oxford and Cambridge
Gardens of England
Literary Britain and Ireland
Victorian Architecture
  in Britain
Churches and Chapels
  of Northern England
Churches and Chapels
  of Southern England
Channel Islands
USA
New York
Boston and Cambridge

Yugoslavia

The restless expressionist frontage of the Scheepvaarthuis

BLUE GUIDE

Amsterdam

Charles Ford

Photographs by Susan Benn

A & C Black
London

WW Norton
New York

First edition 1993

Published by A & C Black (Publishers) Limited
35 Bedford Row, London WC1R 4JH

Cartographic work by John Flower, Doug London, Andras Bereznay and Thames Cartographic Services Ltd.

A CIP catalogue record of this book
is available from the British Library.

ISBN 0-7136-3228-3

Published in the United States of America by
WW Norton and Company, Inc
500 Fifth Avenue, New York, NY 10110

Published simultaneously in Canada by
Penguin Books Canada Limited
2801 John Street, Markham, Ontario L3R 1B4

ISBN 0-393-31041-8 USA

The author and the publishers have done their best to ensure the accuracy of all the information in Blue Guide Amsterdam; however, they can accept no responsibility for any loss, injury or inconvenience sustained by any traveller as a result of information or advice contained in the guide.

Please write in with your comments, suggestions and corrections. Writers of the best letters will be awarded a free Blue Guide of their choice.

Charles Ford lectures in the History of Art at University College London. He has published many articles, reviews and translations on matters relating to the history of Dutch painting and art theory. He is presently preparing a book on Dutch writings on art during the seventeenth century. He is also the author of *Blue Guide Holland*.

Printed and bound in Great Britain by
Butler & Tanner Ltd, Frome and London

INTRODUCTION

This book is intended to serve as a practical guide as you plan your trip to Amsterdam and as a source of reference during your visit. It is, however, principally a cultural handbook in the Blue Guide tradition, introducing you to the history and monuments of a remarkable city. The Walks will take you around the most famous traditional scenery and, it is hoped, introduce you to some new Amsterdams; for example, the 19C and 20C suburbs are given a great deal of attention. The hotel, restaurant, shopping and entertainment sections are inevitably the product of personal responses; I should be pleased to receive your comments and suggestions for future editions.

Amsterdam is not a museum. It is a hard, busy modern city with all the trappings of a developed capitalist economy—junkies, racists, casinos and pornography, one-parent families, green activists, yuppies, cable TV and dogs. The most abiding and definitive memories will be those for which this book cannot prepare you—a market at closing time, rain coming at you sideways as you cross a bridge, eccentric garden houses in the *volkstuinen* (allotments) seen on a summer's evening from the train. If this book convinces you to go to Amsterdam and if you have a wonderful time never even using it (having, of course, bought it!), then so much the better. You cannot walk down safer city streets, you will not find more humanely run public services, you will not travel on more thoughtfully-designed public transport, you will not come across a population more friendly or considerate. These things count ... Who needs museums?

Deciding when to go to Amsterdam is not so much of a problem; it has its appeal whatever the season. Here are some dates and events to consider when you are making up your mind.

The year starts with a bang; New Year is the Dutch firework night, but imagine fireworks with champagne. The Dutch confusingly call New Year's Eve *Oudejaarsavond* (Old Year's Eve) but the business of enjoyment is much the same as in that other great Calvinist stronghold, Scotland. The place to be is the old city centre at the Dam or the Nieuwmarkt.

In **February**, on Mardi Gras, there is a Carnival. The Carnival is a recent innovation and not yet a guaranteed fixture; if you are in the country at this time of year you should make for the southern, Catholic provinces to see the real thing. On 25 February the Wartime General Strike is commemorated at a solemn ceremony on the J.D. Meijerplein (near the Waterlooplein) by the statue of the *Dokwerker*.

In **March** on the Sunday closest to 15 March the ancient *Stille Omgang* (Silent Procession) commemorates the Amsterdam Miracle and follows its traditional route from the Heiligeweg (which means sacred way) to the St Nicolaaskerk. Roman Catholics from all over Europe crowd into Amsterdam for this event. There is a Blues Festival out west at De Meervart Centrum and a Boat Show down south at the RAI Congresgebouw.

One high point of the year, possibly *the* high point, is *Koninginnedag* (Queen's Day, Queen Juliana's birthday) on 30 **April**; it actually starts at midnight on the previous night. The whole city turns out to buy, sell and dance, playing host to some two and a half million of their compatriots in Europe's most appealing street festival. Bars and restaurants are tax-free and the city is one big market. The third weekend in April is National Museum Weekend when all admission prices are waived and museums are packed full of visitors; perhaps this is not the weekend to visit the Netherlands. Meanwhile, during late April and May the World Press Photo Exhibition is held at the Nieuwekerk on the Dam.

May starts off with National Remembrance and Liberation Days on the 4th and 5th. 4 May sees a ceremony led by the Queen at the National Monument on the Dam (starts at 19.30); Liberation Day is celebrated across the city, especially in the Vondelpark, with events and markets.

The whole of **June** is dominated by the Holland Festival with all arts represented in performances and exhibitions held throughout the Randstad; a large version of the Edinburgh Festival. For details it is best to contact the VVV on arrival, or your nearest tourist office before you leave. There is also a parallel fringe event called the Off Holland Festival. At the beginning of the month is Kunst RAI, a contemporary arts fair held at the RAI Congresgebouw. On the second Sunday in June the canals are taken over by athletes in varying conditions of fitness for the annual Echo Grachtenloop, a canalside run organised by a newspaper. If you have your gear with you then register at the Stadsschouwburg in the Leidseplein and jog along too. Around the corner at the Melkweg is the World Roots Festival of reggae and world music. The dates vary from year to year and the event lasts nine days (see Entertainment listings for address and telephone number).

The Summer Festival in **July** is usually more avant-garde than the Holland Festival, eschewing normal venues and formats for artistic events (contact VVV for details and AUB for tickets).

August is a quiet month; the Dutch leave for the duration unless they are at home servicing the tourist trade. During the last week of August there is the strange phenomenon of the *Uitmarkt* (Entertainment Market) when all kinds of performers from all over the country preview their forthcoming seasons in the theatres and on outdoor stages throughout the city. Also, on one evening during late August, there is an outdoor classical music concert in front of the Pulitzer Hotel at Prinsengracht 315–31.

On the first Saturday in **September** there is a grand parade of flowers (the *Bloemen Corso*) from Aalsmeer to Amsterdam. This will coincide with the opening of the Jordaan Festival, the most exuberant of the various neighbourhood festivals held during this time of the year throughout the city. The talent contests are the best/worst of the events. On National Monuments Day, usually the second Saturday in September, many of the nation's listed buildings are opened to the public; visit a canal house or a windmill.

You can tell winter is coming when the little ice rink is set up in the Leidseplein. In mid **November** Sinterklaas (St Nicholas) arrives in a steamboat, he disembarks by the Centraal Station and parades through Amsterdam on a white horse, accompanied by his servant Swart Piet (Black Peter—there are several Black Peters in fact), who distributes sweets to children. He is officially received by the mayor and given the keys to the city before setting off on a grand tour. Tradition has it that he comes from Spain. The legend is all very confusing as St Nicholas was originally a Turkish bishop; each year there are long explanatory articles in the newspapers. St Nicholas was one of the most popular medieval saints and the patron of the city.

St Nicholas' Day is 5 **December**. It is a delightful entertainment. Children go to school as normal (my children went to their friends' school one year coming out at playtime to find Sinterklaas, complete with white beard and bishop's robes, on the roof), and when they return home the whole family sits around and sings songs at the tops of their voices. The songs (should they be loud and tuneful enough) are answered by a bang on the door, a shower of sweets and gifts on the doorstep. Then more gifts, with witty verses attached, are exhanged. Traditionally (that is, since the fall of Catholicism) there has been little emphasis upon the popish feast of Christmas, Sinterklaas and Oudejaarsavond replaced it. In recent years, and especially following the example seen on imported TV, there has been an increasing emphasis upon Christmas and Christmas presents and the tendency has been to double-up.

The tourist theme for 1993 will be the Golden Age of Amsterdam with exhibitions at the Rijksmuseum, Historisch Museum, Rembrandthuis, Amstelkring Museum, Bijbels Museum, Royal Palace, Nederlands Scheepvartsmuseum, Universiteitsmuseum De Agnietenkapel, Trippenhuis, Nieuwe Kerk, Zuiderkerk and Westerkerk. Information on these events and special attractions in subsequent years will be available through the agencies listed in the first chapter.

If you want to find out more about the city and its culture you might find the following books of interest. Bob Haaks' *The Golden Age, Dutch Painters of the Seventeenth Century* (London, 1984) is a wide-ranging and accessible introduction to the period 1578–1700, and general readers have enjoyed Simon Schama's *An Embarrassment of Riches* (London, 1987) which gives an engaging account of social life in Rembrandt's Holland. For an historical overview since the French Revolution, Gerald Newton's *The Netherlands: an Historical and Cultural Survey* (London, 1978) has yet to be matched. If you can obtain a copy of Tim Killian's *Amsterdam Canal Guide* (Utrecht/Antwerp, 1978) you will have an invaluable companion for city walks—it shows every building on the 17C concentric canals.

Dutch literature is not much translated—Penguin has recently recently published Multatuli's *Max Havelaar* set in mid 19C Java and Amsterdam, a brooding indictment of colonial corruption. Louis Couperus' novels enjoyed a vogue in England at the end of the last century and they read well—try in your local library for *Of Old People and Things Past*. Contemporary Dutch novelists in translation include Harry Mulisch (*The Assault* and *Last Call* both in Penguin), Cees Nooteboom (*Rituals, In the Dutch Mountains, A Song of Truth and Semblance*) and Jan Wolkers. The *Diary of Anne Frank* has been a best-seller for a generation.

A Note on Blue Guides

The Blue Guide series began in 1915 when Muirhead Guide-Books Limited published 'Blue Guide London and its Environs'. Finlay and James Muirhead already had extensive experience of guidebook publishing: before the First World War they had been the editors of the English editions of the German Baedekers, and by 1915 they had acquired the copyright of most of the famous 'Red' Handbooks from John Murray.

An agreement made with the French publishing house Hachette et Cie in 1917 led to the translation of Muirhead's London guide, which became the first 'Guide Bleu'—Hachette had previously published the blue-covered 'Guides Joannes'. Subsequently, Hachette's 'Guide Bleu Paris et ses Environs' was adapted and published in London by Muirhead. The collaboration between the two publishing houses continued until 1933.

In 1933 Ernest Benn Limited took over the Blue Guides, appointing Russell Muirhead, Finlay Muirhead's son, editor in 1934. The Muirhead's connection with the Blue Guides ended in 1963 when Stuart Rossiter, who had been working on the Guides since 1954, became house editor, revising and compiling several of the books himself.

The Blue Guides are now published by A & C Black, who acquired Ernest Benn in 1984, so continuing the tradition of guidebook publishing which began in 1826 with 'Black's Economical Tourist of Scotland'. The Blue Guide series continues to grow: there are now more than 50 titles in print with revised editions appearing regularly and many new Blue Guides in preparation.

'Blue Guides' is a registered trade mark.

CONTENTS

Maps and Plans

Ceramics, metalwork and inventive treatment of stone and brick on the façade of the American Hotel

PRACTICAL INFORMATION

The Netherlands are easily reached from all parts of the world and entry for English-speaking visitors (British, North American, Australian and New Zealand) is uncomplicated. If you have chosen to travel with a package deal, which is obviously less troublesome, then this section will still be useful as it contains information which you would do well to study before you set off. If you are making your own arrangements (a traveller rather than a tourist) then much of what is listed here under 'Planning your trip' and 'Getting there' should be considered essential.

Planning your trip

There are three important organisations for the intending visitor: the NBT, the NRC and the VVV.

The **Netherlands Board of Tourism** (National Bureau voor Toerisme: NBT) is the central organisation charged with the encouragement of tourism. It is the best starting point for prospective visitors planning their tour and requiring information before leaving their own countries. The Board publishes maps and brochures, covering topics such as watersports, cycling, facilities for young people, museums, castles and architecture, annual events, facilities for the handicapped, fishing, bird sanctuaries and golf and tennis (prices and postal charges from the addresses below).

NBT offices also market the *Holland Leisure Card*, a wallet which inclu.. .s a map, a calendar listing major events, a booklet setting out useful hints, a 'Good Time Guide' and a Holland Leisure Credit Card. Valid for the calendar year of purchase, the card entitles the holder to a wide range of discounts.

NBT addresses. You can write to the NBT in the Netherlands at Vlietweg 15, 2266 KA Leidschendam, but you may find it more useful to contact local offices. *United Kingdom*: 25–28 Buckingham Gate, London SW1E 6LD, tel: 0891 200277, fax: 071 828 7941. *USA (East)*: 355 Lexington Avenue (21st Floor), New York, NY 10017, tel: 212 370 7367, fax: 212 370 9507. *USA (West)*: Suite 305, 90 New Montgomery Street, San Francisco, CA 94105, tel: 415 543 6772, fax: 415 495 4925. *Canada*: Suite 710, 25 Adelaide Street East, Toronto, Ontario M5C 1Y2, tel: 416 363 1577, fax: 416 363 1470. *Australia*: 6th Floor, 5 Elizabeth Street, Sydney, NSW 2000, tel: (2) 247 6921, fax: (2) 223 6665.

The **National Reservations Centre** (NRC) is a joint booking organisation of the Netherlands' hotel trade. If you simply turn up in Amsterdam at the height of the season (July–August) you will certainly find somewhere to stay, but it will not be in the elegant seventeenth-century canal house you had hoped for, it may not even be in Amsterdam. To forestall such disappointment you should book early. It is remarkably simple: reservations may be requested in writing, by telephone, fax or telex. As well as arriving in good time, your requirements should be clearly and fully stated (e.g. where you want to be, your arrival and departure dates, your preferred price range, the number of people and number of rooms, whether you want a private bath or shower). Contact the National Reservations Centre, Postbus

404, 2260 FK Leidschendam, tel: 070 320 2500, telex: 33755, fax: 070 320 2611. Opening hours are Monday–Saturday, 08.00 to 20.00. This service is especially useful if you intend visiting more than one city in the Netherlands. For information on the varieties of hotels in Amsterdam see the section on Accommodation, below.

The **VVV (Vereniging voor Vreemdelingenverkeer)** serves visitors and travellers within the Netherlands. VVV (pronounced *vay-vay-vay*) offices can be found throughout the Netherlands—they are clearly sign-posted with the blue VVV triangle and are usually to be found near railway stations. VVV offices are generally open weekdays, 09.00–17.00, Saturday 10.00–12.00, but in summer many are open for longer hours as well as on Sunday afternoons. Here you will find staff who all speak English and who are able to provide full local and much national information. They will also help with local accommodation providing lists of hotels and prices, bookings for travel and entertainment and suchlike. Amsterdam's main VVV office (see below) will change money for you. In the larger centres the VVV offices bear the additional sign 'i-Nederland', such offices provide information, reservation and other services for any part of the country.

Amsterdam's main VVV office is opposite the Centraal Station at Stationsplein 10, tel: 020 626 6444. The Amsterdam office is open weekdays 09.00–23.00 in the summer months and 09.00–18.00 between October and Easter; Saturday, 09.00–23.00 in the summer months and 09.00–17.00 between October and Easter; Sunday, 09.00–21.00 in the summer months (except during July and August when weekday hours obtain) and 10.00–13.00 and 14.00–17.00 between October and Easter.

There is another office at Leidsestraat 106 (Leidseplein), possibly easier for motorists and conveniently close to the Rijksmuseum. Open daily, 09.00 to 22.30 in the summer months and 09.30–19.00 between October and Easter; Saturday, 10.30–21.00; Sunday, 10.30 to 18.00.

A third office is located at the A2 entrance to the S of the city just S of the bridge over the Amstel (the Utrechtsebrug) and is open on weekdays between Easter and September, 10.30–14.00 and 14.30–18.30.

For **ANWB**, the national motoring club which provides many services for travellers, see below in 'Getting around, Motoring'.

Getting there

There are many ways of travelling to the Netherlands. If you wish to take a car then you must use the ferry. The sea crossings are long and can be arduous. Rail and coach services also use the ferry at some point. If you are not taking a car or a bicycle then you might consider that the small amount saved by electing for surface transport will barely offset the costs of meals and sleeping accommodation and opt for a short flight. Anything other than travelling by air for a long-weekend visit is unthinkable.

For stays of up to three months no visa is required for EC nationals, Australians, Canadians, New Zealanders and US citizens. United Kingdom citizens can use a temporary British Passport, available at post offices for £7.50. If you intend staying longer you should get your passport stamped as you enter the country (insist upon this, it is your proof of duration of residence); you will need a Residence Permit if you are a non-EC citizen.

Car Ferry Services. The following services, all carrying motor vehicles and bicycles, cross between the United Kingdom and the Netherlands. Addresses and telephone numbers of operators are given, but annual brochures with up-to-date information on timetables and fares are obtainable through motoring clubs and travel agents.

Harwich to Hoek van Holland. Crossing 6¾ hours (day) to 8¾ hours (night). Contact Sealink UK Ltd, Charter House, Park Street, Ashford, Kent TN24 8EX. Tel: 0233 47047 or 0255 240980.

Sheerness to Vlissingen. Crossing 7 hours (day) to 8½ (night). Contact Olau Line Terminal, Sheerness, Kent ME12 1SN. Tel: 0795 660776.

Hull to Rotterdam. Crossing 13 hours (night). Contact North Sea Ferries, King George Dock, Hedon Road, Hull HU9 5QA. Tel: 0482 795141.

Shorter crossings may be made from Dover to the Belgian ports of Ostend (4 hours) or Zeebrugge (4½ hours). This approach can be recommended for those wishing to visit Belgium, Zeeland and the delta region en route to Amsterdam. Contact P&O European Ferries, Channel House, Dover, Kent CT17 9TJ. Tel: 0304 203388.

In due course the Channel Tunnel will permit quicker crossings—the journey all the way from the Pas de Calais will be a gruelling one, however.

Air services. For the United Kingdom traveller there is a choice of air services, the principal airlines being British Airways, KLM, NLM and British Midland all operating between London (City, Heathrow and Gatwick) and Amsterdam (Schiphol). Other services link Scotland, Wales, Ireland and English provincial centres with Amsterdam and Rotterdam. Ticket information is available from travel agents, airports and the companies themselves. The average price for a scheduled return flight is from £120 upwards. There are many cheaper flights offered by charter companies—travellers on a budget are advised to consult the travel advertisements in the press (for example London's *Time Out* and *Evening Standard*; the quality Sunday press is also good for this). The trip from Heathrow to Schiphol takes about 45 minutes, from the centre of London to the centre of Amsterdam takes about three hours in all.

North American and Australian travellers flying directly to the Netherlands should consult airlines or travel agents for information about flights direct to the Netherlands.

Schiphol is the Netherlands' principal international airport and serves all the Randstad towns. It has its own railway station and flanks the A4 motorway (which, in fact, tunnels below one of the runways) so communications are excellent by rail, coach and car; it is some 10km from central Amsterdam, 40km from The Hague and 50km from Rotterdam. Schiphol is also the home of the Netherlands' national airline, KLM. The initials stand for Koninklijke Luchtvaart Maatschappij, literally Royal Aviation Company but normally known as Royal Dutch Airlines. Founded in October 1919, on 17 May 1920 KLM inaugurated between Amsterdam and London the world's first scheduled international air service.

Travelling from Schiphol to Amsterdam could not be more simple. The railway station is situated below ground next to the main terminal, tickets to Amsterdam cost about f5. Trains depart every 15 minutes to one or another Amsterdam terminus (once an hour between 01.00 and 05.00). Alternatively you can take a taxi but at about f60 it is an expensive option. The KLM Hotel Bus which departs at half-hourly intervals is available to all air passengers whoever they flew with and costs f15. There are two services: the yellow line goes to the south central area and stops at the Ibis, Amsterdam Hilton, Barbizon Centre, Parkhotel and Amsterdam Apollo; the orange line goes to the north central area and stops at the Pulitzer, Sonesta, Victoria, Krasnapolsky and Barbizon Palace.

Train services from the United Kingdom. There are two routes, both out of London: from Victoria via Dover and Ostend and then via Belgium to Amsterdam; from Liverpool Street via Harwich and the Hook of Holland to Amsterdam. Especially in winter the Harwich–Hook journey is recommended only for good sailors. Either way the journey will take about 12 hours. Both journeys can be done overnight and cabins are available on the Harwich–Hook route at an extra cost. The present standard return fares are about £80 to £90. Youth and Student discounts and special fares for excursions are available on both routes. British Rail European Enquiries will give up-to-date information on fares and timetable (tel: 071 834 2345, credit card bookings, tel: 071 828 0892). Alternatively you can enquire at any British Rail station. Travellers beginning their journeys in Scotland and the North of England might consider travelling via Hull and Rotterdam, picking up a train or coach from there to Amsterdam.

Coach services. The journey by coach takes about the same time as by rail but is cheaper, averaging £50 to £60. In the past there were many small companies working this route but the market has declined. National Express/Eurolines provide two services per day (tel: 071 730 0202).

Getting around in Amsterdam

This section considers your options, first under your own power by car (here the advice holds good for motorcyclists) and bicycle, and then by public transport. Of course, most of the attractions described in this book can be reached on foot as like most of the Randstad towns, Amsterdam is compact and pedestrian-friendly. But one word of warning, beware of stepping out under trams (listen for the bell!) and if you are British, look both ways—the traffic is on the 'wrong' side of the road (it is easy to forget when you tumble out of a nice, warm pub).

Bus, Tram and Metro. Amsterdam's bus and tram services are run by the Municipal Transport Authority (GVB). All enquiries are best directed to their headquarters at Stationsplein 15 (tel: 627 2727; office open weekdays, 07.00–22.30, Saturday, 08.00–22.30, Sunday, 08.30–16.30; telephone enquiries daily, 8.00–23.00). You can buy day and season tickets and browse through the wide range of brochures in English.

Bus and tram services are organised locally in the Netherlands although in the Randstad they can provide the means for travelling between cities and tickets hold good across the boundaries as well as for either bus or tram. Each regional service provides a map of the zones, timetables and information in English as well as Dutch. However long you intend staying you might consider the daily, weekly or monthly tickets available—see above.

Strippenkaarts (the long strip-tickets obtainable from bus and tram drivers as well as at the station—see above) are a sensible option for an outing and are available in a variety of lengths costing up to about f10. With the strippenkaart you have to calculate the number of panels or units needed for a journey, fold at the appropriate point and 'ping' the card in one of the machines standing by the doors of the vehicles. More than one person can travel on a strippenkaart, simply double or treble the number of units.

Amsterdam is divided into five zones which are clearly marked on the itinerary maps shown above the windows in all vehicles. To travel within any one zone you should fold back two units and stamp the card, for two zones three units, for three zones four units and so on. If you are not sure of the number of units any one journey might cost then you can hand the card to the driver—if you enjoy the cut and thrust of controversy ask your fellow passengers and watch them argue the matter out between themselves.

Metro. The Metro is perhaps the least used form of public transport for visitors, its function is to service the commuter traffic between the city centre (Centraal Station) and the suburbs to the east and the south-east.

Coach services. One option for journeys out of Amsterdam is to travel by coach. The Netherlands enjoys an extensive network of interurban coach services, town terminals normally being close to railway stations. It would be wise to call the VVV (see above) to enquire about services and to find a convenient pick-up point.

Cycling. In the Netherlands, a flat country with a network of special cycle tracks which to a large extent traverse country inaccessible to motorists, cycling is not only a national means of transport and a national recreation but also increasingly popular with visitors as a relaxed means of touring (cycle track maps are available from ANWB, Netherlands Railways and VVV offices). Tours may be an independent venture, or alternatively use may be made of one of the several package arrangements available. Details are set out in an NBT annual publication.

Bicycles can be hired in many towns, including from a large number of railway stations. There are a number of cycle hire firms in Amsterdam, the cost is usually about f10 a day with a deposit which can be as high as f200, and you may be asked to leave your passport. Shop around for a good price, the following are listed as being convenient to the city centre.

The Bulldog, Oudezijds Voorburgwal 126, tel: 628 8248, open 10.00–18.30—f100 deposit plus passport; daily rate is f7.50. Rent-A-Bike, Pieter-Jacobsdwarsstraat 11, tel: 625 5029, open 09.00–18.00—they take major credit cards and ask for a f50 deposit plus passport; daily rate is f9. Take-A-Bike, Centraal Station, Stationsplein 6, Tel: 624 8391, open 08.00–20.00—deposit f200; daily rate is f7.

Intending cyclists should take great care that their lights are as visible for right-hand drive conditions as they are for British roads. A very secure lock is recommended; and when securing your bicycle you are recommended to take away all removable parts (lights, saddles and wheels with quick-release mechanisms) as there is a lively trade in exotic machinery (most British machines qualify as this). Every other street has a bicycle shop, it seems, so a puncture or a dented wheel need only be a temporary disaster.

Cycling in Amsterdam will demand all your attention. First and obviously, if you are British, traffic comes from the 'wrong' direction. Another hazard is trams—not only because they whizz around silently, but also because as trams run on rails most roads are treacherously grooved for this purpose. Cobbles and brick mosaic surfaces do not provide good adhesion in the wet and beware, eccentric cambers can set you sliding towards the water. Be sure that you understand the brakes and gears on your bike if it is hired, some have rear brakes operated by back pedalling. Outside the city centre cycle-tracks run alongside the roads and shorter trips through the suburbs and into the countryside are most enjoyable and well worth the effort.

Motoring. The Netherlands has an excellent network of motorways and other roads, the traffic laws and signs generally following western European continental practice, though there is perhaps more emphasis on road surface signs (arrows, route numbers and pictograms of bicycles) than in many other countries. Motorways (Autosnelweg) are indicated by an 'A' symbol in red; other main roads bear yellow signs and the letter 'N'.

It is advisable to be a member of a home motoring organisation (e.g. British Automobile Association or Royal Automobile Club; or American Automobile Association), such membership conferring use of the facilities of the Dutch motoring club (ANWB), while home clubs' specialised publications contain detailed information on local Dutch facilities, regulations and much else. The Dutch motoring club is the *Koninlijke Nederlandse Toeristenbond (ANWB),* founded in 1883 as a bicycling association, ANWB standing for Algemene Nederlandse Wielrijdersbond or General Netherlands Bicyclists' Association. The club's headquarters are at Wassenaarseweg 220, The Hague, and there are many local offices throughout the country. Offices are normally open Monday–Friday, 08.45–16.45 and Saturday, 08.45–12.00. Traffic information (24 hour service) can be obtained by telephoning 070 331 3131. Most of ANWB's facilities are available to visiting motorists on proof of membership of an affiliated club.

In addition to the wide range of activities normally covered by motoring clubs, ANWB has organised signed Tourist Routes through particularly picturesque or interesting districts. These routes are marked by hexagonal signs bearing the appropriate name, and detailed maps and descriptions (some only in Dutch) can be obtained from ANWB or VVV offices.

Useful though a motor car may be in getting to Amsterdam it can be more of a liability than of benefit if you are intending to spend the greater part of your time in the city itself. Parking is restricted in the centre of the city and restrictions are enforced by clamping and towing away. This will cost you at least f200, and they do not accept credit cards. The Dutch, and Amsterdammers in particular, are rather less enthusiastic about the benefits of individual car ownership than we are, not least because their ancient cities are simply unsuited to heavy traffic. A recent referendum looks set to restrict motor vehicle access to the city radically. One of the pleasures of Amsterdam and other Dutch cities is the relatively car-free environment; quieter, cleaner and safer for pedestrians, cyclists and bus and tram travellers. In Amsterdam foreign visitors' cars have beome the target for auto-theft—if you are determined to take your car you are advised to ensure that you take every precaution to secure your valuables.

Much of the inner city is one-way traffic; a useful thing to remember is that when you are driving in the canalised central area of Amsterdam the water ought to be to your left.

Accidents and breakdowns. In the event of an accident of any significance, and invariably if there is any question of personal injury, the police must be called before any vehicle involved is moved. Warning triangles, which must be carried in all cars, should also be placed as quickly as possible. For Police and Ambulance in Amsterdam or The Hague, tel: 22 22 22; in Rotterdam, tel: 14 14 14. Elsewhere, emergency numbers will be found in the front of local telephone directories. Alternatively contact the State Police Emergency Centre, tel: 034 381 4321.

In the event of a breakdown the motorist should first try to manoeuvre the car to the edge of or off the road and then place a warning triangle to the rear of the vehicle to warn following traffic. ANWB 'Wegenwacht' road patrols operate along main roads throughout most of the country between 07.00 to midnight and, if one does not soon turn up, may be contacted by telephoning 070 3147714. Before receiving free breakdown service, foreign motorists will usually be asked to provide evidence of affiliated club membership or of the breakdown cover provided by, for example, the AA's Five Star or the RAC's Travellers Bond schemes.

Bicycles, from a motorist's point of view, can be a hazard. Bicycle tracks, indicated by signs and painted lines, frequently run along one or both sides of the road and even, at intersections, into the middle of the road. Be aware also when you are turning that cyclists continuing ahead normally have priority. Parking is never allowed on bicycle tracks.

Documents. For most foreign motorists the only documents required are passport, driving licence and vehicle registration. Additionally, all vehicles must display an approved national disc (e.g. GB) identifying the country of registration.

Car hire. The leading international companies all have agencies at Schiphol Airport. Many more are to be found in Amsterdam (see below). You will need your passport and (preferably) a credit card for deposit. The local hirers are very much less expensive.

Adam's Rent-a-Car, Nassaukade 344-347, tel: 685 0111.

Avis Rent-a-Car, Nassaukade 380, tel: 683 6061.

Budget, Overtoom 121, tel: 612 6066.

Diks, Van Ostadestraat 278–280, tel: 662 3366.

Europcar, Overtoom 51–53, tel: 683 2123.

Hertz, Overtoom 333, tel: 685 2441.

Kaspers & Lotte, Van Ostadestraat 232, tel: 679 9809.

Kuperus, Middenweg 175, tel: 693 8790.

Insurance. Most British motor policies should provide sufficient Third Party cover to meet the Dutch minimum legal requirement, but this does not necessarily mean that full home cover is automatically extended abroad. Motorists should consult their insurance broker or company, and will in any case be wise to arrange for a Green Card extending the home policy to use abroad for a contracted period. If a caravan or other trailer is towed, the Green Card must be endorsed to this effect. Motorists are also strongly advised to travel under the protection of one of the special breakdown, get-you-home or other insurance packages offered by motoring clubs and some other organisations (e.g. AA Five Star; RAC Travellers Bond).

Lights. Dipped (low beam) headlights must be used between dusk and dawn and whenever visibility is poor. It is forbidden to drive showing only parking or side lights. Headlights must be adjusted (e.g. by fitting converters or deflectors) so that the dipped beam does not light the incorrect side of the road and thus possibly dazzle oncoming drivers.

Priority from the right is the basic rule, but an increasing number of roads are marked as priority roads (white diamond with yellow centre), roads feeding in to these having Stop or Give Way signs.

Seat belts must be worn by the driver and front passenger. Children under the age of 12 may only occupy the front seat if over the age of four and wearing a hip type safety belt; if under four, then they must be in an approved safety seat.

Speed limits. In built-up areas, 50kph (31mph), such areas normally extending between place name signs; walking pace in residential areas indicated by a white house on a blue background. Motorways, maximum 100kph (62mph). Other roads, 80kph (49mph). The limit with a trailer or caravan is 80kph (49mph). The above are the general rules, but frequently there are special speeds signed for particular places or circumstances.

Traffic Signs. The following are some of the wordings likely to be seen on traffic signs—this can only be for reference as you are not advised to use this glossary while on the move.

Alle Richtingen = All Directions (i.e. to all destinations)
Bromfietsen = Mopeds
Bushalte = Bus Stop
Doorgaand Verkeer = Through Traffic
Fietsen = Bicycles
Fietsers Oversteken = Cycle Crossing
Fietspad = Cycle Track
Filevorming = Get into Lane
Geen = No
Gestremd = Forbidden, Obstructed
Gevaar = Danger
Inhaalverbod = No overtaking
Langzaam Rijden = Drive slowly
Pas Op! = Attention!
Rijwielpad = Cycle Track
Tegenliggers = Two-way Traffic
Tussen = Between (usually with parking times)
Uit = Exit
Voetpad = Footpath
Weg Omlegging = Diversion
Werk in Uitvoering = Road Works
Woonerven = Ramps, 'Sleeping policeman'

Warning triangles must be carried by all cars and, in the event of a breakdown or accident, placed behind a stopped vehicle at such a distance and in such a position as to give adequate warning to traffic approaching from the rear.

Rail. The first train in the Netherlands ran between Haarlem and Amsterdam in 1839, the great expansion took place during the reign of William III (see History). The present national railway company is the *Nederlandse Spoorwegen (NS)*, founded in 1917, with its headquarters at Utrecht.

NS operates a dense network commonly regarded as one of the most modern and most efficient in the world, the trains being clean, well maintained, frequent and, despite numerous stops, remarkably fast. So good is the service that NS boasts that few people find it necessary to study a timetable since an early departure for any destination in the country can be relied upon. Travel is made easy by means of the timetable (Spoorboekje), published annually in May or June and containing a series of maps; excellent yellow departure boards at stations, showing destination, time of departure and platform, and giving route diagrams; automatic indicators over platforms; and destinations marked on coaches. However, passengers should be careful to board the correct portion of trains since some consist of two or more parts going to different places.

Among the many special facilities offered are Rover tickets of various types and periods; season tickets; reduced fare concessions for senior citizens and for young people; family tickets; bicycle hire; and a particularly

P.J.H. Cuypers' Centraal Station—Amsterdam's steam age triumphal entrance viewed from in front of the VVV office

good range of reduced fare combined rail, bus, and boat excursions. If you are basing yourself in Amsterdam but would still like to visit some other parts of the country you should go to the station, or the VVV, and collect the booklet of excursions; such excursions will often be cheaper than travelling by car and the experience of the train journey itself might well be one of the highlights of your stay.

For further information British travellers can apply to Netherlands Railways at 25–28 Buckingham Gate, London SW1E 6LD, tel: 071 630 1735. Information is also available at NBT offices (see above).

Taxis cannot be hailed in the street, you must either call the 24-hour number (677 7777) or find a cab rank. If you are in a restaurant or bar the staff will call one for you. You need not worry about being cheated, although it is sensible to ensure that the meter shows only the minimum charge at the start of your journey. Rates are presently about f2.50 per kilometre and higher after midnight.

Water transport within Amsterdam is, if anything, on the increase. There are the tripper boats which plough back and forth, their polyglot commentaries echoing across the water (see A Day Out in Amsterdam). More purposeful, though by no means speedy, is the Canal Bus or Museum Boat (see below) which links the Centraal Station and the Rijksmuseum stopping at the Anne Frankhuis and other points en route; departures at intervals of 45 minutes, one and two day tickets are available (f12.50 and f20).

There are *water taxis* which are expensive (about f2 per minute); they can be hailed from the canal side or you can call the Water Taxi Centrale, Stationsplein 8, tel: 622 2181.

With children to tire out you might consider the canal bikes or pedalos (f18.50 to f27.50 per hour, f50 deposit, no credit cards). These can be picked up and left off at a number of sites: to the south side of the American Hotel off the Leidseplein, on the Stadhouderskade between the Rijksmuseum and the Heineken Brewery, by the Westerkerk on the Prinsengracht, on the Keizersgracht at the crossing of the Leidse-straat and near the Centraal Station.

Accommodation

(See also sections on Hotels and Hostels below.) Amsterdam has the complete range of *hotels* that the visitor would expect, NBT's annual 'Hotel Guide' listing most of these. Hotels are given both a national classification (stars) and also a category-numbered Benelux classification (one to five); prices (which include VAT and service) are indicated, while further information is provided by symbols. The guide also advises on how to make reservations—it is advisable to book well in advance (see NRC above, under 'Planning your trip').

Rather fuller local lists are obtainable from VVV offices, these lists also including *guest houses* and *private homes* with rooms to let; such accommodation, usually with something of a family atmosphere, offers an opportunity to meet local people. *Apartments* can be rented from about f500 per week from Amsterdam Apartments, Nieuwezijds Voorburgwal 63, 1012 RE Amsterdam, tel: 626 5930, and from GIS Apartments, Keizersgracht 33, 1015 CD Amsterdam, tel: 625 0071. The range is from the modest to the magnificent, with prices to match.

There are two 'official' *Youth Hostels* in Amsterdam: The Vondelpark, Zandpad 5, 1054 GA Amsterdam, tel: 683 1744 and the Stadsdoelen, Kloveniersburgwal 97, 1011 KB Amsterdam, tel: 624 6832 (full details are given below). Information from visitors' home organisations or from Stichting Nederlandse Jeugdherberg Centrale, Prof. Tulpplein 4, 1018GX Amsterdam, tel: 626 4433. For other hostels and budget facilities see also below.

Camping and caravan sites. NBT publishes annually a list detailing a large number of selected sites for the country as a whole. This, however, represents only a fraction of the sites available, lists of local sites normally being obtainable from VVV offices. You can stay at a campsite near the coast or in the countryside and travel into Amsterdam. There are two campsites convenient for the city. At Het Amsterdamse Bos, Kleine Noorddijk 1, 1432 CC Amsterdam, tel: 641 6868, open April–October, on bus routes 171 and 172 and at Vliegenbos, Meeuwenlaan 138, Amsterdam 1022 AM, tel: 636 8855, open April–September, on bus route 32. The former is a little further out but has excellent facilities, the latter, no less well-equipped has the subtitle 'Youth Campsite'.

General Information

Admission charges. Most Dutch museums charge for entry, and the fee can often be surprisingly high. Any tourist proposing to visit several museums should consider buying a Museum Card. The cost is reasonable if you intend going to more than two museums during your stay; there are three age-related bands (under 26, between 26 and 64, and 65 or over) and, once bought, the card, which is valid for the calendar year, allows entry without further payment to some 300 museums. A booklet listing those organisations recognising the card can be obtained when you purchase the card itself. Cards are available at NBT offices, principal VVV offices and also at most of the museums and galleries.

Baby-sitters. Hotels will advise guests on their own provisions. Otherwise try Babyzitcentrale Babyhome (tel: 616 1119, bookings taken between 15.00 and 17.00 on Monday and Thursday) or Oppascentrale Kriterion (tel: 624 5848, 24 hour service). Prices are upwards of f5 per hour; you should expect to provide refreshments and transport costs after midnight.

Consulates and embassies
Australia, Koninginnegracht 23, The Hague. Tel: (070) 363 0983.
Canada, Sophialaan 7, The Hague. Tel: (070) 361 4111.
Eire, New Zealand, Mauritskade 25, The Hague. Tel: (070) 346 9324.
United Kingdom, Koningslaan 44, Amsterdam. Tel: 676 4343.
United States, Museumplein 19, Amsterdam. Tel: 664 5661.

Cycling. See under 'Getting Around', Cycling, above.

Disabled travellers will no doubt be experienced at making enquiries from organisations in their home countries. The following guides and addresses may be useful. *Access to the World: A Travel Guide for the Handicapped*, Louise Weiss, available from Henry Holt & Co., Box 30135, Salt Lake City, Utah 84130, USA; the pamphlet *Incapacitated Passenger's Air Travel Guide*, available from the International Air Transport Association, 2000 Peel Street, Montreal, Quebec H3A 2R4, Canada; The Society for the Advancement of Travel by the Handicapped (SATH), 26 Court Street, Penthouse Suite, Brooklyn, NY 11242, USA publishes a list of commercial tour operators who arrange travel for the disabled; help is available from the Travel Information Service, Moss Rehabilitation Hospital, 12th Street and Tabor Road, Philadelphia, PA 19141, USA.

In Britain the Royal Association for Disability and Rehabilitation (RADAR), 25 Mortimer Street, London W1N 8AB, tel: 071 637 5400, gives advice on these matters, as well as recommending specialist holidays; Mobility International, 228 Borough High Street, London SE1 1JX, tel: 071 403 5688, can also help.

Amsterdam is not an ideal city for those disabled visitors who might find the cobbled streets and narrow, stepped doorways inaccessible. Trams are out of the question if you cannot mount the step. People and organisations are in every way helpful and there are few museums, monuments, cinemas or restaurants which do not offer wheelchair access. The railways are especially enlightened and provide a guide in English called *Rail Travel for the Disabled* (see above for NBT and NS addresses); timetables are available in Braille (despite the boast that trains are so frequent that timetables are unnecessary). Many places have special facilities for the visually impaired and hard of hearing. The NBT and VVVs (addresses above) have lists of accommodation, restaurants and places of interest with facilities for disabled people.

Electricity runs at 220v 50 cycle AC which will run British equipment. American visitors will need either to convert equipment (check your manuals) or buy a transformer. Take an adaptor with you.

Emergency phone numbers. Ambulance: 06 11
Credit cards lost/stolen: American Express, 642 4488; Diners Club, 627
9310; Mastercard (Access), 01 04 57 0887; Visa (Barclaycard) 520 5534.
Fire: 06 11
Motor accident: 22 22 22
Police: 06 11

Lost property. For articles lost on the transport system there are lost
property offices at the Centraal Station and at the GVB Head Office at Prins
Hendrikkade 108–114 (open weekdays, 09.00–16.00). For items lost elsewhere there is a lost property office at Waterlooplein 11 (weekdays,
11.00–15.30).

Money. The Dutch monetary unit is the Guilder (Gulden), confusingly
sometimes also called a Florin, prices usually being marked as such with a
f or fl. The guilder divides into 100 cents. There are six notes, values (in
guilders) 1000, 100, 50, 25, 10 and 5. There are five coins, all nickel except
for the 5 cent which is bronze; the coin values are f5, f2.50 (rijksdaalder),
f1 (guilder), 25 cents (kwartje), 10 cents (dubbeltje) and 5 cents (stuiver).

There are no foreign exchange restrictions. Visitors may either carry
travellers' cheques or use the Eurocheque system. The latter, which has the
merit of avoiding the outlay involved in buying travellers' cheques, involves
obtaining from your bank a Eurocheque Card (valid only for the year
printed on it) and as many special Eurocheques as may be needed. You
make out a cheque in the normal way (max. equivalent to c £100) and
present it at any bank or other exchange displaying (as most do) the
Eurocheque sign. Eurocheques have the further advantage of being widely
used by the Dutch themselves and are accepted at all shops, restaurants
and (even) bars. For purchases greater than the limit two or more cheques
can be made out. You may be asked to provide evidence of identity.
Cheques and currency can often be exchanged other than at banks—at
some VVV offices (see above under 'Planning your trip'), bureaux de
change and hotels. The rate of exchange may be the same wherever you
are but commission rates can vary, bureaux de change are often more
expensive than banks, but then they are open at unsocial hours—the same
goes for hotel exchange facilities.

Some familiar names for English-speaking visitors are: American
Express, Amsteldijk 166 and Damrak 66; Barclays Bank, Weteringschans
109; Citibank NA, Herengracht 545; Thomas Cook, Dam 23–25, Damrak
1–5 (open until 22.30 on weekdays, Sunday, 09.30–19.00), Leidseplein 31
and Muntplein 12a; Lloyds Bank, Leidseplein 29.

All the main credit cards (some with cash facilities) are widely accepted,
but not so widely as in North America and the United Kingdom, so look for
the signs, or ask.

Motoring Organisations. See under 'Getting Around', Motoring, above.

Museum Card. See admission charges, above, and Museums, below.

Police. For emergency numbers see above. All road accidents should be
reported to the police and this is absolutely the case where personal injury
is involved (call 22 22 22 for police or ambulance). If you are the victim of
theft or assault the emergency number (06 11) will put you in touch with
an English-speaking telephonist. For insurance purposes you should report
stolen property to the police. The main police stations in Central Amster-

dam are at Elandsgracht 117 and Warmoesstraat 44. Even readers of the *Blue Guide* might get into trouble with the police (by mistake, no doubt) and you should know that the Dutch police are not obliged to grant you that famous phone call; they can hold you for 24 hours in isolation. It is unlikely that they will and you will more than likely be allowed to phone your consulate (see above) or whoever else can help you.

Post offices. You can buy stamps at all tobacconists and postboxes are frequently to be seen. If you specifically need a post office then ask for the nearest one or look for the sign—a red background with the letters 'ptt post'. Post offices are generally open 08.30–17.00 on weekdays. Amsterdam's Main Post Office (Hoofdpostkantoor ptt) is at Singel 250, 1012 SJ Amsterdam, tel: 556 3311; it is open 08.30–18.00 on weekdays (on Thursday until 20.30) and from 09.00–12.00 on Saturday. If you are sending a parcel home you should either bring it here or to the Sorting Office near the Centraal Station at Oosterdokskade 3 (opening hours as above, no late-opening on Thursday).

Public holidays. The following are to a greater or lesser extent public holidays:
New Year's Day
Good Friday. Many shops remain open
Easter Sunday and Monday
Queen's Day (30 April)
Liberation Day (5 May). Most shops open
Ascension Day
Whit Sunday and Monday
Christmas Day and Boxing Day

Religious services. *Christian*. Anglican Church, Groeneburgwal 42, tel: 624 8877, Sunday services at 10.30 and 19.30. Catholic, SS John and Ursula (an old clandestine church), Begijnhof 30, tel: 622 1918, Sunday service at 12.15. (Latin High Mass is celebrated at the Onze Lieve Vrouwekerk, Keizersgracht 220, on Sundays at 11.15.) English Reformed/Scots Presbyterian Church, Begijnhof 48, tel: 624 9665, Sunday service at 10.30. Religious Genootsch der Vrienden (Quakers), Vossiusstraat 20, tel: 679 4238, Sunday service at 10.30. Russian Orthodox, St Nicolaas, Utrechtsedwarstraat 5, tel: 622 5385, services Saturday 17.30, Sunday 10.30 (please phone for details).
   Jewish. Times of services vary so call or write. Liberal Community, Jacob Soetendorpstraat 8, tel: 642 3562. Orthodox Community, PO Box 7967, Van der Boechorstraat 26, 1008 AD Amsterdam, tel: 646 0046.
   Muslim. THAIBA Islamic Cultural Centre, Kraaiennest 125, tel:698 2526. Daily prayer at 13.30 and 14.30 (please phone for details).

Shopping hours. On weekdays generally 09.00–18.00, Saturday 09.00–17.00. This is the case with the larger shops and those shops on main shopping streets. Smaller shops can be closed at the most frustrating time, it is as well to check by looking at the small yellow sign, displayed as a legal requirement at the front of all shops, to see when the shop will next be open.

Telephones. Telephone boxes are green and display the 'ptt telecom' sign. If you have not bought a phonecard (available at railway stations and post offices) you will need 25c, f1 or f2.50 coins. The instructions are very clearly laid out in English, as well as in other languages. The ringing tone is confusingly similar to an engaged tone on British phones—a long high-pitched whine. The engaged tone is rather like the 'put your money in' pips on the British system. If you are trying to get through to a busy number such as Schiphol you may find yourself listening to a Dutch-speaking computer telling you that you are in a queue. Some useful numbers are:

Directory Enquiries: 008

International Directory Enquiries: 06 0418

International Operator (necessary if you want to reverse charges,

i.e. make a collect call): 06 0410

You can dial directly, the international codes are generally displayed in phone-boxes (for example USA: 09 1; UK 09 44) but remember to drop the zero at the beginning of the area code of the number you are calling, also pause after dialling 09 and listen for the change of tone. All calls are cheaper between 20.00 and 08.00. There is the Telehouse at Raadhuisstraat 46–50 which offers a 24 hour telephone, fax, telex and telegram service with the added advantage for those making a long-distance call of showing you the metered costs as you speak; a similar range of services is offered at the Main Post Office (see above). If you are not in Amsterdam on an expense account beware of phoning directly from your hotel room—people only do it in films because they do not have to pay.

Time. Dutch time is Central European time and is therefore one hour ahead of British time.

Tipping. As elsewhere in Europe, service and VAT are included on bills in Dutch restaurants and bars—round up to the next whole guilder or put a little something on top if you have been especially spoiled. Taxi drivers expect anything up to 10 per cent.

Travel insurance and health. Foreign tourists are entitled to medical help when they originate from a country with which the Netherlands has signed a health treaty, when treatment cannot be delayed, or if covered by internationally valid insurance. A health treaty has been concluded between all EC countries and eligible United Kingdom travellers should obtain leaflet SA30 from their Department of Health office, or from the leaflets office at PO Box 21, Stanmore, Middlesex HA7 1AY; this explains eligiblity and contains an application for Form E111 certifying entitlement to medical treatment throughout the EC. Visitors may well judge that the cover provided is not sufficient—it does not, for instance, cover repatriation and the importance of good travel insurance cannot be overemphasised.

Hotels

As stated above, it is advisable to book your hotel room well in advance. This selection of hotels and hostels (see below) is meant to help you to make your choice. For details of how to obtain a comprehensive list of hotels, see under Accommodation, above.

Amsterdam has about 270 hotels with some 20,000 beds. Most visitors will want to stay in the centre of town. This will not make a great deal of difference to the price, since this is determined by the hotel's facilities according to the Benelux star system (from one to five). If you cherish ambience above fax machines then you can start looking at the cheaper end—ambience does not get graded whereas telecommunications do. The best hotels have both ambience and facilities. Be sure to note that your absolute minimum requirements are catered for; for example, you might need a lift to get to an upstairs room.

If you arrive in the country without making a reservation then you should go immediately to the nearest VVV office. They will charge you a small fee (the NRC service, of course, is free). You can phone around the hotels yourself if you prefer—but, why? If when you arrive there are no places in the centre of the city then you can book into a hotel in the outskirts. You might prefer to try for a hotel in a nearby town. Wherever you end up you are unlikely to be disappointed at the cleanliness and efficiency of the service or the hospitality of the staff.

Stated prices are only approximate but do show the differentials between the hotels, which remain absolute. Unless otherwise stated prices include breakfast. Breakfasts vary. A 'traditional' Dutch breakfast can mean anything from an elaborate pancake to a boiled egg. Most common is bread and/or toast with a plate of sliced meats and cheeses, jams and tea or coffee. At the top end of the market breakfast is whatever you want it to be, often with a very special view to gaze at while you eat.

CLASS A HOTELS. These are international hotels orientated principally toward business and expense account travellers. Few are in very old buildings. Expect *en suite* bathrooms and the rest.

The American Hotel, Leidsekade 97, 1017 PN; tel: 624 5322, fax: 625 3236, telex: 12545 CBO NL. Tram 1, 2, 5, 6, 7, 10. Prices: single from f300; double from f390; breakfast extra.

The 'American' was designed by W. Kromhout and built between 1898 and 1902 (see Walk 1). The ground-floor café was later redecorated in an art deco style and has always been one of the trendier meeting places in the city; if you cannot afford to stay here then have a coffee or a drink here. The rest of the hotel interior is merely handsome, a European/Hollywood blend, but with some class. Rooms are large and quiet and very luxurious.

Facilities include the art deco café, conference rooms, dry-cleaning, gift shop, gym, lifts, limited parking, 24-hour room service and valet. Expect to find a hairdryer, telephone, TV, drinks cabinet and clock radio in your double-glazed room.

Amstel Hotel Inter Continental, Professor Tulpplein 1, 1018 GX; tel: 622 6060, fax: 622 5808, telex: 11004. Tram 6, 7, 10. Prices: single from f425; double from f550; breakfast extra.

The Amstel Hotel, built between 1863 and 1867, was commissioned by Dr Samuel Sarphati to play a key role in his plans for a new and cosmopolitan Amsterdam as its first Grand Hotel. His architect, Outshoorn, produced a building on a scale more familiar in Paris or London. The entire building has been renovated recently. It remains the hotel against which all others in the city must be compared, it is the most expensive. A little further out than some, it has its own motor launch in which customers can sweep up and down the broad river as if they were in Venice. For the easily sea-sick there is a Rolls Royce. Facilities include bar, brasserie, business centre, car (Rolls Royce), conference rooms, health centre, library, lifts, the motor launch, parking, restaurant, room service, secretarial services, shops, swimming pool, wheelchair access and assistance. Your room will contain a drinks cabinet, telephone and TV.

Amsterdam Hilton, Apollolaan 138–140, 1077 BG; tel: 678 0780, fax 662

6688, telex: 11025. Tram 5, 24. Prices: single from f375; double from f450; breakfast extra. Children may sleep in their parents' room for free.

Some way out and set in an elegant, modernist suburb (see Walk 5), this is a typical Hilton—quiet, unassuming and a little dull. It is also very large, with 263 rooms. Most famous for being where John Lennon and Yoko Ono staged their 'Bed-In' in 1969, you can rent the very suite (which has been 'lovingly restored' in a high camp seriousness) for f1500 a night.

Facilities include airport bus, banqueting for up to 600, bar, business facilities, conference rooms, dry-cleaning, hairdresser, laundry, lifts, parking, restaurants, shops, water taxi service, wheelchair access and help. Rooms contain hairdryer, drinks cabinet, telephone, TV and are double-glazed.

Grand Hotel Krasnapolsky, Dam 9, 1012 JS; tel: 554 9111, fax: 622 8607, telex: 12262 KRAS NL. Tram 1, 2, 5, 13, 14, 16, 17, 24, 25, 49. Prices: single from f325; double from f400. Children under 12 half-price in parents' room, children under 2 free.

This certainly looks the goods with its imposing presence on the Dam across from the Royal Palace. The hotel takes its name from its Polish founder. There are over 300 rooms and a convention centre (the Winter Garden) for 2000. Rooms are decorated in various styles.

Facilities include a bar, coffee shop, the convention centre, airport bus, shops, restaurant, wheelchair access. Rooms have air conditioning, coffee and tea making facilities, drinks cabinet, radio, telephone, TV with in-house videos.

Hilton International Schiphol, Herbergierstraat, 1118 ZK; tel: 603 4567, fax: 648 0917, telex: 15186. Prices: single from f375; double from f430.

This hotel is in the middle of the Schiphol complex, reached by shuttle bus from the main airport buildings. A luxurious business hotel. Facilities include bar, business facilities, conference rooms, gift shop, laundry, lifts, parking, restaurant, room service, sauna, swimming pool, wheelchair access with help. Rooms are equipped with drinks cabinet, telephone and TV.

Holiday Inn Amsterdam, De Boelelaan 2, 1083 HJ; tel: 646, fax: 646 4790, telex: 13647. Tram 4. Prices: single from f325; double from f400.

Being next to the RAI Congresgebouw and World Trade Centre to the S of the city, and therefore convenient for the airport, this is very much a businessman's hotel. Facilities include bars, business facilities, conference rooms, lifts, parking, restaurant, 24-hour room service and wheelchair access with help. In your room you will find coffee and tea making facilities, drinks cabinet, telephone, trouser press and TV with in-house videos.

Holiday Inn Crowne Plaza, Nieuwezijds Voorburgwal 5, PO Box 2216, 1000 CE; tel: 620 0500, fax: 620 1173, telex: 15183 HICPA NL. Tram 1, 2, 5, 13, 17. Prices: single from f350; double from f450, breakfast extra.

A Holiday Inn, with all that means, in the heart of the city—though not quite the classiest part of the old city. Facilities are very much directed at the younger business person and include airport bus, bar, business facilities, coffee shop, fitness centre, parking, photo developing service, restaurant, room service, sauna, solarium, swimming pool and limited wheelchair access. Rooms are double-glazed and have air-conditioning, hairdryer, drinks cabinet, telephone and trouser press.

Hotel de l'Europe, Nieuwe Doelenstraat 2–8, 1012 CP; tel: 623 4836, fax: 624 2962, telex: 12081. Tram 4, 9, 14, 16, 24, 25. Prices: single from f350; double from f475.

Situated in an historic building designed by Hamer in 1895 (see Walk 2) this hotel has a delightful ambience—large, well-furnished rooms and a terrace on the river Amstel. Try to get a room overlooking the water, though other views are just as pleasant.

Facilities include bar, business facilities, coffee shop, fitness centre, lifts, limousine service, restaurant, sauna and a swimming pool. Rooms have hairdryer, drinks cabinet, telephone and TV.

Hotel Pulitzer, Prinsengracht 315–331, 1016GZ; tel: 523 5235, fax: 627 6753, telex: 16502. Tram 13, 14, 17. Prices: single from f310; double f355; suite f820, breakfast extra.

For its location, if nothing else, this is the pick of the luxury hotels. The Pulitzer spreads through 24 canal houses between the Prinsengracht and the Keizersgracht near the junction of the Raadhuisstraat with these two canals. Deep inside the complex is the hotel garden and you should try to get a view over this. The nature of the hotel means that there are long corridors and strange turnings, but it all adds to the charm. The 18C dining room is very handsome.

Facilities include airline reservation service, airport bus, art gallery, bar, bureau de change, coffee shop, conference rooms, dry-cleaning, gift shop, laundry, lifts, photo developing service, restaurant, 24-hour room service, valet parking (extra). In your room you will find a hairdryer, drinks cabinet, safe, telephone and TV.

Hotel Victoria, Damrak 1–12LG; tel: 623 4255, fax: 625 2997, telex: 16625 VIC NL. Tram 4, 9, 14, 16, 24, 25. Prices: single from f300; double from f375.

The Damrak is not the most salubrious of streets and the Victoria has sought to create a haven with its Victoria Gallery, full of greenery. Its central location makes it very attractive for both business visitors and tourists. Facilities include bar, business facilities, fitness centre, parking, residential apartments and restaurants. Rooms have hairdryer, drinks cabinet, telephone and TV.

Marriott Hotel, Stadhouderskade 21, 1054 ES; tel: 683 5151, fax: 607 5555, telex: 15087. Tram 1, 2, 5, 6, 7, 10. Prices: single from f425; double from f500; weekend discounts, children under 18 free in parents' room; breakfast extra.

A remarkably unappealing building across the Singelgracht from the Leidseplein, conveniently situated, however, for the museums and the centre. Facilities include bar, coffee shop, dry-cleaning, laundry, lifts, parking, restaurant, 24-hour room service, shop, valet, wheelchair access. Rooms are air-conditioned and have drinks cabinet, telephone and TV.

CLASS B HOTELS. These are often set in converted canal houses, many on the grander canals, or in the area to the SW of the city centre close to the museums and the Vondelpark. They are all very comfortable in every sense of the word but do not necessarily provide the range of facilities, especially business facilities, found in Class A hotels.

Agora, Singel 462, 1017 AW; tel: 627 2200, fax: 627 2202, telex: 12657. Tram 1, 2, 5. Prices: single from f140; double from f160. Family room available.

Recently completed in an early 18C building and close to the centre. Handsome antique furniture makes for a very attractive ambience. All rooms have telephone and TV.

Ambassade Hotel, Herengracht 335–53, 1016 AZ; tel: 626 2333, fax: 624 5321, telex: 10158. Tram 1, 2, 5. Prices: single from f175; double from f200.

A genteel hotel, quite and well-appointed. Not all the houses are inter-connected so that the quality of Golden Age living is retained, an illusion reinforced by the furnishing and decorating. Facilities include a bar, lifts and room service. All rooms have telephone and TV.

Het Canal House, Keizersgracht 148, 1015 CX; tel: 622 5182, fax: 624 1317, telex: 10412. Tram 13, 14, 17. Prices: single from f160; double from f180.

This hotel is the work of an enthusiastic American. The 17C houses have been carefully and tastefully restored and filled with interesting and well-chosen antique furniture. This hotel is exceptionally popular with discerning travellers and you must book well in advance. Facilities include a bar, a garden and lift. Rooms have baths or showers and telephones but (quite rightly) do not have television.

Cok First Class Hotel, Koninginneweg 34–36, 1075 CZ; tel: 664 6111, fax: 664 5304, telex: 11679 COK NL). Tram 2. Prices: single from f225; double from f275; 'Junior suite' f450, 'Senior suite' f550; extra bed f50.

This is the prestige hotel in this trio of Cok Hotels, all very well situated for the Vondelpark and the Concertgebouw and Museums districts. Rooms are spacious and agreeable. This is a mini-luxury hotel reaching into the market dominated by the hotels listed above. All three Cok hotels show that the management have a clear, if derivative, notion of what people want. Self-catering units are available.

Facilities include bar, conference rooms, dry-cleaning, gift shop, laundry, lift, parking, restaurants, room service, secretarial services. Each room has a hairdryer, drinks cabinet, safe, telephone, TV and trouser press.

Cok Superior Tourist Class, Koninginneweg 34–36, 1075 CZ; tel: 664 6111, fax: 664 5304, telex: 11679 COK NL). Tram 2. Prices: single from f180; double from f220; extra bed f50.

A few years ago the much loved Cok Student Class hotel was refurbished to cover the 'Superior Tourist' market. One step down in all particulars from the First Class sibling. Facilities include bar, conference rooms, gift shop, ironing facilities, kitchen facilities, lift, parking, restaurants. Rooms have tea and coffee making facilities, drinks cabinet, safe, telephone, TV and trouser press.

Cok Tourist Class, Koninginneweg 34–36, 1075 CZ; tel: 664 6111, fax: 664 5304, telex: 11679 COK NL. Tram 2. Prices: single from f130; double from f175; triple from f195; quad from f220.

The rooms are less well-appointed than those in the other Coks, but you share the facilities which include bar-restaurant, conference rooms, gift shop, ironing facilities, kitchen facilities, lifts and parking. All rooms have safe, telephone and TV.

Hotel Dikker and Thijs, Prinsengracht 444, 1017 KE; tel: 626 7721, fax: 625 8986, telex: 13161; Tram 1, 2, 5. Prices: single from f225; double from f290, extra bed f70; breakfast extra.

A small hotel, attractively finished in art deco style. The restaurant is excellent and the attached delicatessen is where to eat breakfast. Very popular and you should book well in advance.

Facilities include bar, brasserie, conference room, lifts, limited parking, first-class restaurant, room service (not 24 hour). Rooms have bath/shower, drinks cabinet, radio, TV and (it is near the Leidseplein!) double-glazing.

Estherea, Singel 303–9, 1012 WJ; tel: 624 5146, fax: 623 9001, telex: 14019; Tram 1, 2, 5. Prices: single from f125; double from f155.

Eight canal houses recently refurbished for comfort and neatness with a traditional Dutch atmosphere. Facilities include bar, lift, lounge, wheelchair access with assistance. Rooms are double-glazed and have hairdryer, safe, telephone and TV.

Ibis Amsterdam Airport, Schipholweg 181, 1171 PK Badhoeverdorp;

tel: 02968 91234, fax: 02968 92367, telex: 16491; 68 bus from airport. Prices: single from f155; double from f200.

Large and comfortable business or stop-over hotel. Facilities include bar, conference rooms, laundry, restaurant, secretarial services, shops. Rooms have telephones and TV.

Jan Luyken Hotel, Jan Luykenstraat 58, 1071 CS; tel: 676 4111, fax: 676 3841, telex: 16254. Tram 2, 3, 5, 12. Prices: single from f230; double from f260.

Jan Luyken was a late 17C artist who produced moralistic books (incidentally, almost all the streets in the Concertgebouw and Museums district are named after artists). Facilities include bureau de change, lifts, lounge and wheelchair access. Rooms have drinks cabinet, hairdryer, radio, telephone and TV.

Novotel Amsterdam, Europaboulevard 10, 1083 AD; tel: 541 1123, fax: 646 2823, telex: 13375. Tram 4. Prices: single from f240; double from f290.

A spacious business hotel in the southern Amsterdam RAI Congresgebouw area. Facilities include bar, conference rooms, gift shop, laundry, lifts, restaurant, wheelchair access with help. Rooms have drinks cabinet, telephone and TV.

Park Hotel, Stadhouderskade 25, 1071 ZD (PO Box 50600, 1007 DC); tel: 671 7474, fax: 664 9455, telex: 11412. Tram 1, 2, 5, 6. Prices: single from f220; double from f275, extra bed f60; breakfast not included.

A large and recently refurbished hotel well placed for the museums, park and city centre. Good view from top floor. Facilities include airport bus, bar, business facilities, conference rooms, hairdresser, lifts, parking, restaurant, secretarial service, tax-free shopping. Double-glazed rooms with hairdryer, telephone, trouser press and TV with in-house videos.

Schiller Karena, Rembrandtsplein 26–36, 1017 CV; tel: 623 1660, fax: 624 0098, telex: 14058. Tram 4, 9, 14. Prices: single from f200; double from f250.

The Rembrandtsplein was a fashionable part of town in the late 19C when this building was designed by the painter Schiller—his paintings hang throughout the hotel where Amsterdam's literati once met and gossiped. The bar is still a fashionable place to meet although the area has come down a little. A characterful and unusual location for a chain hotel. The emphasis nowadays is upon business.

Facilities include business facilites, café, lifts, restaurant and room service. Rooms have hairdryer, telephone, trouser press and TV.

CLASS C HOTELS. These can be spartan but always provide a good basic service—some are the most pleasant places to stay in the city. *En suite* bathrooms and WCs, if available, might cost extra. Not all will accept credit cards and few have fax or telex facilities, though doubtless many more will be adopting services of this kind over the next few years. A number of these hotels are ideal for small groups who can club together and rent a shared room at rates not much different from the hostels.

Abina, Amsterdamsweg 193, 1182 GW Amstelveen; tel: 641 2261. Bus 173. Prices: single from f60; double from f90.

Although half an hour from the centre of town, this hotel is situated next to the attractive parkland of the Amsterdamse Bos to the S of the city. Facilities include a bar and restaurant.

De Admiraal, Herengracht 563, 1017 CD; tel: 626 2150. Tram 4. Prices: single from f70; double from f90.

A homely and well-situated family hotel on a pretty section of the canal. Rooms have a safe.

Amsterdam Wiechmann, Prinsengracht 328–30, 1016 HX; tel: 622 5410. Tram 1, 2, 5. Prices: single from f75; double from f150.

Quiet, though near the Leidseplein—canal views. Facilities include lift and lounge. Rooms are double-glazed and have telephone and TV.

Concert Inn, De Lairessestraat 11, 11071 NR; tel: 675 0051. Tram 16. Prices: single from f110; double from f140.

Well situated near the Concertgebouw and museums. Expensive for what it is but all rooms have baths and the whole place is clean and pleasant. Facilities inlcude lift and wheelchair access with assistance. Rooms have telephone and TV.

De Gouden Kettingh, Keizersgracht 268, 1016 EV; tel. 624 8287. Tram 12, 14, 17. Prices: single from f110; double from f150; luxury from f180.

One of the luxury rooms is on the ground floor and is suitable for someone who would find the stairs difficult. The highish price is justified by the hotel's situation and the spaciousness of the rooms. Facilities include a bar. Rooms have alarm clock radio.

Granada Hotel, Leidsekruisstraat 13, 1017 RH; tel: 623 6711. Tram 1, 2, 5, 6, 7, 10. Prices: dormitory f40; single from f75; double from f85; triple from f130; quad from f160.

A hotel popular with gay men and women providing a pleasant, quiet, easy-going atmosphere for a range of budgets. Facilities include a bar, a nearby car park, laundry, sitting room.

De Harmonie, Prinsengracht 816, 1017JL; tel: 625 0174. Tram 4. Prices: single from f60; double from f90; triple from f125; quad from f150.

No facilities and not much space, but central and especially suitable for a small group not wishing to confront a large dormitory.

Hotel Engeland, Roemer Visscherstraat 30, 1054 EZ; tel: 612 9691, fax: 618 4579. Tram 1, 2, 3, 5, 6, 12. Prices: single from f70; double from f100.

I was once dragged to this street by an enthusiastic Amsterdammer friend to see a row of fantastical houses, seven of them in a row, each designed in a 'national style'. They provide no great insight into national styles of architecture but they are certainly fascinating insights into late-Victorian Dutch whimsy. The English House is now a very pleasant hotel, convenient for the Vondelpark and museums as well as for the centre of town.

Hotel de Filosoof, Anna van den Vondelstraat 6, 1054 GZ; tel: 683 3013. Tram 1, 6. Prices: single from f65; double from f85.

Each of the rooms is named after a philosopher and decorated accordingly. The bar is a meeting place of philosophers and the hotel can arrange meetings for visitors grappling with existential, phenomenological or whatever problems with real, live philosophers. This hotel is very soon booked up during the season so apply early.

Hotel Mikado, Amstel 107–11, 1018 EM; tel: 623 7068, fax: 623 7068. Tram 9, 14. Prices: single from f80; double from f80.

Quiet though only a short walk from the Rembrandtsplein.

Hotel New York, Herengracht 13, 1015 BA; tel: 624 3066, fax: 620 3230. Tram 1, 2, 5, 13. Prices: single from f80; double from f130; triple from f275.

A classy hotel for gay men with rather better facilities than the others, including a bar, café, laundry and room service.

Orfeo Hotel, Leidsekruisstraat 14, 1017 RH, tel: 623 1347, fax: 620 2348. Tram 1, 2, 5, 6, 7, 10. Prices: single from f65; double from f100; twin from f105; studio apartments available from f130.

A gay men's hotel, very centrally situated. Facilities include bar, laundry, parking and sauna.

Hotel Prinsenhof, Prinsengracht 810, 1017 JL; tel 623 1772/627 6567. Tram

4. Prices: single from f60; double from f90; triple from f140; quad from f185.

Half of the rooms have private bathrooms. Good value, quiet hotel. Rooms have clock radio and telephone.

Hotel Seven Bridges, Reguliersgracht 31, 1017 LK; tel: 623 1329. Tram 4. Prices: single from f60; double from f90.

A very pleasant hotel set on one of the most attractive canals in the city. Breakfast is served in your room. Rooms have TV.

Hotel Terdam, Tesselschadestraat 23, 1054 ET; tel: 612 6876, fax: 683 8313, telex: 14275. Tram 1, 2, 3, 5, 6, 12. Prices: single from f110; double from f152; extra bed f40.

Accommodates groups on package visits. In an attractive street in the 'poets' district across the Singelgracht from the Leidseplein and handy for the museums. Facilities include bar, bureau de change, restaurant, room service. Rooms have telephone and TV.

Unique Hotel, Kerkstraat 37, 1017 GB; tel: 624 4785. Tram 1, 2, 5. Prices: single from f70; double from f95; twin from f125.

Gay men's hotel. Facilites include a bar and TV lounge.

Hotel Verdi, Wanningstraat 9, 1071 LA; tel: 671 1941. Tram 2, 3, 5, 12. Prices: single from f70; double from f90.

Near the museums. Bright and pleasant small hotel. Facilities include a telephone in reception and a TV lounge.

Parkzicht, Roemer Visscherstraat 33, 1054 EW; tel: 618 1954/0897. Tram 1, 2, 3, 5, 6, 12. Prices: single from f55; double from f120.

An attractive, old-fashioned hotel near the Vondelpark and museums. Most rooms have en suite showers and WC, all have telephone and some have TV. Not suitable for wheelchairs.

P. C. Hooft, P. C. Hooftstraat 63, 1071BN; tel: 662 7107. Tram 3, 12. Prices: single from f60; double from f85.

In the very chic P. C. Hooftstraat—near the museums and the Vondelpark. Nothing more than the basics, but good value for money. The hotel has its own café.

International Travel Club, Prinsengracht 1051, 1017 JE; tel: 623 0230. Tram 4. Prices: single from f65; double from f105; twin from f145; triple from f190; Luxury Suite from f175.

The ITC is an English-owned, very friendly and moderately quiet hotel for gay men; popular too with gay women. Rooms have shower and WC. Thoughtfully, breakfast is served until noon for dedicated ravers.

Quentin Hotel, Leidsekade 77, 1017PM; tel: 626 2187. Tram 1, 2, 5, 6, 7, 10. Prices: single from f55; double from f65; breakfast extra.

Popular with musicians and performers at the nearby Melkweg; also popular with gay women visitors.

Slotania, Slotermeerlaan 133, 1063 JN; tel: 613 4568, fax: 613 4565, telex: 17050. Tram 13. Prices: single from f70; double from f100.

In the suburbs to the W of the city near to the Sloterpark and only 20 minutes from the city centre. Facilities include a bar, conference rooms, lift, restaurant and TV lounge. Rooms have a private bathroom.

Toren, Keizersgracht 164, 1015 CZ; tel: 622 6352/6033. Tram 13, 14, 17. Prices: single from f75; double from f125.

An elegant 17C canal house near to the Jordaan. Quiet and very agreeable atmosphere enhanced by the elegant rooms with well-chosen antiques. All rooms have bathrooms. Facilities include bar, dining room and room service. Rooms have telephone.

Hostels

Hostels are cheap but not *very* cheap. They can be very noisy, which, depending on how you look at these things might strike you as being cheerful. You are sure to meet plenty of new people though.

Amstel, Steiger 5, De Ruijterkade; Tel 626 4247. Prices: from f25.

The Amstel is the last remaining boatel. It is moored behind the Centraal Station at Pier 5. Boats are astonishingly small when you get onto them and the Amstel is no exception, but it is perfectly clean and an attractive and interesting option.

Adam and Eva, Sarphatistraat 105, 1018 GA; tel: 624 6206. Tram 6, 7, 10; Metro Weesperplein. Prices: f20 in dormitories, sheets f6.

The 90 beds are distributed between mixed and single-sex dormitories of up to 20 beds each. No curfew. Facilities include bar-restaurant (16.00–02.00), garden, TV room.

Bob's Youth Hostel, Nieuwezijds Voorburgwal 92, 1012 SG; tel: 623 0063. Tram 1, 2, 5, 13, 17. Prices: f19 in dormitories (sheets included).

This is in the heart of the red light district and can be noisy. 160 beds distributed in rooms from 4 to 18, some mixed, some women only. Curfew at 03.00. Facilities include a bar (08.00–03.00), lockers and showers in all rooms.

Eben Haezer (Christian Youth Hostel), Bloemstraat 179, 1016 LA; tel: 624 4717. Tram 13, 14, 17. Prices: f13.50.

Situated near the Jordaan, very clean and quiet (for a hostel). Open 08.00 to 24.00 Monday to Thursday and Sunday, 08.00 to 01.00 Friday and Saturday. Dormitories are single sex with 18 to 20 beds in each. The Christian element is not disguised and you are given a leaflet when you arrive—you do not, however, have to be a Christian. Alcohol is strictly forbidden, as is any drunkenness. Age limit is 35. Facilities include a bureau de change and a snack bar (07.30–11.30).

Greenwich Village Hotel, Kerkstraat 25, 1017 GA; tel: 626 9746. Tram 1, 2, 5. Prices: single (dormitory) f35; double f95.

A gay men's hotel and hostel. There is a bar and rooms have TV. Life can be very busy here so this is definitely for outgoing types.

Hans Brinker Budget, Kerkstraat 136–8, 1017 GR; tel: 622 0687, fax: 622 0687, telex: 12127. Tram 1, 2, 5, 16, 24, 25. Prices: single from f55; double from f100; dormitory from f27.

Facilities include a café, lifts and wheelchair access with help.

Hotel Kabul, Warmoesstraat 38–42, 1012 JE; tel: 623 7158, telex: 15443. Tram 4, 9, 16, 24, 25. Prices: in 10-bed dorm f20; in 6-bed dorm f23; in 4-bed dorm f65; double from f65; triple from f100.

Lively and very central—the Warmoesstraat is at the edge of the red light district. Live music is sometimes performed in the bar. As well as the bar there is a restaurant. Lockers are available.

The Shelter (Christian Youth Hostel), Barndesteeg 21, 1012 BV; tel: 625 3230. Tram 1, 2, 4, 5, 9, 13, 16, 17, 24, 25. Prices: f13.50.

In the red light district. Open 08.00 to 24.00, Monday to Thursday and Sunday, 08.00 to 01.00, Friday and Saturday. Dormitories are single sex with up to 40 beds in some. The Christian element is not disguised and you are given a leaflet when you arrive—you do not, however, have to be a Christian. Alcohol is strictly forbidden, as is any drunkenness. Age limit is 35. Facilities include bureau de change, café (07.30–11.00), left luggage (during daytime), lifts.

Sleep-In Mauritskade, 's Gravesandestraat 51, 1092 AA; tel: 694 7444. Tram 6, 10; Metro Weesperplein. Prices: f12.50, sheets f3; breakfast extra (f1.50).

Open weekends only from Easter to 1 July, open daily until 1 September, closed September to Easter. Dormitories take up to 90 people, some mixed, some single sex. The hostel closes 12.00–16.00 for cleaning. There is no curfew and the bar remains open 16.00–02.00. No individual lockers are provided; you use a luggage room.

INTERNATIONAL YOUTH FEDERATION HOSTELS. There are two Youth Hostels in Amsterdam. To be admitted to either you must be a member of the IYHF. If you are not a member you can join the Dutch federation (about f30); it is cheaper to join in your native country. Temporary membership is available. Further information from NJHC, Professor Tulpplein 4, 1018 GX Amsterdam or telephone 551 3155. The Youth Hostels are:

Vondelpark, Zandpad 5, 1054 GA; tel: 683 1744, telex: 11031. Tram 1, 2, 5. **Stadsdoelen**, Kloveniersburgwal 97, 1011 KB; tel: 624 6832. Tram 4, 9, 14, 16, 24, 25. Prices: f18.50 (non-members f23.50), sheet and pillowcase f5.50. Full board (inlcuding breakfast, packed lunch and supper) is f35 (non-members f40). Prices rise by f2.50 in summer months.

If you are bringing a group you should book well in advance. All accommodation is in dormitories except for a few 2- and 4-bed rooms intended for group leaders. Curfew is at 02.00. The Vondelpark site is leafy and (moderately) quiet, the Stadsdoelen is in the red light district and is probably less appealing for, say, families with children.

Eating and Drinking

Restaurants

A number of the bars listed in the section which follows this one would count as restaurants as far as quality and variety of food are concerned and you are advised to check through those as well.

There is all the variety to choose from that you might expect in a major city. Dutch food is not as boring as people say and the jaded palete of the modern traveller might find new delight in such dishes as *stamppot*, a meat and vegetable stew, or *erwtensoep*, a pea soup. The ingredients are invariably fresh (for example, the ubiquitous *haring* (herring), Dutch sushi!) and in winter traditional Dutch fare is nourishing and filling. The Dutch pancake (*pannekoek*) comes with all manner of toppings/fillings and they are addictive. The Dutch tourist board is promoting Dutch cuisine and restaurants displaying the red, white and blue *Neerlands Dis* sign are worth investigating. Indonesian cookery is a 'Dutch' speciality and you should definitely try a *rijsttafel* (lit. rice table, a selection of spicy dishes forming a complete meal) if you have not done so before.

Although a number of Dutch restaurants are listed, the appeal of eating out in Amsterdam rests ultimately upon the variety of foreign cuisines, many of which combine with Dutch to great and memorable effect. Amsterdam is a beautiful city in which to dine out and many of the places listed below are full of character—an excellent sauce in itself. Ambience has been an important consideration in making the listings. Restaurants are grouped by price, prices change but relative prices are likely to be the same over the longer term. 'Expensive' means above f75 a head, 'Moderate' means above f30 a head and 'Cheap' often means well below f30 a head. Look for signs advertising 'Tourist Menus'; these will be set meals, but will usually provide value for money. Prices do not include drinks, but they give a guide to what a starter, main course and dessert would cost. Amsterdammers dine earlier than the British or Americans so restaurants are most crowded in the early evenings. You are advised to call and book wherever a telephone number is included.

All the major museums have bars—this one is in the Stedelijk Museum; the mural is by Karel Appel

Ten expensive restaurants

Beddington's, Roelof Hartstraat 6–8; tel. 676 5201. Tram 3, 5, 12, 24. A rather aggressively modern setting for a very modern combination of French, English and Far Eastern elements. Recommended.

Christophé, Leliegracht 46; tel. 625 0807. Tram 13, 14, 17. A very fashionable restaurant within hailing distance of the Jordaan. Basically French with a typically Dutch treatment.

Le Ciel Bleu, Okura Hotel, Ferdinand Bolstraat 333; tel. 678 7111. Tram 12. For a formal occasion (jackets and ties are obligatory) this could not be bettered. Japanese and French cuisines on the 23rd floor.

Excelsior, Hotel de l'Europe, Nieuwe Doelenstraat 2–8; tel. 623 4836. Tram 4, 9, 14, 16, 24, 25. An eclectic menu based upon French classics; riverside splendour near to the Opera; a huge wine cellar to please the Michelin. Jacket and tie at dinner, please.

Dikker en Thijs, Prinsengracht 444; tel. 625 8876. Tram 1, 2, 5. The upper restaurant is traditional haute cuisine, the ground floor is a brasserie with a wide selection of dishes, the basement specialises in game in season. During the day you can visit their delicatessen next door.

De Graaf, Emmalaan 25. Tram 2. Closed Sunday. A relative newcomer near to the Vondelpark in an attractive 19C house. The eclectic cuisine, not to mention the pastries, make this another Michelin star winner for the eponymous owner.

De Kersentuin, Garden Hotel, Dijsselhofplanstoen 7. Tram 16. Closed Sunday. A very fashionable eating place; nouvelle cuisine in a Japanese Cherry Orchard. Jacket and tie.

De Silveren Spiegel, Kattengat 4–6; tel. 624 6307. Tram 1, 2, 4, 5, 9, 13, 16, 17, 24, 25. Situated in a house dating back to 1614, close by the Lutheran Church. An imaginative menu. Recommended.

't Swarte Schaep, Korte Leidsedwarsstraat 24; tel. 622 3021. Tram 1, 2, 5. A long established and very handsome restaurant that plays host to royalty, among others, and has an excellent wine list. The food will appeal to all. Recommended.

Tout Court, Runstraat 13; tel. 625 8637. Tram 7, 10. Closed Sunday and Monday. Another very fashionable Jordaan restaurant, more nouvelle than the rest.

Twenty middle-price restaurants

1e Klas, Platform 2b, Centraal Station; tel 625 0131. The former First Class waiting room has been renovated in Edwardian style and houses a surprisingly good restaurant for Dutch and nouvelle cuisines.

Aphrodite, Lange Leidsedwarsstraat 91; tel. 622 7382. Tram 1, 2, 5, 6, 7, 10. Not an instantly appealing place from the outside but the Greek food is excellent and the place is full of people who have come expressly to eat rather than to see or be seen.

Café Americain, American Hotel, Leidseplein 28–30. Tram 1, 2, 5, 6, 7, 10. As has been mentioned elsewhere, this is one of the monuments of late-Victorian Amsterdam, an art nouveau palace. Best to dine from the buffet which, on its own, is nothing astonishing.

Cajun Louisiana, Ceintuurbaan 260. Tram 3. An attractive setting and no surprises (nor disappointments) with the food—this is an ethnic restaurant, after all. Cajun food is as trendy here as elsewhere.

Crignon Culinaire, Gravenstraat 28. Tram 1, 2, 4, 9, 14, 16, 24, 25. This is one of Amsterdam's curiosities, a former cheese house in a 16C building right in the centre of the town (behind the Nieuwe Kerk) now a small restaurant specialising in cheese, though there is a broader menu than that.

De Gouden Reael, Zandhoek 14 (Westerdok). Tram 3. A very relaxed and attractive place, in a 17C house overlooking the water. French food in great variety. Recommended.

Hemelse Modder, Oude Waal 9. Metro Nieuwemarkt. Closed Mondays. This restaurant gets its name from its chocolate mousse ('heavenly mud')—or perhaps it is the other way around.

De Impressionist, Keizersgracht 312; tel. 627 6666. Tram 13, 14, 17. A wide range of dishes (English, American, Oriental and Italian) in a very popular, small cellar restaurant.

Jean Jean, 1e Anjeliersdwarsstraat 12–14; tel. 627 7153. Tram 3, 10. Closed Monday. Excellent French-based cuisine at an affordable price.

Mayur, Lange Leidsedwarsstraat 91; tel. 623 2142/625 0776. Tram 1, 2, 5, 6, 7, 10. A very good Indian restaurant in a city not known for Indian food.

Het Melkmeisje, Zeedijk 19. Tel 625 0640. In an old dairy. Fish soup is the speciality here. The décor is interesting too, with a fairground organ for a bar.

Orient, Van Baerlestraat 21; tel. 673 4928. Tram 10. Indonesian food in a small restaurant with an authentic atmosphere.

Oshima, Prinsengracht 411; tel. 625 0996. Tram 1, 2, 5, 7, 10. Japanese cuisine, at the expensive end of the moderately priced group.

Pier 10, De Ruijterkade Steiger 10; tel 624 8276. Steiger 10 is Pier 10 on the waterfront just to the N of the Centraal Station. A fine view of the harbour as you eat Dutch and French food.

Salad Garden, Weteringschans 75; tel. 623 4017. Tram 6, 7, 10. Good solid fare in an attractive restaurant near the Leidseplein.

Sluizer Visrestaurant, Utrechtsestraat 45; tel. 626 3557. Tram 4. This is a fish (*vis*) restaurant, next door is the Sluizer meat restaurant. The menu is dictated by what is in the market, but the stylish 30s setting is always there to be enjoyed.

De Smoeshaan, Leidsekade 90; tel. 627 6966. Tram 1, 2, 5, 6, 7, 10. (Restaurant closed Sunday) Downstairs a café, upstairs a restaurant; the food is good in both. Recommended.

Speciaal, Nieuwe Leliestraat 142; tel. 624 9706. Tram 10, 13, 14, 17. One of the most popular and respected Indonesian restaurants in Amsterdam.

Tempo Doelo, Utrechtsestraat 75; tel. 625 6718. Tram 4. Indonesian; reputedly the hottest sauces in Amsterdam—but only if you ask. Recommended.

Vivaldi's, Van Baerlestraat 49; tel. 679 8888. Tram 2, 3, 5, 12, 16. Closed Monday. A well-situated dinner spot for the Concertgebouw. On Sundays there is a surprise menu and this is the evening to go for.

Twenty inexpensive restaurants

Anda Nugraha, Waterlooplein 339; tel. 626 6046. Tram 9, 14. Indonesian food at a budget price.

Baldur, Weteringschans 76; tel. 624 4672. Tram 6, 7, 10, 16, 24, 25. A range of vegan and organically grown foods elegantly prepared and presented. (Probably) the best vegetarian restaurant in Amsterdam, despite being unlicenced and closing so early (21.00).

De Blauwe Hollander, Leidsekruisstraat 28; tel. 623 3014. Tram 6, 7, 10. A proper Dutch restaurant—a cultural and culinary experience which all visitors should try. Recommended.

Bloemberg Vis Specialiteiten, Van Baerlestraat (opposite the Concertgebouw). Tram 2, 3, 5, 12, 16. Closed Sunday and Monday. Not a restaurant at all, this is a herring bar where you can lunch on fresh and smoked fish delicacies during office hours (near museums). The weather adds an extra dimension to your enjoyment, or not.

Bolhoed, Prinsengracht 60; tel. 626 1803. Tram 13, 14, 17. Vegetarian food in a licenced restaurant. Laid-back atmosphere would appeal to meat eaters and vegetarians alike.

Casa de David, Singel 426; tel. 624 5093. Tram 1, 2, 5. Pasta made in the kitchen and excellent pizzas from the wood-fired ovens. Remarkably cheap and therefore highly popular.

The Egg Cream, St Jacobsstraat 19; tel. 623 0575. Tram 1, 2, 5, 13, 17. Vegetarian food, some vegan choices. Only open 11.00–20.00 so get there early.

Joodse Studenten Mensa, De Lairessestraat 13. Tram 3, 5, 12, 16. Open evenings 17.45–19.15. Budget kosher refectory; a friendly place with plenty of good food.

Keuken van 1870, Spuistraat 4. Tram 1, 2. Very good value for money—it originated as a soup kitchen for the poor in 1870, hence the name.

Marakech, Nieuwezijds Voorburgwal 134; tel. 623 5003. Tram 1, 2, 3,

13, 17. An excellent and affordable Moroccan restaurant; enjoy the couscous, but just wait for the cakes!

Moeders Pot, Vinkenstraat 119. Tram 1, 2, 5, 13, 17. The name means 'Mother's cooking' which sums it up. Tasty and filling fare at bar food prices.

Pancake Bakery, Prinsengracht 191; tel. 625 1333. Tram 13, 14, 17. Excellent pancakes, see how many you can eat.

Le Petit Restaurant, Kadijksplein. Bus 22. A co-operative set up by squatters and serving very good food, when it arrives. Recommended.

Pizzaria Capri, Lindengracht 63; tel. 624 4940. Tram 3, 10. Affordable Italian food and home-made ice cream.

Rose's Cantina, Reguliersdwarsstraat 38; tel. 625 9797. Tram 16, 24, 25. Mexican food in a very busy, not to say crowded setting. Good value.

Rum Runners, Prinsengracht 277; tel. 627 4079. Tram 13, 14, 17. A lively Caribbean bar/restaurant which offers good, filling food with a view of parrots. At the top end of the price range.

De Schutter, Voetboogstraat 13–15. Tram 1, 2, 5, 14, 16, 24, 25. This could have been listed under bars as readily as under restaurants. The smaller bar is a dining room between 18.00 and 21.00. Formerly the headquarters of a militia company, it is a very pleasant place to spend a whole evening.

Tandoor, Leidseplein 19. Tram 1, 2, 5, 6, 7, 10. A long-established Indian restaurant serving a wide variety of Indian dishes as well as tandoori.

Het Trefcentrum Atrium, Oudezijds Achterburgwal 237. Tram 4, 9, 14, 16, 24, 25. One of a number of student self-service dining halls which are open to the public and which are a godsend to families (or anybody) surviving on a budget. Good food for less than f10 each.

Upstairs Pannekoekenhuis, Grimburgwal 2; tel. 626 5603. Tram 4, 9, 14, 16, 24, 25. Closed Monday. A tiny upstairs room with space for ten. An excellent view as you eat.

Bars, cafés: 'Browns' and 'Whites'

There are, apparently, some 1500 or so bars and cafés in Amsterdam. There is no need for the visitor to die of thirst or faint for lack of food. Many of the museums and galleries listed elsewhere have places to eat and drink and they have not been included here.

Bars fall into, or between, two categories—'white' and 'brown'. The whites are modernistic and bright and are considered the places to see and be seen in. Brown cafés range from the 'traditional' Jordaan drinking places with bare floors, carpets on the tables and smoke-stained walls to high-ceilinged art deco palaces. On the whole, women might feel that the whites (or coffee shops, see below) are more sympathetic—brown culture is very male.

There are many sub-types, for example 'designer cafés', often but not always whites, '*rariteitencafés*' which feature unusual furnishings and 'grand cafés' which are what you might expect from the name. All serve a wide variety of beers and spirits, coffee and tea. All, usually, supply food; you can expect brown cafés to offer the more traditional fare and expect more eclectic selections of food in the white cafés. Drinks are more expensive than in England or America, but the food is usually well prepared and attractively presented and compares well on price—you might find bar meals sufficient for all your needs. Bar snacks offer new delights for visitors—for example *bitterballen*, deep fried balls of meat paste in breadcrumbs. Bars have a more clubby atmosphere than pubs, not only does everyone seem to know each other but newspapers and magazines (all languages) are left around, some bars have reading tables, a number provide chess. You will not be hurried over your drink.

Beer (*bier*), unless you specify otherwise, is always *pils*, or lager. It is served very cold, with a deep head on it, in remarkably small glasses. The better establishments have menus listing other beers available and it is not a bad idea to experiment with the range of imported Belgian beers—Belgian stout, or brown beer, is good; the flavoured beers (lemon, cherry, raspberry) are drinkable. British, Australian and American beers are widely available but can be expensive.

White cafés might look like wine bars but there is rarely a wide range of wine on offer. Spirits, however, are another matter. The Dutch spirit is *jenever*, known as 'Dutch gin', an oily form of gin flavoured with juniper. It comes in two types, *oud* (old) which is often brownish in colour, and more popularly *jong* which is transparent. You drink it neat; it is best when freezing cold (keep your duty-free bottle in the freezer when you get home) and you do not have to do anything heroic like throwing it down your throat in one go, you can sip it gently. Flavoured *jenevers* are popular, though having tasted them, I cannot say why that should be. Some people like *advocaat*, a traditional Dutch treat for those who like it; not this author.

Coffee is a dense black liquid, usually served with a neatly wrapped little biscuit. The Dutch drink it black or with processed milk—if you want cappuccino or espresso you must ask if it is available. Tea is served black or with lemon; if you want milk you may be offered processed milk.

Browns

Some browns are open at noon, some are closed until teatime—all of these will be open between six and midnight. Food is not usually served after nine and credit cards are rarely accepted. Do not bother trying to breakfast in one of these places—unless you get up late.

Aas van Bokalen, Keizersgracht 335. Tram 1, 2, 5. Good value for its food; youngish and arty-alternative clientele.
Int Aepjen, Zeedijk 1. Tram 4, 9, 16, 24, 25. A rariteitencafé which is worth the visit just to have seen it (see Walk 2).
Belhamel, Brouwersgracht 60. Tram 1, 2, 5, 13, 17. A beautiful art nouveau café with a pretty view. Food is a little pretentious. Recommended.
Bern, Nieuwmarkt 9. A very authentic Wallen district brown, the food is excellent.
Café Nol, Westerstraat 109. Tram 10. If you want to see a Jordaan brown then you should try this one; very jolly and noisy in the evenings, quieter during the day.
De Doffer, Runstraat 12. Tram 1, 2, 5. Lunches as well as suppers; popular with students.
De Druif, Rapenburgerplein 83. Tram 1. A dockland bar in an out-of-the-way corner.
Dulac, Haarlemmerstraat 118. Tram 1, 2, 5, 13, 17. A 'grand café' with decor inspired by the eponymous artist. You should see this (call in on Walk 3).
Engelbewaarder, Kloveniersburgwal 59. Tram 4, 9, 14, 16, 24, 25. A 'literary café' popular with students and resident Anglo-Americans.
Frascati, Nes 59. Tram 4, 9, 14, 16, 24, 25. Good, cheap food near the theatres; popular with students.
Gollem, Raamsteeg 4. Tram 1, 2, 5. Closed during the day and very much a drinker's bar which gets crowded at weekends.
Heuvel, Prinsengracht 568. Tram 1, 2, 5, 16, 24, 25. A very pretty location

for pavement drinking during the afternoon.

Het Hok, Lange Leidsedwarsstraat 134. Tram 1, 2, 5. A very quiet chess bar near to the Leidseplein.

Hoppe, Spui 18–20. Tram 1, 2, 4, 5, 9, 14, 16, 24, 25. This is the bar that everyone knows about. Business types make the weekday happy hour too crowded. Try it on a Sunday morning (buy a book or a newspaper at the Athenaeum bookshop opposite).

Huyschkaemer, Utrechtsestraat 137. Tram 4. This trendy café is at the light end of brown.

De IJsbreker, Weesperzijde 23. Tram 3, 6, 7, 10. This is a bar in a music venue overlooking the Amstel river.

De Kalkhoven, Prinsengracht 283. Tram 13, 14, 17.

Koophandel, Bloemgracht 49. Tram 10, 13, 14, 17. Open from four in the evening until dawn but nothing happens until midnight.

De Kroon Royal Café, Rembrandtsplein 7. Tram 4, 9, 14. A sedate and spacious 'grand café' on the first floor with a balcony overlooking the Rembrandtsplein. Posh(-ish) but not expensive.

Luxembourg, Spuistraat 22. Tram 1, 2, 5, 13, 17. A very attractive bar, this is a trendy place to be seen; excellent food served all day.

Het Molenpad, Prinsengracht 653. Tram 1, 2, 5, 7, 10. Worth a visit for the food and the calm atmosphere (though not when there is a jazz band).

Nieuwe Lelie, Nieuwe Leliestraat 83. Tram 10, 13, 14, 17. A quiet Jordaan brown—probably the best one to check out if you are in the district during the afternoon or evening.

L'Opera, Rembrandtsplein 19. Tram 4, 9, 14. Quiet art deco café; watch life go by on the square outside.

Orangerie, Binnen Oranjestraat 15. Tram 3. A quiet, old-fashioned brown with interesting customers.

De Pieter, St Pieterspoortsteeg 29. Tram 4, 9, 14, 16, 24, 25. A 'night café' like the Koophandel–does not open before eleven at night. Live music from time to time.

De Prins, Prinsengracht 124. Tram 13, 14, 17. Popular with students, good cheap food.

Van Puffelen, Prinsengracht 377. Tram 1, 2, 5, 7, 10. A very attractive evening's destination combining a bar and restaurant. Recommended.

De Reiger, Nieuwe Leliestraat 34. Tram 10, 13, 14, 17. Good food in a fashionable setting.

Scheltema, Nieuwezijds Voorburgwal 242. Tram 1, 2, 5, 13, 17. This is the first brown I ever went to so it holds a special place in my heart. The walls are covered with mementoes of its journalistic past. Closes early.

Schiller, Rembrandtsplein 26. Tram 4, 9, 14. Another of this square's art deco backwaters, this with a theme attached to the painter Schiller whose works are displayed here.

't Smackzeyl, Brouwersgracht 101. Tram 1, 2, 5, 13, 17. A very authentic brown popular with the (surprisingly large) Irish emigrée community, for a reason that is obvious when you see the list of draught beers.

't Smalle, Egelantiersgracht 12. Tram 10, 13, 14, 17. Food all day from eleven; a quiet terrace in good weather.

Smoeshaan, Leidsekade 90. Tram 1, 2, 5, 6, 7, 10. Busy eating place in the theatre district.

De Tuin, 2e Tuindwarsstraat 13. Tram 3, 10, 13, 14, 17. A more bohemian option in the Jordaan; chess and backgammon played here.

Twee Prinsen, Prinsenstraat 27. Tram 3, 10. Another comfortable and laid-back Jordaan bar.

Twee Zwaantjes, Prinsengracht 114. Tram 13, 14, 17. A traditional Jordaan brown, with sing-alongs for those that dare.
Vergulde Gaper, Prinsenstraat 30. Tram 3, 10. A posh(-ish) Jordaan brown over the road from the Twee Prinsen.
De Wetering, Weteringstraat 37. Tram 6, 7, 10, 16, 24, 25. A very homely brown popular with students.
Wildschut, Roelof Hartplein 1. Tram 3, 5, 12, 24, 25. A busy art deco bar.

Whites

Properly speaking, a white should have been designed not to look like a brown; i.e. you should be able to see to the bottom of your drink. When the term 'designer bar' is used an ambiguity arises, for a number of the browns listed above are 'designed'. You can, however, do some serious posing in the whites.

De Beiaard, Herengracht 90. Tram 1, 2, 5, 13, 14, 17. Every beer you have ever heard of, and then some more, served in very pleasant surroundings.
Café Americain, American Hotel, Leidseplein 28–30. Tram 1, 2, 5, 6, 7, 10. Expensive but worth every cent for the flamboyant art nouveau surroundings. Find a corner and enjoy watching others worry how they look.
De Jaren, Nieuwe Doelenstraat 20. Tram 4, 9, 14, 16, 24, 25. Bar with snacks downstairs, restaurant upstairs. A 'grand café' worth visiting, perhaps for lunch (when the media people are there).
Kapitein Zeppos, Gebed Zonder End 5. Tram 4, 9, 14, 16, 24, 25. Evenings only, with heavy music.
Land van Walem, Keizersgracht 449. Tram 1, 2, 5. One of the original whites which has remained trendy, but not dedicatedly so. The food is expensive. The garden is a big draw.
Morlang, Keizersgracht 451. Tram 1, 2, 5. Next door to the Walem; there is talk that the one is trendier than the other—go to both and make up your own mind.
Paris Brest, Prinsengracht 375. Tram 1, 2, 5, 7, 10. A very hi-tech white set next door to the Van Puffelen (see above). A good place to eat at any time of day.
Tisfris, St Antoniesbreestraat 142. Tram 9, 14. Busy with a vaguely arty clientele. Food recommended.
Waterloo, Zwanenburgwal 15. Tram 9, 14. Part of the Stopera complex with beautiful view over the Amstel river—which is as well because the bar itself is rather over-flashy.

Proeflokalen

Proeflokaal means 'tasting house'; these were originally counters where distillers would allow prospective customers to taste their wares. The term is now used to describe bars owned by distillers, or is employed by bar owners who have taken over a proeflokaal and continue to run it as a bar. These places are for serious (or foolish) drinkers only.

De Admiraal, Herengracht 319. Tram 1, 2, 5. A large, comfortable bar with easy chairs. Run by Ooiyevaar, the only remaining independent distillery in the city.
De Drie Fleschjes, Gravenstraat 16. Tram 1, 2, 4, 5, 9, 13, 16, 24, 25. Often packed, leaving nowhere to sit. The regulars, you will note, have their own supplies reserved.

Het Hooghoudt, Reguliersgracht 11. Tram 4, 9, 14, 16, 24, 25. Really a brown which clings to the dubious distinction of proeflokaal.
House of Liquors, Damstraat 36. Tram 1, 2, 5, 13, 14, 16, 17, 24, 25, 49. Probably the nearest to the original real thing, cluttered with barrels.

Coffeshops

You can get coffee in any bar, but a coffee shop is where you can drink coffee or tea and eat cakes and light meals. Hours are usually closer to shop hours and unless otherwise stated they are closed on Sundays.

Artemis, Keizersgracht 676. Tram. 4, 16, 24, 25. Opens 10.30. Situated in a converted church this coffeeshop serves a dance centre—you can see the dancers through a glass wall.
Backstage Boutique, Utrechtsedwarsstraat 65–67. Tram 4. An off-beat coffee shop which doubles as a knitwear shop with a gay and female clientele. Recommended.
Berkhoff, Leidsestraat 46. Tram 1, 2, 5. Open from 09.00–18.00 on weekdays, closes one hour earlier on Saturdays. Excellent cakes.
Caffé Esprit, Spui 10a. Tram 1, 2, 4, 5, 9, 14, 16, 24, 25. The coffeeshop is open 10.00–22.00 on weekdays, except on Thursdays when it remains open until midnight and Saturdays when it closes at 21.00. This place is owned by the fashion store next door and is a very stylish place to pass the time.
Greenwoods, Singel 103. Tram 1, 2, 5, 13, 17. An English-run coffeeshop which is also a tearoom.
Langskroon, Singel 305. Tram 1, 2, 5. Open 08.30–17.30, closed Mondays. Probably the best cakes in the city.
Metz, Keizersgracht 455. Tram 1, 2, 5. Open 09.30–17.30, open until 20.30 on Thursdays. Situated on the roof of the Metz department store in a conversion designed by Gerrit Rietveld. Pricey food.
Patricia's, P.C. Hooftstraat 128. Tram 2, 3, 5, 12. Open 10.00–18.00. Posh but not hideously expensive.
PC, P.C. Hooftstraat 83. Tram 2, 3, 5, 12. Open 10.00–19.00 on weekdays, 10.00–17.30 weekends. A shopping street retreat.
Pompadour, Huidenstraat 12. Tram 1, 2, 5. Open 08.30–18.00, closed Monday. Excellent chocolatey things in a decadent French 18C interior.

Smoking coffeeshops

Marijuana is not exactly legal in the Netherlands, but possession and use are not prosecuted by the police forces in certain controlled circumstances. When this loophole was first exploited dozens of 'smokings' opened up, marijuana leaf signs hanging outside, where customers could choose between various kinds of dope, hash cookies and the rest. The numbers have now declined substantially and smokings no longer display leaf signs—they might put up a blank sign, or a question mark.

The Bulldog, Leidseplein 13–17. Tram 1, 2, 5, 6, 7, 10 (also at Oudezijds Voorburgwal 90, Oudezijds Voorburgwal 132 and at Hekelveld 7). Open daily 09.00–01.00. The original established on the OZ Voorburgwal, its own distinctive style of Victorian fairground-cum-Carnaby Street wackiness on the façade makes this one to see. They also rent bikes, which seems a bit risky if you are stoned.
Fancy Free, Martelaarsgracht 4. Tram 1, 2, 4, 5, 9, 13, 16, 17, 24,25. Open 10.00–midnight. Rather clean and 'high street' for this sort of trade, with an aggressive branding policy.

Prix d'Ami, Haringpakkersteeg 5. Tram 1, 2, 4, 5, 9, 13, 16, 17, 24, 25. Open 09.00 to midnight. Another 'high street'-ish operation.
Rusland, Rusland 16. Tram 4, 9, 14, 16, 24, 25. Open 11.00–21.00, opens at noon on Sunday. More like a brown, which seems about right.
So Fine, Prinsengracht 30. Tram 13, 14, 17. Another brownish refuge from the world which seems always to have been around and never to have changed.

Entertainment

One great advantage for the English-speaking visitor is that much of the entertainment in Amsterdam is readily accessible. In your hotel room the television provides all the British and satellite stations; most films are shown in the original language, which is generally English; many touring theatre companies and even some Dutch companies perform in English; dance and music, be they modern or classical, are above language anyway.

With entertainment some of the most interesting events are of the moment and you should rely on word of mouth, the advice of Amsterdammers or listings publications such as *Uitkrant* to bring them to your attention. *Uitkrant* is available at most arts venues, VVV offices and hotel foyers and an English-language monthly listing guide, *What's On*, can be bought in hotels, restaurants, venues and information outlets for a couple of guilders. The **AUB Uitburo** at Leidseplein 26, tel. 621 1211, is open from Monday–Saturday 10.00–18.00 and provides information, handles ticket purchases, advises on discounts and much else.

The following suggestions are intended as much to put you where you can find out more as to put you where you can be entertained.

Cinema. There are notably fewer cinemas per square metre in Amsterdam than in other capital cities, which is strange, because the Dutch are enthusiastic cinema-goers. The proportion of 'art' or second-run venues is high, indicating that the cinema public is also relatively discerning. Amsterdam remains the most important Dutch cinema town (the Film Museum is here, for instance) despite Rotterdam's recent claim to being cinema capital with its international festival each January. Although there are a number of Dutch stars, and Dutch companies are involved in film-making (Peter Greenaway makes his films here), there are few Dutch feature films made. Government sponsorship is not generous but has produced some successes—Fons Rademakers' *The Assault* won a foreign film Oscar recently and Paul Verhoeven came through the system to direct *Robocop* and *Total Recall* in America. There is a film department at the city's art school and many technicians have emerged to find work in Hollywood and elsewhere.

For a visit to the cinema you should know a few things. In the mainstream houses programmes change each Thursday ready for the weekend trade; prices are about f12.50 with reductions on some evenings and shows run twice a day (matinée and evening) as elsewhere; late-night showings are usually Friday and Saturday only. There are some cinemas which allow smoking in all or part of the auditorium. When you are sitting watching your film, be prepared for the interlude (the *pauze*); heaven only knows why the Dutch do this.

Cinemas interesting in themselves include the Tuschinski, the Cineac, the Desmet and De Uitkijk. The **Tuschinski** (Reguliersbreestraat 26–8, tel. 626 2633; Tram 9, 14) is Amsterdam's prestige first-run cinema; it is where the openings happen. It was built in 1918, designed by H.L. de Jong and its owner Aram Tuschinski in the then still very salubrious Rembrandtplein area. The façade is an ebulliently overripe mixture of late art nouveau/deco and Expressionism in brick and ceramic with very interesting metalwork and stained glass. The interior, now converted into six smaller units, retains the original lobby with its fully integrated decoration and furnishings; note the carved wood on the stairs. You can tour the building at 10.30 and 11.45 on Mondays and Sundays in July and August (ask at the box office). The Tuschinski's seventh screen is across the road in J. Duikers severely modernist **Cineac** (Reguliersbreestraat 31–3, details as Tuschinski) of 1933–34. Should you enter note the subtle shift of axis of the interior from that of the street front allowing a more economical use of the limited space. The **Desmet** (Plantage Middenlaan 4a, tel. 627 3434; Tram 7, 9, 14) is another beautiful deco cinema; this is an 'art house' with late screenings every night and a programme of gay interest films at weekends. Another interesting arty cinema is the **Uitkijk** (Prinsengracht 452, tel. 623 7460; Tram 1, 2, 5), Amsterdam's oldest cinema, opened in 1913. As well as the regular programme this is often a venue for old and unusual films in conjuction with the Film Museum—there are two pianos in the auditorium (one apparently unplayable bu t too large to remove) to accompany silent films. Films are also shown at such art/music venues as the **Melkweg** (Lijnbaansgracht 234a, tel. 624 1777; Tram 1, 2, 5, 6, 7, 10) and the **Film Museum** (Nederlands Filmmuseum, Vondelpark 3, tel. 683 1646; Tram 1, 2, 3, 5, 6, 12) is worth visiting for anyone interested in film and cinema (see Museums and Galleries, and Walk 4b).

Inside the lobby of the Tuschinski cinema

Dance. The Netherlands has been gaining respect internationally for its dance during the last dozen years or so. The two great companies, the Nationale Ballet in Amsterdam and the Nederlands Dans Theater in The Hague, still dominate the scene, but for the visitor there is also a range of small venue, low budget dance which is as exciting, novel and experimental as the dance scene anywhere. The **Nationale Ballet** has, since 1985, been based at the prestigious Stopera complex (The Muziektheater, Waterlooplein 22, tel. 625 5455; Tram 9, 14; Metro Waterlooplein), one of the sights of contemporary Amsterdam (see Walk 2 for information on guided tours of this controversial building). The repertoire is classical, the audiences large (1500 seats) and in comparison to some London venues a visit here is a bargain. The Muziektheater also houses the Nederlandse Opera and plays host to touring productions. The Nederlands Dans Theater has, since 1987, been based at the fabulous AT&T Danstheater, Schedeldoekshaven 60, The Hague, tel. 070 360 9931. NDT's younger dancers have their own company, NDT2, and both companies perform from time to time in Amsterdam. Each alternate September (in 1993, 1995) there is the Holland Dance Festival at the AT&T Danstheater which attracts many visitors.

The best place to go to find out about dance events, over and above those sources of information listed in the introduction to this chapter, is the **Artemis Kunstcentrum** in a converted church at Keizersgracht 676 (tel. 623 2655; Tram 4, 16, 24, 25) which is open from 10.30 until late every day except Sunday. The café here affords a view onto the practice floor. You can even enlist for classes yourself. If you are feeling reckless enough to experiment and see a performance come what may you could do worse than contact the **Danslab** at Overamstelstraat 39 (tel. 694 9466; Tram 8, 15; Metro Wibautstraat); it will cost less than a cinema seat and you will see young performers strutting their stuff in a Fringe atmosphere.

Classical Music. The Netherlands has seen the number of its major professional orchestras cut from 13 to eight since 1980. Government sponsorship continues, but at a much lower level and it is not clear exactly what, apart from reducing costs, the strategy was intended to achieve. Amsterdam's two great orchestras are the **Concertgebouworchest** at the Concertgebouw, Jacob Obrechtstraat 51 (tel. 679 2211; Tram 3, 5, 12, 16) and the **Nederlands Philharmonisch Orkest** now based in the handsomely revamped Beurs van Berlage, Damrak 213 (tel. 627 0466; Tram 4, 9, 16, 24, 25) which it shares (along with personnel) with the Nederlands Kamerorkest (Chamber Orchestra). The Concertgebouw is reckoned to have the finest acoustics in the world and the Beurs is possibly one of the handsomest buildings in the world. Whereas the Concertgebouw Orchestra has been in existence for over a century, has exclusive access to its own building and has an ambitious new director/conductor, the Philharmonisch was recently assembled out of the city's Symphony, Opera and Chamber orchestras, works on a variety of repertoires and has yet to sort out conducting. The Beurs is divided into two halls, one sponsored by a computer company and the other by a household appliances manufacturer and if you phone up and wait you will get a listing of programme details in both English and Dutch. Orchestral and ensemble music is performed at a number of the city's churches, where you can also get to here organ music (a strong Dutch tradition).

Free **lunchtime concerts** are given at the Concertgebouw, at the Muziektheater in the Stopera (except July and August), in the **Engelsekerk** in the

Begijnhof (tel. 624 9665; Tram 1, 2, 4, 5, 9, 14, 16, 24, 25) during July and August, all year round except July and August at the **Sweelinck Conservatorium** at Van Baerlestraat 27 (tel. 664 7641; Tram 2, 3, 5, 12) and it is worth checking in *Uitkrant* whether there are any others. The **IJsbreker** (the name is a pun) at Weesperzijd 23 (tel. 668 1805; Tram 3, 6, 7, 10) is one of Amsterdam's most enviable institutions, a meeting place and performance centre for contemporary music and jazz (see below). A visit here cannot be wasted because the café is always open at least from 10.00–02.00. There are many concerts each week, often linked thematically.

The Netherlands Opera Foundation shares the Stopera Muziektheater with the Nationale Ballet and the critical reception has tended to focus as much upon the unhappy acoustics of the new hall as upon anything else.

Popular Music. During the summer months rock and pop music is hard to escape if you are walking through the city. Open air combos can be found on the Dam, in the parks and squares. This is the level at which popular music is best enjoyed in Amsterdam. There is nowhere for the international pop superstars to play and Amsterdam is not quite on the beautiful peoples' circuit, nor is it tremendously up-to-date with the frequent shifts even the quality Sundays report in England. It is possible that you may hit upon a promising new band (many young British groups doing Europe in a Transit pass through Amsterdam), and you are assured of finding much ethnic/world, folk and jazz music if you like your sounds live; there is a bright disco scene led by the self-confident gay community. If you want to know what is happening at the very minute get a copy of the music listings magazine *Oor* (in Dutch but self explanatory) or call in at **WILD!** boutique at Kerkstraat 104 (Tram 1, 2, 5) and get a copy of their own magazine.

Venues and fashions come and go but places to check out include the **Melkweg** (Lijnbaansgracht 234a, tel. 624 1777; Tram 1, 2, 5, 6, 7, 10), at one time a ravers' haven but now a proper arts centre (though dope is still sold and used openly). Friday nights for live World Music, Saturday for indie bands. The Melkweg is closed on Mondays (like the Rijksmuseum!); it opens at 19.30 otherwise and there is a nominal membership fee to get in. It publishes a listing sheet each month which you can pick up in the foyer. The **Paradiso** (Weteringschans 6–8, tel. 626 4521; Tram 6, 7, 10) is only a short walk across the Leidseplein in a converted church. This remains one of the better venues for live music and again there is a small monthly membership fee over and above the price of admission. Nearby also is the **Korsakoff** at Lijnbaansgracht 161 (tel. 625 7854; Trams as Melkweg) which is a place to be, be seen and see local indie bands. **PH31** at Prins Hendricklaan 31 (tel. 673 6850; Tram 2) is open every night and has live music (at least) every Thursday.

Jazz is well served in Amsterdam as in many north European cities. Jazz bars include the **Jazzcafé Alto** at Korte Leidsedwarsstraat 115 (Tram 1, 2, 5, 6, 7, 10) which has live jazz every night; you can eat and hear jazz at **Gambrinus**, Ferdinand Bolstraat 180 (Tram 3, 12, 24, 25) which has live music on Sunday evenings and the **Odeon Jazz Kelder** at Singel 460 (Tram 1, 2, 4, 5, 9, 14, 16, 24, 25) which is open every night except Tuesday and Thursday. The **Bimhuis** (Oudschans 73, tel. 623 3373; Tram 9, 14) is Amsterdam's premier jazz venue; Monday and Wednesday are free; for other nights tickets are available at AUB (see above) and on the door; arrive early to sit down. Trad fans might like to check out the **Joseph Lam Jazz Club**, Van Diemenstraat 8 (Tram 3) which has jazz till late at weekends, Sundays free. A good place to find out what's going on is the **Jazz Inn** record shop at Vijzelgracht 9 (tel. 623 5662/620 4313; Tram 6, 7, 10, 16, 24, 25; Monday to Friday 10.00–18.00, Saturday 10.00–17.00), useful information is also to be found at the **IJsbreker** (see above, Classical Music). In July the Drum International Jazz Festival occupies a number of venues, and there are jazz events associated with the Holland Festival at the same time. There is a Blues Festival each March at De Meervart Centrum (Osdorpplein 205, tel. 610 7393; Tram 1, 17).

There is plenty of folk and world music around, even an Irish pub with live music on Friday and Saturday nights (**Mulligans**, Amstel 100; Tram 4, 6, 7, 10). The most interesting and distinctive music on offer is Latin—choose between **Canecao**, Lange Leidsedwarsstraat 68 (Tram 1, 2, 5, 6, 7, 10), a bar with music (at weekends), and the nearby **Iboya** at Korte Leidsedwarsstraat 29 which is a cultural centre and restaurant with programmes which might include theatre or live music. Latin with reggae is a frequent mixture, try **Royal Star** at Paardenstraat 9 (Tram 4, 9, 14) if you want a 'classy' scene, or **Roothaanhuis** at Rosengracht 133 (Tram 13, 14, 17). If you want to try some Amsterdam folk music there is the **Rembrandt Bar**, Rembrandtsplein 3 (Tram 4, 9, 14).

Discos and clubs come and go. At the smarter end of the market are the **Boston Club**, Kattengat 1 (no admission charge; Tram 1, 2, 4, 5, 9, 13, 16, 17, 24, 25) and **Julianas**, Apollolaan 138 (admission charge; Tram 16), both are linked to large hotels and both like their customers to dress nicely. At the bottom of the market is the student club, **Dansen Bij Jansen** at Handboogstraat 11 (admission charge, and if you are not a student you must convince them that you are; Tram 1, 2, 5) which is fun but remarkably unsophisticated. The **Roxy**, Singel 465–467 (admission charge; Tram 1, 2, 4, 5, 9, 14, 16, 24, 25), a converted cinema with lots of atmosphere, is generally considered the best disco in Amsterdam. It is members only—try turning up early and do look your best; you should get in. **Homolulu**, Kerkstraat 23 (Tram 1, 2, 5) is a gay disco popular with men and women as well as many straights who like to dance. The same goes for **The iT**, Amstelstraat 24 (no admission charge, Thursday to Saturday only; Tram 4, 9, 14) which has the best music of them all and occasional bizarre cabaret acts.

Theatre has a long and distinguished history in the Netherlands, the playwrights of the Golden Age (Vondel, Hooft, Bredero) are still performed regularly and Vondel's *Gijsbrecht van Amstel*, the great celebration of the city's foundation, is performed at the Stadsschouwburg each January.

Theatre in the Netherlands was traditionally a popular art, many burgers were members of the so-called Guilds of Rhetoricians, amateur poetry and dramatic societies, which performed plays new, traditional and translated for a highly literate populace. The professional theatre arrived late and it was not until the 19C that a 'modern' theatre environment arrived. There is no national theatre nor any theatre company of the order of the RSC anywhere in the Netherlands; the principal company at the Stadsschouwburg is the Toneelgroep Amsterdam (Amsterdam Theatre Group). As in the other arts, the Provo years of the mid to late 1960s were marked by the arrival of a generation of baby-boomers; this produced a culture of outrage and confrontation which has been swept away not only by the attrition of age but also by the government cut-backs of the late 1980s. Without a large indigenous culture of theatre at least actors in employment, are few and far between.

You can find out what is on at the information sources listed at the beginning of this chapter. For more on both history and contemporary developments you should visit the **Nederlands Theater Museum** at Herengracht 168–170 (Tram 13, 14, 17) which is open everyday except Monday 11.00–17.00. During the summer months it is possible to tour the **Stadsschouwburg** (Leidseplein 26, tel. 624 2311; Tram 1, 2, 5, 6, 7, 10).

Shopping

It was always the proud boast of Amsterdam that you could buy anything you wanted and that everything was for sale. By about 1600 the city had succeeded Antwerp to the title of Emporium to the World and, although there have been many competitors since then, Amsterdam remains the place where the long sought after antique or the out-of-print book is likely to be unearthed. All the familiar names can be found on Amsterdam's streets—Benetton, Body Shop and the rest. Familiar brand names, or the Dutch equivalents, are everywhere in streets such as the Kalverstraat.

High-class shopping is focused in the P.C. Hooftstraat and the Van Baerlestraat SW of the Rijksmuseum. If you are looking for nothing in particular then you might try wandering the Beethovenstraat or the area around the Rozengracht for gifts, or window shopping for antiques around the Looiersgracht and (very scenically) in the Spiegelkwartier. Markets are especially good places for finding the unusual and cheap gift and in and around the markets there are often very interesting shops for the visitor with time to spare. The larger shops will accept credit cards, everyone accepts Eurocheques.

Antiques. As stated above, the best area for seeking out antiques is along the Spiegelgracht and in the Nieuwe Spiegelstraat, both just to the north of the Rijksmuseum, and around the Looiersgracht in the Jordaan. The Rokin remains an important centre for antiques, where prices are high with the quality to match. The Amsterdam Antiques Gallery (Nieuwe Spiegelstraat 34; weekdays 11.00–18.00) has a number of dealers together under one roof and the range of goods is typical—19C and 20C paintings, bronzes, silverware and ceramics. Furniture and quality household goods and decorations are the particular strength of the Amsterdam antique trade. See also Markets, below.

Auctioneers include branches of Sotheby's (Rokin 102, tel. 627 5656) and Christie's (C. Schuytstraat 57, tel. 575 5255), Amsterdam is on the international art map. L. Gijselman (Overtoom 197, tel. 616 8586) is one of the oldest Dutch auction houses and the monthly sales of household articles are popular with collectors of 20C antiques.

There are so many **bookshops** in Amsterdam, selling both new and second-hand books, that a comprehensive list would fill a book (there is in fact a guide to the city's second-hand book trade). On the Kalverstraat there are three general bookshops, starting from the Dam end: De Slegte (Kalverstraat 48–52) is the most famous and the largest, all languages new and second-hand as well as antiquarian; the American Discount Book Center (Kalverstraat 185) deals mainly in new paperbacks and magazines but some second-hand, too; W.H. Smith (Kalverstraat 152) stocks only new books in English. Other shops worth visiting include The Book Exchange (Kloveniersburwal 58) for second-hand books, mainly in English. The

English Bookshop (Lauriergracht 71) and Lambiek (Kerkstraat 78) which has specialised in comics since 1968. Also worth dropping into if you are passing: N.C. van den Berg (Oudeschans 8–10); the Canon Bookstore, specialising in photographic books (Leidsestraat 79); Robert Premsela, art books (Van Baerlestraat 78).

Specialist and academic bookshops worth visiting include the Athenaeum (Spui 14–16) which has, it seems, every newspaper published anywhere as well as a huge range of new books in all languages on all subjects, and Architectura & Natura (Leliegracht 44) which was a resource of first and last resort in the compilation of this guide. Antiquariaat Lorelei (Prinsengracht 495), Vrouwen in Druk (Westermarkt 5) and Xantippe (Prinsengracht 290) are specialist women's bookshops, the first two having good selections of second-hand books; all three function as information centres for women. Intermale (Spuistraat 251) and Vrolijk (Paleisstraat 135) are bookshops with a wide range of literature, fiction and non-fiction, for gay men and women, as well as magazines and information on up and coming events. Antiquarian bookshops can be found anywhere, especially in and around the University district, notably at the Oudemanhuis Book Market (S end of Oudezijds Achterburgwal).

Camera equipment might need replacing if you leave it in a parked car or drop it into a canal. Foto Professional (Nieuwendijk 113) handles all the major manufacturers' products and is open late on Thursdays. Film and videotape (all formats) are widely available.

Children's needs are well catered for in high street shops, department stores and the like, try Prénatal (Kalverstraat 42). A doting parent with time to spare (i.e. having left the children at home) might try looking for a special book or toy at The Bell Tree (Spiegelgracht 10)—although there is nothing here that cannot be found in one of the modern-olde-worlde shops at home. De Speelmuis (Elandsgracht 58) has toys and gifts and caters too for childlike adults. De Kinderboekwinkel (Nieuwezijds Voorburgwal 344, around the corner from the Athenaeum in the Spui) has an excellent range of books, many in English.

Clothes are much the same price as in Britain, which is to say more expensive than in North America. Amsterdam is not a known centre for fashion, although the Benelux origins of much recent dance music have made some youth styles influential. For the gentleman wishing to buy the Anglo look The English Hatter (Heiligeweg 40) is more English than Bond Street and sells sweaters, ties and scarves as well as headgear. If the man in your life likes sexy underwear (for him) try Tothem (Nieuwezijds Voorburgwal 149); sexy lady's underwear, not quite the type of stuff in porno-shops, is classily presented at Tony Tolo (Kinkerstraat 161) as well as pretty frocks, similar styles more expensively at Victoria's Secrets (Leidsestraat 32). Classic haute couture at Edgar Vos (P.C. Hooftstraat 134) and Frank Govers (Keizersgracht 500). Designer fashions at Antonia (Gasthuismolen-steeg 12) and Modegalerie Summat (Zeedijk 39); both of these are showcase shops for young designers, in November the Modegalerie has recently focused on menswear (both are closed on Mondays). Far-out fashions, and a good range of T-shirts, can be seen at WILD! (Kerkstraat 104) which specialises in Clubwear (also closed Mondays). At WILD! you can get hold of information on dance, music and club events in WILD! magazine. There are many interesting second-hand shops S of the Raadhuisstraat inside the Keizersgracht where good clothes can be found. Daffodil (Jacob Obrecht-straat 41; closed Mondays) and Rose Rood (Kinkerstraat 159) sell quality second-hand women's clothes; at Daffodil the emphasis is on haute couture, shoes and jewellery; at Rose Rood you will find vintage costume from c 1700–1992. See also Markets, below. Specialist shoeshops include Jan Jansen (Rokin 42) which sells its own designs.

The major **department store** is De Bijenkorf (Dam 1) which is also the city's oldest department store (see Walk 1). The name means 'The Beehive'. It is not as classy as Harrods, more like the Army and Navy, but is well worth a visit for, among other things, lunch in the restaurant. Metz & Co (Keizersgracht 455, off the Leidsestraat) is good for gifts; its speciality is furniture. The rooftop restaurant has a staggering view of the city. Vroom & Dreesman (Kalverstraat 201) is one of a chain, something below De Bijenkorf in prices and quality. There are a number of Hema stores throughout Amsterdam and the Netherlands, for example at Reguliersbreestraat 10, these all offer a service something between Woolworths and Tesco.

The art of **diamond** cutting and polishing was introduced to Amsterdam in 1576 or 1586 by Louis de Berguem of Bruges, a refugee from the Spanish Netherlands, and for long remained a Jewish monopoly. The trade received a boost early in the 18C when the United Provinces was granted a monopoly for handling the newly discovered Brazilian diamonds, and again after 1867 as the result of the opening of the South African fields. Such famed stones as the Cullinan and the Koh-i-Noor were cut here and it is estimated that during the 1920s as many as 20,000 people, most of them Jewish, were working in the industry.

Until the Second World War diamond workshops were concentrated in the district around Waterlooplein, but firms are now in various parts of the city. Arrangements may be made through VVV, but listed below are some firms offering guided tours. All are normally open Monday–Saturday, but there are seasonal variations to Sunday opening.

Amsterdam Diamond Centre, Rokin 1–5, tel. 624 5787.

AS Bonebakker, Rokin 86, tel. 623 5972.

Coster Diamonds, Paulus Potterstraat 2–4, tel. 676 2222.

Samuel Gasson, Nieuwe Uilenburgerstraat 173–5, tel. 622 5333.

Holshuysen-Stoeltie, Wagenstraat 13–17, tel. 623 7601.

Van Moppes, Albert Cuypstraat 2–6, tel. 6761242.

Dutch specialities, Delftware, clogs and the rest, are available in numerous souvenir shops, for example and especially in the Leidsestraat. When the first East India Fleet ships returned from the Orient with Chinese porcelain Dutch potters, in Delft and elsewhere, started imitating the distinctive blue designs. Properly speaking *Delftware* has to be made from Cornish clay, baked, painted by hand and glazed. Most touristware is decorated with transfer or printed.

You can see this traditional process being carried out still at the Rinascimento Gallerie d'Arte (Prinsengracht 170); the prices are very high, but the quality of goods in the showroom is also high. De Porceleyn Fles (Rotterdamseweg 196, Delft) is still in business having manufactured authentic Delft Delftware for 300 years; if you do not have time to go there their goods are sold through Focke and Meltzer (P.C. Hooftstraat 65–7) and Holland Gallery De Munt (Muntplein 12, actually in the Munttoren).

The other Dutch ceramic speciality is *Royal Makkum* from Friesland, a beautiful and richly coloured ware made with local clay, also sold at Focke and Meltzer and Holland Gallery De Munt. The most famous manufacturer is Tichelaar (Tichelaar's Royal Makkum Faience, Turfmarkt 61, Makkum, Friesland) who make a range of different products. Antique and contemporary ceramics, glassware and small-scale artworks can be seen at

Hogendoorn and Kaufman (Rokin 124). The work of contemporary potters can be viewed and bought at Kleikollectief (Hartenstraat 11; open Wednesday to Saturday, 13.00–17.00).

Glassware is another celebrated Dutch product; Royal Leerdam is one of the oldest manufacturers. A wide range can be seen at Focke and Meltzer. Modern glassware from all over Europe is to be seen at Glasgalerie Kuhler (Prinsengracht 134).

Dutch *pewter* can be found in many gift shops and department stores, the traditional designs are very attractive and popular. The Rotterdam Historical Museum at the **Zakkendragershuisje**, Delfthaven, Voorhaven 13 is a functioning pewterer's workshop and pewter can be bought there (see Days Out at the back of the book).

See *clogs* being made at De Klompenboer (Nieuwezijds Voorburgwal 20) and buy yourself a pair of *klompen* (clogs), but will you dare wear them?

Flowers are everywhere in this city. Florists are as commonplace as building societies in the UK. For a good selection of cut flowers, potted flowers and seeds visit the Bloemenmarkt (Singel, N side, between the Leidsestraat and the Muntplein).

The Flower Market (Bloemenmarkt) on the Singel near the Muntplein

Food, that is Dutch specialities to bring home with you. *Cheeses* to look out for include the three famous hard cheeses: Goudse (from Gouda, the most popular cheese in the Netherlands); Leidse (from Leiden, flavoured with cumin seeds); and Edammer (from Edam). Cheeses are sold as *jong*, that is mild, *belegen* and *extra belegen* being more matured versions. Take advantage of the offers to taste cheeses. Wegewijs Kaas (Rozengracht 32) has been at this address for a century and they sell more than 100 types of Dutch cheese as well as many imported varieties. They will send cheese home for you. Kef (Marnixstraat 192) has the largest selection of French cheeses in the city. Both shops also sell wines, filled rolls, etc.

Bakeries are everywhere. There are two kinds: *warme bakkers* who sell bread and biscuits and *banketbakkers* who sell the cream cakes and chocolates doctors warn us about. Pool (Ceintuurbaan 278) and Paul Anneé (Runstraat 25) are good and very popular examples of the former; Harrison's

(Kinkerstraat 339), Hendrickse (Overtoom 472), Macrander (Vijzelstraat 125) and Oldenburg (P.C. Hooftstraat 97) are the most famous of the latter. Macrander serve excellent Dutch lunches as well as tea or coffee and cakes.

In the run-up to St Nicholas' Day it was traditional for marzipan figures and chocolate or pastry and marzipan letters (*banket staffen*) to be bought as gifts. These are now available at any time of year; shop-made examples (from *banketbakkers*) are infinitely better than factory-made. *Speculaas*, a kind of mild gingerbread with almond is widely available, often moulded into amusing shapes. Dutch licorice, known as *drops*, is an acquired taste. They are available *zoet* (sweet) or *zout* (salty); do not ever buy them for children, unless you do not like children. The Dutch are also major exporters of teas and coffees, and Keizers (Prinsengracht 180), who have been here since 1839, is the place to visit; especially interesting and desirable are the tea- and coffee-making utensils.

Tobacco is another Dutch speciality, although it has been noticeable how much less commonplace smoking is now even than it was ten years ago. The traditional Dutch tobacconists P.G.C. Hajenius, Rokin 92–6 (founded 1826) were recently bought by Gallaghers and the interior has been restored to look like an Edwardian shop. Cigars, pipes, tobacco and cigarettes (in Holland all much cheaper than elsewhere, and not much more expensive than at the Duty Free shops) can be bought and shipped as gifts.

Markets can be general or specialist. The times given are approximate, no one ever missed a bargain by turning up earlier than advised. The most popular market in the city is the Albert Cuyp Markt (weekdays, 09.00–16.30) in the Albert Cuypstraat. Between them the stalls and the shops sell most things necessary to support life and make it interesting. The Lapjesmarkt (Westerstraat; Monday, 09.30–13.00) is good for clothes and fabrics. There is a good small Saturday market on the Lindengracht (09.00–16.00); organic foodstuffs are available at the Boerenmarkt beneath the Noorderkerk (Westerstraat and Noorderkerkstraat; Saturday, 10.00–15.00).

At the same place on Mondays (07.30–13.00) the Noordermarkt is the best of the in-town flea markets; be prepared to roll up your sleeves and dig through the piles of junk. The Sunday market at the Nieuwmarkt (May to September only, 10.00–17.00) has well laid out, often good quality antiques. The most famous of the flea markets is the Waterlooplein market (weekdays, 10.00–16.00); this has the status of a tourist sight now. There are some serious bargains, especially if your taste in clothing runs to squatter chic; do not allow yourself to be bullied. For books there is the Oudemanhuis Book Market, see above, Books. The Stamp Market is near the Nova Hotel (Nieuwezijds Voorburgwal 276; Wednesdays and Saturdays, 11.00–16.00). For the Bloemenmarkt, Flower Market, see above, Flowers.

The Zwarte Markt (Saturday 07.00–17.00) bills itself as the largest indoor flea market in Europe, next door to it the Oosterse Markt (Saturday and Sunday, 08.00–18.00) deals in all manner of oriental produce, including food; both are very popular with Amsterdammers and bargains abound. They are held outside the city at the Industriegebied aan de Buitenlanden, Beverwijk-Oost (train to Beverwijk, or by car N202 to A9, exit Beverwijk). See also Shopping Centres, below.

Recorded music is cheaper in the Netherlands—new CDs, for example, are a bargain. Interesting shops (i.e. those with holdings of second-hand and hard to get hold of releases often at very low prices) include, for all kinds of music, Concerto (Utrechtsestraat 54–60). Jazz and Blues are much more popular on the continent and you will find obscure and deleted gems at Jazz Inn (Vijzelgracht 9) as well as a comprehensive range of contemporary styles; 50s and 60s popular recordings with excellent holdings of black music at Sound of the Fifties (Prinsengracht 669); Forever Changes (Bilderdijkstraat 148; closed Monday morning), as the name suggests, stocks 60s music, also most things since. Second-hand record stalls appear at most of the markets.

Shopping centres in and around Amsterdam include the Amsterdamse Poort (Bijlmerplein); take the Metro or bus to Bijlmer. This is the largest and has many familiar chain-stores. Two smaller shopping centres are at Gelderlandplein and Osdorpplein.

Unusual shops include The Scale Train House (Bildersdijkstraat 94) which is packed with scale models, trains, train set accessories and scenery. Fifties Sixties (Huidenstraat 13) is a wonderland of the kind of things we threw away (or remember our parents throwing away). How did it all get here? It might be that edible condoms are your idea of a safe present—go to Condomerie Het Gulden Vlies (Warmoesstraat 141) to see the entire range. (Most visitors buy the illustrated catalogue.) De Witte Tanden Winkel (Runstraat 5), that is, The White Tooth Shop, has everything you could imagine and some things you could not imagine as necessary for keeping your teeth clean. The Poppendoktor (Reestraat 20) sells dolls and parts for dolls. At The Head Shop (Kloveniersburgwal 39) you can buy every conceivable marijuana smoking device.

Museums and Galleries

There are dozens of museums in Amsterdam, add to these the hundreds of commercial art galleries and antique shops and you have plenty of places to visit and things to see. Most museums charge an admission fee, though a large number accept the **Annual Museum Card** (*Museumjaarkaart*, available at the ticket desk of affiliated museums. There are three rates: full-price, under-18 and senior citizen and the **CJP** (*Cultureel Jongeren Passport*, available at the AUB Uitburo, Leidseplein 26, tel. 621 1211, office open Monday–Saturday, 10.00–18.00). Bear in mind too that Monday is the day when most museums are likely to be closed.

Many museum and gallery descriptions have been included within the Walks, so that even if you do not wish to follow the Walks you will be able to read the descriptions within an immediate topographical context.

There is a **National Museum Weekend** at the end of April when hundreds of museums are open free of any entrance charge.

An enjoyable way of getting to, from and between the attractions is to use the **Museum Boat**. The Museum Boat links 16 museums to the Centraal Station. The main office and starting point is at Stationsplein 8, tel. 622 2181. Boats leave every 45 minutes, 10.00–15.15 daily. The idea is that you buy a day ticket and get on or off the boat wherever it suits you. There is a reduced rate for children under 13 and for holders of the CJP (see above). If you are only spending one day in the city you might opt for the **combination ticket** which gives you a day's travel, plus entrance to three museums. The Museum Boat stops at Prinsengracht/Egelantiersgracht (for the Westerkerk, Anne Frank House and Theatre Museum), Singelgracht (for Rijksmuseum, Van Gogh and Stedelijk), Herengracht/Leidsegracht (for Bible, Fodor, Amsterdam Historical and Allard Pierson Museums), Amstel/-Zwanenburgwal (for Rembrandt House, Jewish Historical),Oosterdok/

Kattenburgergracht (for Dutch Maritime Museum, Werf 't Kromhout, Artis Zoo and Tropical Museum).

Museums are listed alphabetically by their Dutch names; popular English names are included for the purposes of cross-referencing where this seems appropriate.

Agnietenkapel, Oudezijds Voorburgwal 231, tel. 525 3341; Monday–Friday 09.00–13.00, 14.00–17.00, you are advised to call before you turn up. Tram 4, 9, 14, 16, 24, 25. Housed in a 15C chapel this is the historical collection of Amsterdam University.

Allard Pierson Museum, Oude Turfmarkt 127, tel. 525 2556; Tuesday–Friday 10.00–17.00, weekends 13.00–17.00. Tram 4, 9, 16, 24, 25; The University's archaeological collection housed in former National Bank.

Anne Frankhuis/Anne Frank House, Prinsengracht 263, tel. 623 4533; September–May, Monday–Saturday 10.00–17.00, Sunday 10.00–17.00; June–August, Monday–Saturday 10.00–19.00, Sunday 10.00–19.00. Tram 13, 14, 17; The site of the '*achterhuis*', the house at the back, where the Frank family and others evaded the Germans for two years.

Museum Amstelkring/Our Lord in the Attic, Oudezijds Voorburgwal 40, tel. 624 6604; Monday–Saturday, 10.00–17.00, Sunday 13.00–17.00. Tram 1, 2, 4, 5, 9, 13, 16, 17, 24, 25. Clandestine Catholic Church and restored canal house in late-17/18C fashion.

Amsterdams Historisch Museum/Amsterdam Historical Museum, Kalverstraat 92, tel. 523 1822; daily 11.00–17.00. Tram 1, 2, 4, 5, 9, 14, 16, 24, 25. A broad and endlessly fascinating introduction to Amsterdam's history.

Artis Zoo Museum, Plantage Kerklaan 38–40, tel. 523 3400; daily 09.00–17.00. Admission to Zoo and Zoo Museum are on the same ticket. Tram 7, 9, 14. Rather a lot of stuffed animals which look no more miserable than the live ones next door (see Walk 4).

Aviodome, Schiphol Centre, Schiphol Airport, tel. 604 1521; October–May, Tuesday–Friday 10.00–17.00, weekends 12.00–17.00; May–September, daily 10.00–17.00. Train to Schiphol Airport. Located in a futuristic aluminium dome with multi-media displays which extend beyond merely technological issues to environmental and political ones. This museum is not only for the devoted aircraft fan, it is a rewarding place to visit even if you have only half an interest in the subject. The Aviodome is especially good for families—children (and adults) are allowed to climb all over some of the planes. There are more than 30 aircraft on display including a reconstruction of a Wright brothers' original and an early aeroplane by Anthony Fokker (yes, he was a Dutchman). Space exhibits on the first floor include a Mercury capsule.

Bijbelsmuseum/Bible Museum, Herengracht 366, tel. 624 2436; Tuesday–Saturday 10.00–17.00, Sunday 13.00–17.00. Tram 1, 2, 5. There is a characteristically Dutch fascination with the materiality of religion, as well as this museum in Amsterdam there is a biblical theme park, the Heilig Land Stichting, near Nijmegen. The Bible museum sets forth archaeological evidence relating to the Holy Land alongside curiously old-fashioned models and modern audio-visual displays. The collection of bibles is most impressive. The museum dates back 140 years to when the Reverend Leendert Schouten put his own collection on display. Many visitors come to see the two restored houses of 1660–62 which the museum now occupies, both by Philip Vingboons (1608–78); the rear gallery has a ceiling decorated with rather inappropriately pagan paintings by Jacob de Wit of 1717; and there is a stunning spiral staircase.

Bosmuseum, Koenenkade 56, Amsterdamse Bos, tel. 643 1414; daily 10.00–17.00. Bus 146, 147, 170, 171, 172. Not in itself worth the journey, but a useful introduction should you spend a day in the Amsterdamse Bos (see Days Out). Get there via the Tramline Museum's antique tram service on a Sunday (see next entry).

Electrische Museumtramlijn/Electric Tramline Museum, Amstelveenseweg 264, tel. 673 7538; April–October, Sundays 10.30–17.30; July and August, Tuesday–Thursday and Saturday, at 13.00, 14.15 and 15.30. Tram 6, 16. Not a museum in the normal sense of the word as the exhibits run back and forth to the Amsterdamse Bos—the exhibits being trams and trolleys from all over Europe. Exhibits depart every 20 minutes.

Nederlandse Filmmuseum/Dutch Film Museum, Vondelpark 3, tel. 589 1400; Museum open Tuesday–Sunday, 13.00–20.30; Cinema Box Office open Monday–Friday from 08.30, Saturday from 13.00, Sunday from 11.00; Library open Tuesday–Friday 10.00–17.00. Tram 1, 2, 3, 5, 6, 12. The museum, cinema and café should be gleamingly revamped by the time this book is available. There are a variety of prices for the cinema with reduced 10 and 60 visit rates, reductions for students and senior citizens and a membership scheme (see Walk 5).

Museum Fodor, Keizersgracht 609, tel. 624 9919; daily 11.00–17.00. Tram 16, 24, 25. The building itself was a coach house before 1861 when it was reshaped as a museum by Outshoorn, the architect of the Amstel Hotel, in accordance with the bequest of C.J. Fodor. Fodor's original collection has been kept in store at the the Stedelijk Museum since 1948, which is a great shame as it comprised Rembrandt drawings and etchings as well as Dutch Romantic paintings—surely a record of a fascinating episode in the history of taste. The museum now presents the most avant-garde publicly-funded art shows in the city—mostly of contemporary Dutch work. Each summer the city's art acquisitions are put on display. Sculpture is also displayed, in the garden. During much of the time of the currency of this guide the museum will be under renovation.

Van Goghmuseum, Paulus Potterstraat 7, tel. 570 5200; Tuesday–Saturday 10.00–17.00, Sunday and holidays 13.00–17.00. Tram 2, 3, 5, 12, 16. Gerrit Rietveld's building seems never to get overcrowded despite this being one of the most popular destinations in the city; a complete survey of the life and work of Vincent with, usually, interesting temporary exhibitions (see Walk 4).

Hash Info Museum, Oudezijds Achterburgwal 150, tel. 624 0386; Friday, Saturday and Sunday 11.00–21.00. Tram 4, 9, 16, 24, 25. Do not rely on the museum being open when it should be; however, the shop next door, which is just as interesting, is usually accessible. Find out all about the culture and cultivation of dope. Very nice people, too.

Heineken Brewery Museum, Stadhouderskade 78, tel. 523 9239; guided tours, Monday–Friday, at 09.30 and 11.00; between 15 June and 15 October also at 13.00 and 14.30. It is worth phoning to check the times. Tram 4, 6, 7, 10. The history of brewing illustrated out of the history of Heineken beer (see Walk 4).

Hortus Botanicus, Plantage Middenlaan 2, tel. 525 5403; October–March, weekends and holidays 09.00–16.00; April–September weekdays 09.00–17.00, weekends and holidays 11.00–17.00. Tram 7, 9, 14. An island of vegetable calm just minutes from the centre of town. Some 6000 plants in a collection dating back to 1682. There is another Hortus Botanicus, belonging to the Vrije Universiteit (at Van de Boechorststraat 8, tel. 548 4142; weekdays 08.00–16.30; bus 23, 65, 173) which is a much more recent foundation (1967) and emphasises native Dutch flora as well as having the largest collection of ferns in the world.

Joods Historisch Museum/Jewish Historical Museum, Jonas Daniel Meijerplein 24, tel. 626 9945; daily 11.00–17.00, closed Yom Kippur. Tram 9, 14. Amsterdam, or '*Mokkum*' as it was known in Yiddish slang, was one of the capitals of European Jewry until the German invasion. The museum now occupies a complex of former synagogues. The appalling story of a millennium of pogrom and persecution is balanced by stunning artefacts and a lively presentation of the daily lives of ordinary Jewish people in the city (see Walk 2).

Werf 't Kromhout/Kromhout Shipyard, Hoogte Kadijk 147, tel. 627 6777; Monday–Saturday 10.00–16.00, Sunday 13.00–16.00. Bus 22, 28. Here, in a 19C dock and boat-building yard, old marine engines and other machinery are exhibited, various small old vessels are moored alongside. This is a working museum where the technology of the age of stream power and skills that date back to the age of sail are not yet dead. It is probably better to ask for a guided tour if you want to make sense of this fascinating place.

Museum van Loon, Keizersgracht 672, tel. 624 5255; Monday 10.00–17.00. Tram 4, 9, 14. Set in a house designed by A. Dortsman (of Lutheran Church fame), one of the first façades with a balcony. Owned by, among others, Ferdinand Bol after he had quit painting to marry a rich widow. In 1884 Hendrick van Loon purchased it for his son. He stocked it with family portraits dating back to 1602 and Willem van Loon, founder of the family fortune; one very interesting picture is Jan Miense Molenaer's family portrait of the Van Loons which doubles as a representation of the five senses. Paintings, sculptures and other artefacts and furnishings make for an experience not unlike the Wallace Collection in London, or the Frick Collection in New York. The upper part of the house is still inhabited by the family. The garden, which has an exquisite garden house, has been maintained in all its 18C glory. It is open on the day that most other collections are closed.

Maritime Museum, see Nederlandse Scheepvaart Museum/Dutch Maritime Museum, below.

Money Box Museum, see Spaarpottenmuseum, below.

NINT/Nederlands Institute voor Nijverheid en Techniek/Dutch Institute for Industry and Technology, Tolstraat 129, tel. 664 6021; Monday–Friday, 10.00–16.00; weekends and holidays 13.00–17.00. Tram 4. The museum's permanent collections cover all aspects of science and technology and there are plenty of 'hands on' exhibits too. Due to be rehoused near the Centraal Station as a much larger and more prestigious display (see Walk 5).

Rembrandthuis/Rembrandt's House, Jodenbreestraat 4–6, tel. 624 9919; Monday to Saturday 10.00–17.00, Sunday and holidays 13.00–17.00. Tram 16, 24, 25. Rembrandt bought this house (built in 1606, the year of his birth) when he was at the height of his contemporary fame. It has been much altered since then but the museum uses it to great advantage, displaying an almost complete set of his prints (see Walk 2).

Resistance Museum, see **Verzetsmuseum**, below.

Rijksmuseum, Stadhouderskade 42, tel. 673 2121; Tuesday–Saturday 10.00–17.00, Sunday and holidays 13.00–17.00. Tram 6, 7, 10. The name means 'National Museum'; it was founded in the 19C as the Netherlands constructed its modern idea of itself and its history. Along with the building, which is a secular cathedral, the collections provide a fascinating insight into the way in which the Dutch would like to see themselves and would like themselves to be seen. It is also a collection of sacred objects—for

The Rembrandthuis is now set some way below the level of the road—but it is taller than it was in Rembrandt's time

instance the Rembrandts and Vermeers. Prepare yourself for a very full day and lament the second-rate café (see Walk 1).

Informatiecentrum Ruimtelijk Ordening/Town Planning Information Centre, Zuiderkerkhof, tel. 5961357; Tuesday, Wednesday and Friday 12.30–16.30, Thursday 12.30–16.30, 18.00–21.00. Metro, Nieuwmarkt. Town planning is not the most prepossessing topic. It is intended to change the display for one on the restoration of monuments during the 'Golden Age' exhibitions, July to September 1993.

Nederlandse Scheepvaart Museum/Dutch Maritime Museum, Kattenburgerplein 1, tel. 523 2222; Tuesday–Saturday 10.00–17.00, Sunday and holidays 13.00–17.00. Bus 22, 28. In the former Admiralty building. A remarkable collection of craft, including full-sized reproductions of great sailing ships. The museum traces the history of sea travel from classical times to the present (see Walk 4).

Schrijftmuseum J.A. Dortmund, University Library, Singel 425, tel. 525 2284; admission by appointment. Tram 1, 25. The history of writing from the third millennia BC to the present day from the University's collections. You will need to know some Dutch to enjoy this museum to the full.

Sex Museum, Damrak 18, tel. 622 8376; daily 10.00–23.30. Tram 4, 9, 16, 24, 25. I cannot understand why anybody chooses to go here when they can see the 'real thing' (which is not really the real thing anyway) a few streets away. Perhaps the notion of its being a 'museum' dignifies natural curiosity (or prurient fascination) with some show of scientific purpose.

Six Collection, Amstel 218; guided tour at 11.00. Tram 4, 9, 14. Visitors are only admitted by card of introduction from the Rijksmuseum, obtainable on production of a passport at the information desk, or by written application sent to the Six Collection, Amstel 218, 1017 AJ Amsterdam.

The house dates from 1680, it contains the accumulated property of the descendants of Jan Six (1618–1700), Rembrandt's friend and patron. Six was the only burgomaster of Amsterdam—a distinction which came his way long afterwards, in 1691—to be portrayed by Rembrandt. Rembrandt made a very richly worked portrait of him in print (an example is usually on display at the Rembrandthuis) and the celebrated painting of 1654. There are paintings by many 16C and 17C masters including Lucas van Leyden, Cornelis Ketel, Thomas de Keyser, Frans Hals, Pieter Saenredam, Jacob van Ruisdael, Aelbert Cuyp, Gerard Terborch and, of course, Rembrandt. Rembrandt's portrait of Jan Six in the large Drawing Room is the highpoint of the visit. Six is shown toying with his glove, either arriving or departing—there are hardly enough reference points to be sure of anything. Except for the face, which engages us with a quizzical glance, the paint is handled imprecisely. For many critics this is Rembrandt's best portrait and the sight of it is certainly worth the effort of getting to see it. There is also much fine furniture, porcelain and silverware.

Stedelijk Museum, Paulus Potterstraat 13, tel. 573 2911; daily 11.00–17.00 (closes one hour earlier on public holidays). Tram 2, 3, 12, 15, 16. The permanent collection offers a brief survey of Dutch art of the present century as well as a bitty selection of modernist artists' work—notably Malevich. It has huge holdings and you should expect to come across a widely diverse variety of art. During the winter months there are usually temporary and travelling exhibitions. Sunday mornings are pleasant here (see Walk 4).

Spaarpottenmuseum/Money Box Museum, Raadhuisstraat 12, tel. 556 7425; Monday–Friday 13.00–16.00. Tram 13, 14, 17. Of the 12,000 money boxes, piggy banks and the rest belonging to the museum there is only room enough for 2000 to be displayed. You will see extraordinary antiques next to examples you might have owned as a child.

Nederlandse Theatre Instituut/Theatremuseum, Herengracht 168, tel. 623 5104; Tuesday–Sunday 11.00–17.00. Tram 3, 14, 17. Another stunning location—a canal house by Vingboons with early 18C interiors featuring painting by Jacob de Wit, the collection looks rather dull by contrast.

Torture Museum, Leidsestraat 27, tel. 620 4070; daily 10.00–17.00. Tram 1, 2, 5. Instruments of torture, the real things unfortunately, presented in appropriately dismal settings.

Town Planning Information Centre, see Informatiecentrum Ruimtelijk Ordening, above.

Trade Unions Museum, see Vakbonds Museum, below.

Tramline Museum, see Electrische Museumtramlijn, above.

Tropenmuseum/Tropical Museum, Linnaeusstraat 2, tel. 568 8200/8295; Monday–Friday 10.00–17.00, weekends and holidays 12.00–17.00. Tram 9, 10, 14. Within a couple of generations this has been transformed from a celebration of Empire to an ethnographical museum focusing upon life in the tropics. Combined with a visit to the Artis Zoo this is the best family day out in Amsterdam (see Walk 4).

Madame Tussauds, Kalverstraat 156, tel. 622 9949; Daily 10.00–17.30. Tram 4, 9, 16, 24, 25. Three-dimensional reconstructions of Golden Age master-pieces set above the Peek & Cloppenburg store with stunning views over the Dam—this Madame Tussauds is a most bizarre place to visit. Ultimately it is kitsch (as Tussauds always seems to be), probably because it takes itself rather seriously.

Universiteitsmuseum De Agnietenkapel/University Museum, see Agnietenkapel, above.

Vakbonds Museum/Trade Unions Museum, Henri Polaklaan 9, tel. 624 1166; Tuesday–Friday 11.00–17.00, Sunday 13.00–17.00. Tram 7, 9, 14. The history of the Dutch Trades Unions, of more appeal to those with a knowl-edge of Dutch or a grounding in labour history generally. The building, by Berlage, is worth the visit (see Walk 4).

Verzetsmuseum/Resistance Museum, Lekstraat 63, tel. 644 9797; Tuesday–Friday, 10.00–17.00, weekends 13.00–17.00. Tram 4, 25. The museum of the Dutch Resistance housed in an important modernist building, formerly a synagogue (see Walk 5).

Museum Willet-Holthuysen, Herengracht 605, tel. 523 1870; daily 11.00–17.00. Tram 4, 9, 14. A collection of paintings, sculpture, glass, ceramics, silverware and furniture set in a grand mansion dating from 1687. The collection was assembled by Sandrina Luise Geertruida Holthuysen and her husband Abraham Willet, on her death she left the house and its contents to the nation stipulating that it should be called 'Museum Willet-Holthuysen'. There are a number of paintings from the 17C onwards, of particular interest are the 19C paintings (by the Maris brothers, Rochussen and Bouguereau). The appeal of this museum is that it attracts fewer visitors than most, you can frequently linger in the handsome rooms alone.

Commercial art galleries

The **contemporary art** scene's party has been over since 1988. During the 60s and 70s the Dutch government sponsored artists with a salary, a form of artistic CAP where the state bought unsold works and stored them. That money has been stopped and, in 1992, it was announced that the 200,000 or so works of art accumulated during the time the scheme was running are to be distributed to deserving sites—if the hospital canteen or provincial gallery which receives the long-unseen masterpiece does not like it, then the work will be returned to the artist. The consequence is that the whole art scene has been forced to sort itself out. Artists now have to sell their works. Grants are still available, but they have to be competed for. In every way artists have been forced to concentrate upon presenting themselves before the public. One result has been a lively gallery scene, another has been a cautious investigation of art sponsorship from industry and commerce.

The Stedelijk/Fodor Museum is the principal provincial and municipal showplace for contemporary art in Amsterdam; if you are interested in the scene generally you should first go to these. You will be able to pick up a copy of *Alert* at either, which will be much more comprehensive and up-to-date than this brief listing. English is the language of the contemporary art trade—ask questions and follow your interests. Summer is not the best time of year to visit galleries; they are often closed in July and/or August. In late May, early June there is an art fair, the **Kunstrai**, so called because it is held at the RAI exhibition centre (Tram 4).

Apunto, Damrak 30, tel. 620 4384; open afternoons, closed Sunday, Monday. Tram 4, 9, 16, 24, 25. A spacious upstairs gallery with a good line in young artists—all media, including installations.

Art Affairs, Wittenburgergracht 313, tel. 620 6433; open afternoons, closed Sunday–Tuesday. Bus 22, 28. Very much oriented to sculpture of the blocky, 'sincere' kind.

Arti et Amicitiae, Rokin 112, tel. 623 3367; open afternoons, closed Sunday, Monday. Tram 4, 9, 14, 16, 24, 25. The name can be translated to mean 'Artists and Amateurs'. This is a long-standing club with its own exhibition space for both members and visiting shows.

Aschenbach, Bilderdijkstraat 165c, tel. 685 3580; open afternoons, closed Monday, Tuesday. Tram 3, 12, 13, 14. This is the best gallery to see East European and German artists, often before they happen elsewhere.

Barbara Farber, Keizersgracht 265, tel. 627 6343; open afternoons, closed Sunday, Monday. Tram 13, 14, 17. A major gallery for young American talent and young talent generally. Certainly you should check out what is showing here.

Collection d'Art, Keizersgracht 516, tel. 622 1511; open afternoons, closed Sunday, Monday. Tram 1, 2, 5. Compared to the other galleries this is long established (since 1969); this is where many established artists show.

Espace, Keizersgracht 548, tel. 624 0802; open afternoons, closed Sunday, Monday. Tram 1, 2, 5, 16, 24, 25. Another longer established gallery (1960) which has kept faith with the COBRA artists and some of the lesser known but none the less interesting older generation of figurative painters.

Galerie Rob Jurka, Singel 28, tel. 626 6733; open afternoons, closed Sunday–Tuesday. Tram 1, 2, 4, 5, 9, 13, 16, 17, 24, 25. Twenty years ago this was the most outrageous of the new generation of galleries, Mapplethorpe was first shown here. Still a place to visit.

Van Krimpen, Prinsengracht 629, tel. 622 9375; open afternoons, closed Sunday, Monday. Tram 1, 2, 5. Like Barbara Farber (above) definitely a gallery to visit for unusual and/or about to happen art.

The Living Room, Laurierstraat 70, tel. 625 8449; open afternoons, closed Sunday, Monday. Tram 13, 14, 17. Especially, but not exclusively, a showplace for contemporary Dutch artists.

Mokum, Nieuwzijds Voorburgwal 334, tel. 624 3958; open afternoons, closed Mondays. Tram 1, 2, 5. A delightful spot close to the University. This gallery specialises in magic realist and realist painting which you might not get to see anywhere else.

De Selby, Nieuwe Teertuinen 16, tel. 625 0990; open afternoons, closed Sunday, Monday. Tram 3. With its harbour location this gallery has a squatter feel—very laid-back and self-absorbed.

Swart, Van Breestraat 23, tel. 676 4736; open afternoons, closed Monday, Tuesday. Tram 2, 3, 5, 12, 16. The policy is to show young artists (they are cheaper) and since 1964 has been at the front of every fashion.

Time Based Arts, Bloemgracht 121, tel 627 2620; open afternoons, closed Sunday–Tuesday. Tram 13, 14, 17. An exhibition space and information centre for and about media artists. There is a library and archive (open Fridays, 09.00–17.00).

Torch, Prinsengracht 218, tel. 626 0284; open afternoons, closed Sunday–Wednesday. Tram 13, 14, 17. Some top names show here, international stars like Cindy Sherman. All and any media crammed into a rather small space.

W 139, Warmoesstraat 139, Tel 622 9434; open afternoons, closed Sundays. Tram 4, 9, 16, 24, 25. An enormous space where you will see student work and new artists in all media.

Fons Welters, Bloemstraat 140, tel. 622 7193; open afternoons, closed Sunday, Monday. Tram 13, 14, 17. Dedicated to sculpture (including installations) and especially Dutch sculpture. One to visit.

Notes on Architecture

The city was originally built of wood. The most characteristic gable on wooden houses (for example Begijnhof 34, and Zeedijk 1) is the **pointed gable**, a plain triangle. Very few wooden houses survive anywhere in the Netherlands. The pointed gable was the standard façade from c 1200 up to c 1550 when city ordinances, a ready supply of bricks and stone, and increasing affluence, brought about the age of brick and stone. Whatever fancy or decorated wooden façades might have been built in the city during that time, none have survived. During the Middle Ages the city progressively expanded with the Spui, Grimburgwal and two Voorburgwals, all about 1300. At the end of the 14C the two Achterburgwals were dug (as the name implies) beyond the existing town walls. The Singel (meaning belt, or encircling canal) followed soon after c 1425; this waterway was continued to the S and E with the Kloveniersburgwal and Gelderskade. The great 17C expansion was anticipated by the digging of the Brouwersgracht W from the Singel; the Brouwersgracht was begun in the 16C, the wider 17C continuation is readily distinguishable beyond its junction with the Herengracht.

The brick houses of the Renaissance are characterised by an increasing variety of gable types. The earliest surviving are façades with **roll ornaments** (as at Singel 423, and St Annenstraat 12), a type rare in Amsterdam. These are curvaceous stone-dressed patterns which mark the line of relieving arches across the wall surface and which, when exposed at the sides at roof level, were frequently rounded off with pinnacles and globe-like decorations. Roll ornamentation is not found after c 1610, when it was replaced by the **step-gable**, façades which can be as simple as Herengracht 361, or as ornate and mannered as the Huis Bartolotti at Herengracht 170–72. Decorated with crisp white detail, the frontage dramatised with light and shade from brick buttressing and the whole effect enlivened by brighly coloured shutters, these are the gables which everyone recognises as 'typically Dutch'. Step-gables are generally to be found on houses built between 1600 and 1665. In 1620 the earliest **spout-gables** appear; they are triangular with a short rectangular extension at the top looking for all the world like inverted funnels, explaining their name. Spout-gables are found less commonly on the fronts of houses than on the rear, and they are most common on warehouses. The Prinsengracht, which was designated a commercial area, has many such façades.

The 1613 city extension plan quadrupled the size of the city—at 28 metres the Keizersgracht was the widest of the three grand canals, the Herengracht and Prinsengracht were both slightly narrower at 25 metres. The new canals were dug starting at the Brouwersgracht and in the first stage they reached as far as the Leidsegracht; the Jordaan was developed at the same time. In 1658 work started on the eastern extension of the canals, taking them as far as the Amstel. Surprisingly few of the original 17C houses are left, many were replaced in the 18C and 19C, but as rebuilding has usually been carried out with respect for the original scale of the city and in historical styles this is not immediately apparent to modern visitors.

The **neck-gable** (*'halsgevel'* in Dutch—Frans Hals, therefore, means Francis Neck) is one of the most common 17C façades found on the grand canals. The earliest (c 1640–c 1670) neck-gables are 'elevated neck-gables', a developed form of step-gable where the central element, often picked out with pilasters and topped with a pediment, thrusts up from one or more steps. The earliest neck-gable proper, which has only one step, was built at Herengracht 168 in 1638 and was designed by Philip Vingboons; neck-gables come in many varieties and can be of brick or stone, usually a combination of both, they are often flanked by 'claw pieces', elaborate garlands like fancy book-ends. Neck-gables can be found on buildings as late as 1770.

After 1660 the **bell-gable** became fashionable. A bell-gable, as the name suggests, is bell-shaped. The raised central element of brick is continued to the edge of the façade thus eliminating the need for infills of any kind and the 'step' is gone for ever. There are a number of types, some no more than simple arcs, some with complicated, undercut silhouettes. When they were most popular, in the mid-18C, they were often topped with asymmetric crests and slim dressings of stone more familiar in pattern to furniture work.

During the 18C the **elevated cornice** appeared; the majority of older buildings in Amsterdam have straight cornices and during the 18C it became the thing to raise the façade a little, adding an arched element in the middle (as, for example, at Singel 56), and dress the whole extension with fancy, richly three-dimensional stonework; these extensions are referred to as *'attieks'*. Plain, straight **cornices**, often dressed with no more than a medallion or two, had always been popular on façades, though most of those remaining are the result of 19C building or alteration. After the fall of the United Provinces during the French Revolutionary period the plainer kind of cornice became the norm.

Other characterists which are worth looking out for are the **fanlights**, the glazed overdoors. Other houses have **shutters** in various colours—green and rust-red being the most common. **Stoeps**, the raised steps in front of buildings, often have benches fitted into them on older buildings. The grander houses offer steps on both sides of the stoep.

In the Walks described below a number of later kinds of canal house are described in styles as various as Gothic, art nouveau, Modernist and Post-modern. It is remarkable what variety can be brought to the treatment of three-storey, three-bay rectangular structures.

A view off to the left from the Leidsestraat along the Herengracht

Introduction to the Walks

These five walks are meant to introduce you to a variety of districts within the city. I cannot guess how long they will take you to do. At a smart lick you might cover any one of them in a morning. But if you take your time and enjoy your own diversions, mix them and match them and sit down from time to time to read, then you will perhaps take as many years as I have. I should hate to think that you spent too much time looking at the book while you were actually on the move, for one thing you would miss out on your own experience, for another it is dangerous! You might get lost from time to time; do not worry, the maps at the back of the book will see you back onto the route, streets are very well marked and, of course, you can always ask someone the way.

The special emphasis is upon the architecture of Amsterdam but an effort has been made to avoid a mere itinerary and to draw in historical and cultural references, some of which are dealt with at greater length in the other chapters; you might try the index if you want to see if there is more elsewhere on the Provos or William the Silent.

Attention, too, has been paid to providing routes which offer you indoor as well as outdoor sights. All the major museums are on one or another of the Walks. It might be that the weather will drive you into the churches and museums and I cannot think that it would be too much of a pity if that were so. And if you find yourself numbed by the cold or burned by the sun or simply out of breath, then there are bars and cafés every hundred metres of so. Get in the warm/shade and read on.

1

Essential Amsterdam

It is possible to walk from the Centraal Station to the Rijksmuseum down the main shopping streets of Amsterdam without feeling that you are anywhere particularly interesting—which is to say, you could be anywhere. Were it not for the occasional distinctive perspective to right or left, or the half-dozen bridges and stretches of water which might be invisible to the determined shopper, you could believe that you were anywhere in High Street Europe.

Despite its handsome 19C Northern Renaissance exterior, crowded with symbolic decoration in two and three dimensions, the **Centraal Station** is a thoroughly modern railway 'facility'. It was designed in 1876 by P.J.H. Cuypers, 1827–1921, a remarkable and influential architect whose churches mark the rising self-confidence and self-assertion of Roman Catholicism in the southern parts of the Netherlands during the 19C. Cuypers won the commissions for the Centraal Station and the Rijksmuseum simultaneously. Both buildings are at the same time celebratory edifices and component elements of the up-to-date 19C metropolitan city.

It is important to realise that Cuypers was a radical and controversial architect in his day. His inspiration came from the French architect Viollet-le-Duc who had anticipated the 20C dictum that form must follow function.

Viollet-le-Duc was profoundly grounded in the study of medieval church architecture where the integration of form and function in the arrangement of the various elements was taken for granted; he had announced that all form which was not indicated by structure had to be suppressed. This, coupled with a romantic fascination with the particular history of his own nation and a sense that his role as an architect was to celebrate and propagandise that national history, makes Cuypers' selection as the architect of these two most important buildings a most fortunate one.

Decoration, on the other hand, became increasingly deplored in the 20C tradition, but for Cuypers and his contemporaries it was the very stuff of a building, rationalising and emphasising, instructing and illuminating every part and making of every structure a *Gesamtkunstwerk*, a total work of art. In the debates of the time the arguments ranged over whether Amsterdam should have a classical, or a this-period or a that-period medieval station and national gallery, but the principal disputes, and the most bitter, were over Cuypers' Catholicism.

When it was built, between 1882 and 1889, the Centraal Station finally closed off the Amsterdammers' view of their harbour. Symbolically it shut off one great tradition and opened another. Despite the Noordzee Kanaal of the same period which ensures that Amsterdam has remained one of the world's great ports, Amsterdam has since that time increasingly become the 'European' city of the Netherlands, an industrial and financial centre in kind and identity, while Rotterdam has taken on the role of the home of merchanters. The station is built upon an artificial island and railway lines sweep around the limits of the 19C city from east and west to pass beneath its magnificent roofs. It is not a terminus station like those of Paris and London; if you are travelling on somewhere else you do not need to leave the building. Most rail traffic in the Netherlands, or at least in the Randstad, seems to be drawn through it; it is the railway entrepôt of the nation. The profile is busy, at least as busy as the view the station superseded, that of masts and smokestacks. (The best quick way to view the harbour is to go down to the De Ruijterkade on the N side of the Station and take one of the free ferries across to the Zaandam side.) The style is a Northern Renaissance pot-pourri reminiscent of the great town halls of the Flemish cities to the south, though of course the scale is very much larger.

Despite the apparent unity suggested by the central emphasis with flanking wings, the building is a complex which contains the platforms (designed with a high roof for the steam trains of the time), the services for tickets, waiting and information, and the institutional offices of the railway company. To the visitor a striking feature is the way the basically simple solid geometry of the building has been given a coherence through the decorative scheme—the surface is literally encrusted with allegories on the Amsterdam traditions (for the business class) of sailing, trade and industry. This building is an introduction to the history of Amsterdam as conceived of by the city's governors in the late 19C.

The success of the building can be measured by the degree to which it has been successfully adapted to the conditions of one hundred years later. Many readers of this book will have landed at Schiphol airport and travelled to the city by train. After descending from the train you will have passed beneath the platforms in the pedestrian tunnels which disgorge you into the main entrance hall on the S side out of which you will pass to obtain your first views of the city from the edge of the broad square, the **Stationsplein**, which lies in front of the station.

If you have made the necessary arrangements suggested in the earlier chapters of this book you will, depending on your financial resources, take a taxi or a tram to your hotel. The taxi ranks are to the right against the west wing of the building; the tram stops are grouped to the left and the right across the Stationsplein. If you have not yet made the necessary arrangements for accommodation you should, taking due care as trams are silent, cross the Stationsplein and enter the VVV office on the far side to the left. Within a few metres you have all the necessary facilities for transport, accommodation, luggage storage and the rest to set you up for your stay in the city.

For those who now intend walking from Cuypers' station to his Rijksmuseum the prospect can be described in more scenic terms. From the Stationsplein the view directly in front leads across a wide bridge down the Damrak towards the Dam which may just be visible in the distance depending upon the traffic. To the right behind the screen of a grubby little park-cum-traffic island a 19C frontage of shops and offices, not immediately appealing, continues the main harbour front street, the Prins Hendrikkade, as far as the Haarlemmerbrug over the Singel to the W. To the E the Prins Hendrikkade sweeps around and away as far as the eye can see—not far admittedly—towards the Oosterdok. The most striking building on this side is the **St Nicolaaskerk** (1885–87), designed by A.C. Bleys (1842–1912). This Catholic church, in red-brick baroque, has a look more industrial than spiritual perhaps owing to the layers of grime which disguise an elegant if pedantic reworking of a domed basilican church. The interior is well preserved and the high altar, also by Bleys, is very handsome. For the enthusiast of 19C revivalism, the visit is worth the risk to life and limb of a complex journey through the busy traffic.

Walk out of the Stationsplein, take the left-hand pavement, and cross to the **Damrak**. The Damrak was the original inner harbour of the city, it is now used by a number of tour companies as a starting point for canal tours. The Damrak harbour, as well as being cut off by the station, suffered encroachment during the 19C being filled-in for almost half of its original length from the Dam end. There is enough of it left to provide a picturesque setting, the backs of the houses on the far side looking charmingly ramshackle.

The area to that left-hand (E) side of the Damrak is the Oude Zijd, the bank which was first built upon and the houses and warehouses you see face out onto the Warmoesstraat, at one time the most distinguished street in the city. The street now called the Damrak divides the Oude Zijd from the Nieuwe Zijd. It was originally called Windmolen (Windmill) Street, settlement here dates back to the 13C. The Damrak is lively and tacky: fast food, noisy hotels, a 'Museum of Sex' (actually quite interesting, though more prurient than scientific) and half-way along on the right a rather good bookshop with a wide range of books and maps useful for tourists. There are also some distinguished architectural monuments: Damrak 28–30, an American-style steel-framed mini-skyscraper by J.F. Staal and J. Kropholler, built in 1905, has expressionist sculptures of animals on the façade by J. Mendes da Costa; further down on the left is the **Koopmansbuers**, now usually referred to as the **Beurs van Berlage**, of 1898–1903; just beyond that is the De Bijenkorf building. Opposite, at Damrak 62, is the Allert de Lange bookshop occupying a premises designed, as you can tell from the façade decoration, as a bookshop in 1886 by J. van Looy (1852–1911), who also designed the New York/Metz building in the Leidsestraat (see below). Note also the converted Cineac Cinema next door, dating from 1926.

The Koopmansbeurs (the Stock Exchange) was the first major building in the Netherlands to break with 19C revivalism; it was designed by H.P. Berlage (1856–1934) a man who has influenced the whole of Dutch 20C architecture. His building replaced an early 19C exchange on the site of the Bijenkorf, which had in turn replaced a building by Hendrick de Keyser (1565–1621) of 1608 which stood on the Rokin, still home to many financial concerns. De Keyser's building had brought under one roof the numerous dealers in cargoes and commodities who had blocked the streets around the Oudekerk and the Damrak at the end of the 16C.

This earlier building is echoed in the use of the arcade both outside at the front (which faces onto the Beursplein) as well as on the inside. De Keyser's building also featured a tower. It is a simple basilica with attached tower (or campanile, for there is a bell inside), the interior being a large nave or hall flanked by arcaded galleries. The exterior is decorated with a mixture of decorative features in stone and brick, sculpture (by J. Mendes da Costa and L. Zijl) and variations in the style of the windows which creates continually interesting surfaces; the doorways are sunk deep into the façade so that even here in the dull north there is a drama of light and shade.

The tower (towers are a feature of Berlage's and Amsterdam School architecture) is completed by a handsome art noveau clock (although Berlage would not have thought of it as art nouveau, his affiliation at that time was to the Nieuwe Kunst, something more akin to British Art and Crafts); the clock is embellished with sensible encouragements to passersby to 'Duur uw uur' and 'Beidt uw tijd', meaning 'Last (or Dear) your hour', and 'Bide your time'.

The Stock Exchange has long since departed (the Effectenbeurs or Commodities Exchange is now next door) and the building is now used as a concert hall (it is the home of the Netherlands Philharmonic) and exhibition space. You can get a glimpse of the interior by visiting the café at the Beursplein end; visits can be arranged, check at the VVV. The De Bijenkorf (The Beehive) building of 1911–13 is in a grand, Lutyens-like neo-classical revivalist style interesting for its scale (competing with the Royal Palace to dominate the Dam Square) and function (it has always been a department store).

The Damrak terminates at the DAM SQUARE, a space divided into two by the main flow of traffic. To the left the middle-European elegance of the Grand Hotel Krasnopolsky and, in front of that, the **Nationaal Monument** (1956) in undistinguished isolation on the traffic island. This commemorates the nation's suffering during the Second World War. The urns surrounding the monument contain soil from each of the country's provinces and from Indonesia, too.

During the late 1960s and early 1970s the Dam square and the Nationaal Monument became the rallying point of the youth movement, drugs were traded openly and despite the city administrators hosing it down regularly, youngsters flocked from all over Europe, their numbers swelled by backpackers from North America, to sit on the steps and watch each other watching each other. The Vondelpark and large parts of the inner city became hippy campsites, street theatres and marketplaces.

Beyond the Krasnopolsky the Damstraat leads E toward the Wallen and the red light district; directly across the square and concealed by buildings the Rokin, filled-in during the 19C, leads towards the Munttoren and the Rembrandtsplein; just to the right of the Peek and Cloppenburg store (here a **Madame Tussaud's** with remarkable tableaux including, presently, The Night Watch of all things) and parallel to the Rokin the Kalverstraat, a very busy pedestrianised shopping street, leads in the same direction.

Across the cobbled square lies the rectangular bulk of the Koninklijk Paleis (Royal Palace). The large church tucked away to the right is the Nieuwe Kerk. Aross the square from the Kalverstraat, running parallel to the Damrak, is the Nieuwendijk, like the Kalverstraat a pedestrianised shopping street but a little rougher, especially at night. During the summer months the square in front of the Palace is given over to entertainers and buskers of all kinds and nationalities. On a warm evening this can be a very pleasant place to stroll.

The whole of the W side of the Dam is taken up by the **Koninklijk Paleis**, built between 1648 and 1655, designed by Jacob van Campen (1595–1657) and completed by Daniel Stalpaert (?1615–76). (Admission: open daily 12.30–16.00 in July and August; guided tours Wednesday 13.30 during the rest of the year.)

It was originally built as the Town Hall, and succeeded a Gothic building that lay on the N side of the Dam which burned down in 1652. It made an immediate impression upon contemporaries: Constantijn Huygens called it the eighth wonder of the world, Sir William Temple, the English Ambassador, spitefully dismissed it as 'a big little thing'. Big indeed, it must surely have stood out dramatically from the streets of medieval gabled houses around it in its time as well as from the newly erected merchants' palaces on the new canals, the grander of which echoed its stately classicism.

In 1808 the building was commandeered as a Royal Palace by Louis Bonaparte and the heavy French Empire furniture was left there by him; at the establishment of the Orangist monarchy it was handed back to the city by King William I, so that the reigning monarch when in residence became the guest of the city. In 1935 the city sold the palace to the State.

Resting on foundations of no fewer than 13,659 piles, the large square building is designed in a developed Palladian classicist style; the noticeable absence of any formal central doorway was deliberate, the object being to prevent sudden entrance being forced by a mob—there are slits set into the wall for small arms fire by a defending militia. It should be borne in mind that as well as being the administrative headquarters of city government and the principal place for receiving honoured guests, the Town Hall was also the seat of magistracy (the blocks which supported the scaffold are still visible above the entrance) and the city bank.

The building is by any standards a severe and restrained exercise in baroque classicism; the grey ashlar gives the whole edifice a grimness which is quite as imposing as the sober *gravitas* projected in contemporary portraits of the city's elite. The spare external sculptural ornament, most above the roof-line, is by *Artus Quellin the Elder* (1609–68). The pediments show the Maid of Amsterdam, an allegorical and generalised figure representing the city, surrounded by marine deities on the front of the building and by river gods at the back. Above are figures of Peace, between Prudence and Justice; and Atlas, between Temperance and Vigilance. The enormous cupola, visible from far away for sea-borne travellers, has a weathervane in the form of a galleon ('t *Koggeschip*: the 'Dutch cog' of 15–16C English literature).

Inside the palace the first room entered is the rather cramped Vierschaar, or Tribunal, with *sculptures by Quellin—the main piece comprising reliefs of Justice, Wisdom and Mercy, separated by caryatids. The magnificent *Burgerzaal (the Citizens' Hall; for Louis, his throne room) above has a lower part entirely of marble. It was one of the largest covered spaces of the age and has an extraordinary floor. The sculptures here are school of Quellin, while the ceiling paintings date from the early 18C.

Richly decorated galleries surround the Burgerzaal, a feature of the sculptures being that the subjects above the doors relate to the function of the room beyond (for example, Icarus outside the bankruptcy court). Two adjacent reliefs symbolising Fidelity (a dog watching over his dead master) and Secrecy (a figure of Silence) are ascribed to Rombout Verhulst. The large paintings of early Dutch history are by Jan Lievens, Jacob Jordaens, Govert Flinck and Juriaan Ovens.

The painting by Ovens of the Conspiracy of Claudius Civilis was preferred by the municipal authorities to a rendering of the same subject by Rembrandt (the cut-down remainder is now in Stockholm)—the reason for this rejection probably being that Rembrandt did not follow the iconographical programme of the series from its source in an earlier 17C book by Otto van Veen.

The Schepenzaal, the large room in the centre of the W wing, contains a picture of Moses the Lawgiver by Ferdinand Bol, above a rich chimneypiece. There are also fine chimneypieces in the rooms opening off the E wing; here too are paintings from Roman history by Flinck, Bol and Lievens. Whereas the sculpture is tied to explicating the functions of the various parts of the building, the paintings celebrate the values of the ruling group of patricians who saw themselves very much in the character of Roman Senators.

The balcony gallery, offering a view from above of the Quellin reliefs, was used for the reading of proclamations, while it was to the small room next door that the condemned were brought before stepping out to execution. The northern room beyond has scenes from the Old Testament by Flinck and J.G. van Bronkhorst, the Blessing of Moses (1736–38) by Jacob de Wit, and *trompe l'oeil paintings above the doors, also by De Wit.

To the N of the palace stands the **Nieuwe Kerk**, which takes its name from being the church on the Nieuwe Zijd, and was begun in about 1408 (it was twice burnt down and rebuilt during the ensuing century) largely through the benefactions of Willem Eggert, lord of Purmerend, who dedicated it to St Catherine. The north transept was completed in 1538–44, but the whole church was again badly damaged by fire in 1645, one result being that little of the interior furnishing is earlier than that date. It is here that the nation's royal investitures are solemnised.

The church is usually open Monday–Saturday, 11.00–16.00; Sunday, 12.00 to 15.00; closed January and February. As it is much used for exhibitions, concerts and suchlike you might find that features of interest are hidden and you may also be confronted with a stiff entry charge.

The interior contains a number of monuments to admirals, these being, to the left of the W door, Van Kinsbergen (1735–1819) by P.J. Gabriel; in the N transept the tomb by Rombout Verhulst of Jan van Galen, who died in 1653 after a battle at Leghorn; in the choir a monument by Verhulst to De Ruyter (1607–76), who died at Syracuse of wounds received in battle against the French Admiral Duquesne. On a nearby pillar a bust medallion of Admiral Bentinck (1745–1831).

Also noteworthy are the panels of the organ case by J.G. van Bronkhorst; the pulpit of 1648 carved by Aelbert Vinckenbrink on the model of one lost in the fire; a window in the N transept containing all that is left of the stained glass of c 1650 by Bronkhorst (Count William IV granting arms to the city); in the S choir aisle a small painted memorial to Willem Eggert, the church's early benefactor; on a pillar in the S transept the urn of the poet Joost van den Vondel (1586–1679); and the brass and marble choir screen (c 1650) by Johannes and Jacob Lutma.

Just N of the church there is a small street called Blaeuerf (Blaeu's premises); this is where the famous atlases and globes of Johannes Blaeu were produced during the 17C. Behind the Palace across the road at Nieuwezijds Voorburgwal 182 is the former main Post Office built in a fussy town-hall Gothic in 1895–99; it is now converted into a shopping and office complex with a remarkably foolish looking Po-Mo (Post-Modern) entrance. The original decoration can be seen in parts of the interior.

The walk leaves the Dam via the Kalverstraat, an ancient and fascinating road which, if you raise your eyes above the shop fronts, retains many features of interest. For example, a short way down on the right-hand side there is the *Pappegaai* (Parrot) doorway beyond which lies a 19C Catholic church. Further on at 92 there is a cobbled alleyway leading to a decorated entrance. This is the old gateway to the Burgerweeshuis or Orphanage (not for street urchins but for the children of burghers of the city), established in 1520 and moved here in 1578 where it remained until 1960.

Beyond the gateway now lies **Het Amsterdams Historisch Museum** (open daily 11.00–17.00; admission charge), where the story of the city is told. The museum opened in 1975 (on 27 October, precisely 700 years after the first mention of Amsterdam in an official document), moving from the cramped quarters it had occupied in the Waag since 1926. The Kalverstraat entrance is the main one, but there are others from the Begijnhof on the S and St Luciensteeg on the N; the latter gateway dates from the 16C (rebuilt 1634) and alongside there is a collection of façade stones from demolished houses.

At the beginning of the 15C this area was a triangular island enclosed by the Spui on the S, NieuwezZijds Voorburgwal on the W, and a large ditch, the Begijnensloot, on the E (running parallel to and immediately W of Kalverstraat). The S end of the island was occupied by the Begijnhof, and in 1414 a convent (of St Lucy) was built on the N end.

In 1578, when Amsterdam sided with the Protestants, the convent was given to the Burgerweeshuis administrators, a new wing, by Hendrik de Keyser, was built on the E side of the courtyard. Later, c 1630, the orphanage took over an old men's home situated on the E side of the Begijnensloot, using this for orphan boys, and two years later a new gallery, attributed to Pieter de Keyser (son of Hendrik; 1595–1676), was built to run E to W along the side of what was now the boys' courtyard. The orphanage then had two courtyards—one for the boys on the E and one for the girls (the old convent) on the west.

In 1634 the convent buildings were demolished, giving way to new wings, designed by Jacob van Campen, on the N and W sides; the S wing, built rather later than the others, cut the old convent courtyard into two, the smaller part, alongside the Begijnhof, being used as a playground. As a part of this reconstruction, the girls' orphanage was given its own entrance in St Luciensteeg.

The next major change came in 1745 when Hendrik de Keyser's E wing was given external and internal renovation to bring it into harmony with the other wings. At about the same time a start was made with covering the Begijnensloot, which was entirely filled in by 1865. The orphanage was moved to a countryside location in 1960. Recent (1960s and 1970s) restoration and conversion to a museum (by B. van Kasteel and J. Schipper) has, as far as possible, retained the exterior façades, and has also produced one imaginative change, namely the Civic Guard Gallery, running along the former course of the Begijnensloot (as this is a public right of way you can wander through here for free, although the pictures are even more interestingly viewed from inside the museum, through the windows).

The gateway off Kalverstraat (by Joost Bilhamer; 1581) carries figures of a boy and a girl orphan; the later verse carved below (asking for contributions) is by the poet Joost van den Vondel. Beyond the gateway the visitor is in Pieter de Keyser's gallery of 1632, to the right being the restaurant, on the site of the convent cowshed and later of the orphanage carpentry workshop; the restaurant takes its name from carved figures of David and Goliath (c 1650) which until 1862 stood in a maze in the Jordaan.

Opposite is the boys' courtyard, the W wing of which is used for temporary exhibitions. To the left of this is the Civic Guard Gallery which runs as a covered 'museum street' through to the Begijnhof.

The militias of Amsterdam and other Dutch cities were created at the end of the 14C for the purpose of imposing law and order. They were made up of groups of marksmen and following the practice of the time banded together as guilds, e.g. of St George and St Sebastian (two military saints). These guilds merged in 1580, and in 1672 a formal Civic Guard was formed. The practice of commissioning group portraits dates from c 1530 and lasted well over a century (see History and also Rijksmuseum, Night Watch). The oldest groups here are from the first half of the 16C.

The museum is entered via a glazed entrance on the W side of the courtyard. The story of Amsterdam is laid out part chronologically, part thematically on three floors. The displays are explained in Dutch and English and (free) leaflets in English are available at the ticket desk. Immediately to the right of the entrance is the Regentenkamer, the Administrators' meeting room (not normally open), restored as nearly as possible to its 17C state.

On the GROUND FLOOR, **Room 1** is introductory, with a floor plan and an illuminated map together illustrating the growth of the city, while a large, striking painting of the IJ in 1686 by Willem van de Velde the Younger provides appropriate background. **Room 2** (Early History) is, understandably perhaps, somewhat short on material, and it is really only in **Room 3**, devoted to the growth of commerce and industry in the 14C and 15C, that the displays become interesting. Notable here are a huge metal cauldron, possibly used to soften tar in shipbuilding (it was discovered during the excavation of the metro), as well as vitrines displaying shoes, tools, tailoring equipment, etc., all well presented with accompanying reproductions of old pictures showing the articles in use.

A short underground passage reaches **Room 4** and the 16C, with armour, some massive silver drinking horns, pictures by Dirk Barendsz. of The Longbowmen and by Hendrick Vroom of the IJ c 1610, and portraits, all by unknown artists, of Charles V, Philip II, the Duke of Alva and William of Orange (see History chapter for their association with the city). Undoubtedly the most extraordinary exhibit here is a bird's-eye *View of Amsterdam (1538) by Cornelis Anthonisz. This is the oldest known plan of Amsterdam (N is at the bottom). It is striking how the Amstel clearly divides the town, the Dam and the old Stadhuis are clearly visible.

Room 5 illustrates marine development during the 17C and 18C, here being maps and globes by Johannes Blaeu, a portrait of Blaeu (1603) by Jan van Rossum, and several sea scenes. The theme of **Room 6** is the growth of the city and of municipal organisations during the Golden Age. There are various exhibits but the stars are two pictures: one, of 1656 by Johannes Lingelbach, shows the Dam with the new Stadhuis under construction and, in the centre, the old Waag (built 1565, demolished 1808 to improve Louis Napoleon's view), a building of key importance in the days of Amsterdam's supremacy in the commodities trade. The other picture is Adriaan van Nieulandt's *Procession of Lepers on Copper Monday, absorbing for all its

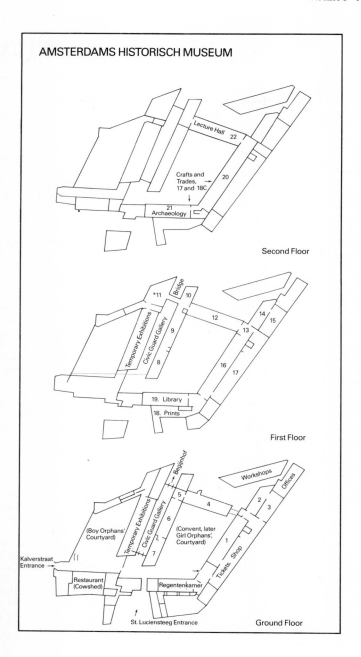

AMSTERDAMS HISTORISCH MUSEUM

Lecture Hall 22

Crafts and Trades, 17 and 18C

20

21 Archaeology

Second Floor

*11 Bridge 10

Temporary Exhibitions

Civic Guard Gallery

9

8

12

14 15

13

16 17

19. Library

18. Prints

First Floor

Begijnhof

Workshops

Offices

5

4

2 3

Temporary Exhibitions

Civic Guard Gallery

6

(Boy Orphans' Courtyard)

(Convent, later Girl Orphans', Courtyard)

1

7

Kalverstraat Entrance

Restaurant (Cowshed)

Regentenkamer

Tickets, Shop

St. Luciensteeg Entrance

Ground Floor

characters and other detail all admirably explained by a video film alongside.

The ground floor ends with **Room 7**, concerned mainly with commerce, exemplified by portraits of the Bicker family, leaders within the Amsterdam oligarchy.

On the FIRST FLOOR, **Room 8** continues the theme of 17C and 18C commerce and finance, the latter emphasised by Job Berckheyde's picture of the courtyard of De Keyser's Beurs (Stock Exchange) in c 1660. (Rooms 8 and 9 both have windows offering good views of the Civic Guard Gallery.)

Room 9 describes the development of the city and daily life during the same period. Here there is another bird's-eye view, this one by Jan Christiaan Micker, c 1620, and again with N at the foot of the picture. Church life in the 17C and 18C is the theme of **Room 10**, of particular interest being pictures of the interiors of the Oude Kerk and the Nieuwe Kerk.

A bridge across the Civic Guard Gallery leads to ***Room 11**, a room which many visitors may well judge to be the museum's most rewarding. The theme here, social welfare in the 17C and 18C or, more popularly and simply, Rich and Poor, is vividly brought home by several large portrait groups of citizens concerned with charitable activities. Each group tells its story, and each reveals facets of contemporary life, particularly moving being two pictures of about 1650 by Jan Victors portraying the clothing and feeding of orphan girls, while a contrast is provided by Adriaen Backer's more stuffily formal group of the Regentesses of the Burgerweeshuis.

Rooms 12 to 15, reached by returning across the bridge, cover further 17C and 18C themes. Elegance is the emphasis of **Room 12**, though a case of lances and muskets seems out of place; **Rooms 13** and **14** are devoted to both fine and applied art with, among them, works by Jan van Huysum and Rachel Ruysch; and **Room 15** looks at Instruction (Learned Institutions) and Amusements, notable here being the Anatomy Lesson of Professor Roëll by Cornelis Troost. **Rooms 16** and **17** bring the visitor to the 19C and 20C; **Room 18** doubles as Print Room and home for temporary exhibitions, and **Room 19** is the Library.

On the SECOND FLOOR there is some archaeological material, but for many visitors the main interest will be provided by **Rooms 20** and **21**, themed as Crafts and Trades of the 17C and 18C and imaginatively presented as a series of divisions devoted to, for example, the baker, the distiller (with some fine old bottles), the silversmith, the brickmaker and the potter. At the top of the building, up a spiral staircase, there is a room where you can listen to recordings of the city's various carillons and even try your hand at playing one taken from the Munttoren.

You can leave the museum by returning to the Kalverstraat entrance or you can pass via the Civic Guard Gallery and the Begijnhof to the Spui.

The Kalverstraat continues as far as the Munttplein, but we shall follow it only as far as the Spui, the first trafficked crossroad. The Spui leads out into an open space, the right-hand side bounded by ancient walls (the backs of the houses facing on to the Begijnhof), the left by first the road and then old buildings and ahead, in the middle distance, the Nieuwezijds Voorburgwal. The Spui was the venue for many of the Provos' happenings in the late 1960s, the site ostensibly chosen because of the small statue of a boy, the so-called *Lieverdje* (little darling), which had been commissioned in 1960 by a tobacco company and had thereafter became the focus of anti-smoking protests which were thinly disguised anti-establishment protests. Each Saturday night the Provos pulled off one prank or other and more often than not the Amsterdam police over-reacted. The dramas were played out in front of Amsterdam's intelligentsia as they sat on the terraces of the Hoppe and Luxembourg cafés.

The **Begijnhof**, reached via a doorway bearing the figure of a *begijn* half-way down on the right (or from the far side if you came directly from the Historical Museum), was founded in 1346. It is a peaceful courtyard of small old houses (mainly 16–18C). The *Houten Huis* (the Wooden House) at 34 dates from c 1470 (restored 1957) and retains its wooden gable. No. 35 is a café and information centre. The church in the centre was granted to the Scottish Presbyterians in 1607 and rebuilt in 1727, while the inconspicuous little Roman Catholic chapel facing it dates from 1671 and functioned as a hidden church until 1795.

Opposite the Begijnhof, beyond the trees, Voetboogstraat leads S from the Spui to reach Heiligeweg. The doorway at the far end, opposite the junction, is the preserved entrance to the Rasphuis, with sculptures in the style of De Keyser (1603) and later (1663); this was once a prison for men where petty criminals had to rasp brazil-wood for use in dyeing, hence the name. (Women were sent to the Spinhuis, see Walk 2.)

From the Spui it is probably better not to cross the Nieuwezijds Voorburgwal, appealing though the canal-side walk along the Singel might seem, as there is no footpath and if a tram and bicycles arrive at the same time you will probably cause an accident. Stay to the left of the Spui and walk past Singel 411, a handsome Lutheran church dating to 1633 (now part of the University), and past Singel 413 to 423, a row of handsomely restored houses, mainly from the 18C and 19C. No. 423 is a beautiful building of 1606 decorated with roll ornaments and pinnacles which has served various functions over the centuries, including being a militia house. Do not gaze up and walk at the same time because the pavement in front of the **University Library** (Monday–Friday 10.00–13.00, 14.00–16.30) at 425 is littered with bicycles. The library houses the Joost van den Vondel Collection and also a Script Museum tracing the story of writing from prehistoric to modern days. (Entry by appointment only, tel. 525 2284.)

Across the water the imposing church is the Krijtberg (chalk mountain) designed by A. Tepe in 1881, on a plot wider behind than in front. The interior decorations are extremely well-preserved and any admirer of Victorian Gothic should make an effort to see them. There are several interesting buildings to the left of the Krijtberg—at 450, two houses along, and at 456 are 17C houses with step-gables, and the very tall house with a neck-gable at 460 (bearing the date 1662) is built to a design by Philip Vingboons.

The bridge to the right leads SW via the Koningsplein to the Leidsestraat, the road to the left is the Heiligeweg which leads N back to the Kalverstraat. The Singel continues as far as the Muntplein—on the far side is the floating **Flower Market**, open every day except Sunday, 09.00–18.00. The market straddles across from barges onto the pavement and at times the way can be blocked with the volume of tourists and office workers. As well as cut flowers you can buy seeds and bulbs. Notice, too, *D'Eendragt*, a picturesque warehouse with six storeys of numbered doors at Singel 516–18.

The Leidsestraat runs from the Singel across the Herengracht, the Keizersgracht and the Prinsengracht before terminating at the Leidseplein; it is one of the busier concourses in the city with pedestrians, trams and service vehicles bustling in both directions. The buildings are substantially modern and many are picturesque and interesting; for example, 455 on the NW corner with the Keizersgracht, the New York/Metz building of 1891, which has the famous roof café (1933, refurbished 1986) by Gerrit Rietveld

(1888–1964) offering excellent views across the city. One of the methods of 'solving' the problem of abutting gable-fronted buildings at corners is to add a corner cupola as with the New York/Metz, or, as at 508, by 'bevelling' the corner and adding a tower ... and perhaps a bust of Rembrandt. There is a Torture Museum at Leidsestraat 27, open daily 10.00–17.00.

The **Leidseplein** is the open space at the end of the Leidsestraat; it is the Amsterdam equivalent of Time Square or Leicester Square though not quite as trashy and certainly not as menacing. It is surrounded with late-Victorian and Edwardian buildings of some interest though advertising hoardings, tram power-lines and the paraphernalia of a tourist trap obscure lines of sight.

As you enter the square on the immediate right there are a number of café terraces surrounding a small open space which during the winter months has an open-air skating rink. The large, neo-Renaissance building on the far right on the far side of this area is the **Stadsschouwburg** (City Theatre) of 1894 designed principally by J.L. Springer who, following the negative response to the building, went into early retirement. It is quite possible that an English-language production will be running here, though tickets are usually sold out well in advance. To the left the E side is dominated by fast-food outlets and the like; there are usually street enter-tainers in the open space here playing to the busy and responsive crowds of tourists and shoppers.

Two of the city's most famous rock venues lie close to the Leidseplein. Behind the Stadsschouwburg at Lijnbaansgracht 234a is **De Melkweg** which has altered its image in recent years becoming far more of an arts centre. The **Paradiso** at Weteringschans 6–8 (the broad street running SE out of the square), although small, remains an important stop-off point on many bands' European tours. It seems apposite that Amsterdam's rock and roll credentials were earned respectively at a converted dairy and a con-verted church.

The Leidseplein proper includes the area to the S of the junction of Marnixstraat and Weteringschans, straddling this thoroughfare and con-tinuing as far as the Leidsebrug which crosses the Singelgracht, the line of 17C defences which were not breached by development until the late 19C. For many enthusiasts of early modern architecture the **American Hotel** on the far SW side at Leidseplein 28 is a place of pilgrimage. It was designed by W. Kromhout (1864–1940) and built between 1898 and 1902. Like Berlage, Kromhout eschewed revivalist styles and took great pleasure in simple masses of forms, surface decoration (note the mixture of brick colour and type) and a somewhat Expressionist reworking of traditional features (note the tower and the oriels below the dormer windows on the façade). One of the pleasures of a visit to Amsterdam is taking tea or morning coffee and cakes in the later art deco café.

Leave the Leidseplein via the Korte Leidsedwarsstraat, a narrow cobbled street lined with restaurants and a solitary sex shop, which opens out at the end on a broad quay beside the Lijnbaansgracht at the junction of the Spiegelgracht, one of the most picturesque stretches of water in the city and at the southern end of the main antique shop area. Cross the bridge to your right and you will see the Rijksmuseum on the far side of two broad traffic streets, first the Weteringschans and then, across the bridge over the Singelgracht, the Stadhouderskade.

The ****Rijksmuseum** (open Tuesday–Saturday, 10.00–17.00. Sunday and holidays, 13.00–17.00), is the Netherlands' national museum and contains the largest and finest collection of Dutch paintings in existence, almost every one of the great Dutch artists being represented. In addition, there is a small selection of Flemish, Italian, and Spanish paintings. The sculpture, applied arts (especially ceramics), Asiatic, and historical collections are in themselves worth a visit, as are the dolls' houses. The museum includes a print room, study collections and library; and there are audio-visual shows with commentaries in English (David Roëll Room, First Floor).

The collection dates from 1808 when Louis Bonaparte decreed the establishment of a Royal Museum. Being housed in the palace (formerly the Town Hall) on the Dam, it at once received a fine collection of paintings on loan from the city, including Rembrandt's Night Watch, none of which, of course, needed to be moved. With the departure of the French and the accession of William I the museum was re-established at the Trippenhuis (Kloveniersburgwal 29). This accommodation was always too cramped and P.J.H. Cuypers, after much dispute and discussion, was commissioned to design today's building, to which the museum moved in 1885. For him, trained for 25 years as a church architect, it was natural to think a building all the way through from the basic ground plan (for the Rijksmuseum he adapted the plan of Van Campen's Town Hall) to the minutiae of decoration. If it were stripped of all its objects, Cuypers' building would still tell the history it was built to display. As we have seen, Cuypers also designed the Centraal Station and the buildings stand at either entrance to Victorian Amsterdam (the Museum looked out over fields) asserting his vision of a national style.

Approached from the S, the visitor is first impressed by the variety of the Gothic silhouette; as you get closer you are presented with a cross-vaulted porch adorned with figures representing the crafts (the building as a whole straddles the road like a triumphal arch). The four façades of the building are all decorated with reliefs, designed by G. Sturm, not only depicting incidents in and aspects of the history of art and craft in the Netherlands but also celebrating the constitution of the nation. From the city side it is difficult to get any distant view, but as you approach up the Reguliersgracht the various masses and towers shift pleasingly in relation to each other. There has been much subsequent extension and alteration, notably in 1898 and 1909.

There are two entrances to the museum, both facing N onto the Stadhouderskade, one on either side of the road which passes under the building. The one usually employed is that on the right-hand side. Access is cramped and when one or another is closed, say for the installation of a large exhibition, you may have a short wait in the cold and the rain—dress up warm. From the main entrance (cloakrooms just inside, the café is on your immediate right as you enter) visitors ascend stairs to the large hall (**Room 237**), where there are information and sales desks. Application may be made at the information desk for introductory cards to the Six Collection of Paintings, for this a passport is required.

The hall has recently been whitewashed, and the stained glass windows now appear more as works of art in their own right rather than mere fenestration. They are by W.F. Dixon of London and carry the date 1884. Together the windows in the hall form a massive triptych synthesising the literary, artistic, constitutional and economic histories of the nation, continuing, therefore, the themes of the decoration of the exterior.

Many visitors come primarily, or even only, to see Rembrandt's Night Watch and the museum's four Vermeers. The former (in Room 224, with explanatory material in 223) can be seen and approached direct from the information desk by way of the broad Gallery of Honour (Rooms 236–229, presently hung with Golden Age masterpieces, see below); as you face the Night Watch, the Vermeers are in Room 221a, to your left. If you have a longer stay in mind glance through the six sections below and then choose which part or parts of the museum to visit. To attempt to visit the whole of the museum in any worthwhile detail could easily absorb several days.

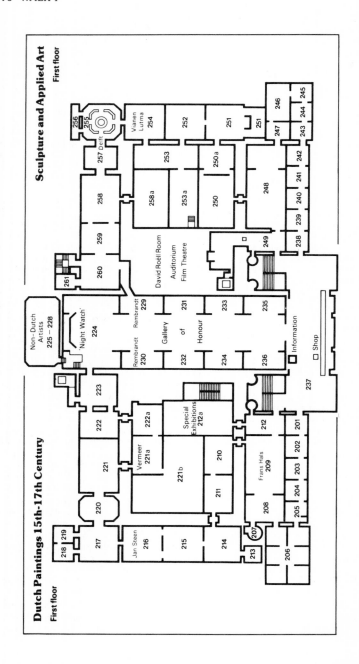

Dutch Paintings 15th–17th Century
First floor

Sculpture and Applied Art
First floor

Dutch Paintings, 15C–17C (First Floor. Rooms 201–224, 229–235)

The principal attraction, the Dutch paintings, are presently being re-hung following the huge 1991–92 Rembrandt exhibition. It is possible that there will be some variation from the listing provided below but the tour of the rooms includes all the pictures you are likely to come across—the most important works, if not out on loan, are always on display. Rooms are in places described in order of convenience of visiting and not necessarily in strict numerical sequence.

In the early years, in a Catholic Netherlands, much art was commissioned by the Church; functionally and iconographically this gives the dominant character to the art of the earlier period. The local, precious, Gothic style came under pressure for change in the early 16C when Dutch artists, most importantly Jan van Scorel, began to visit Italy and absorb Renaissance ideas.

Room 201: Geertgen tot Sint Jans: Adoration of the Magi; Master of the Virgo inter Virgines: Mary and the Infant Jesus with saintly women (c 1490), Resurrection; Dutch School (15C): an interesting series of 18 pictures on the Life of Christ. **Room 202**: Master of Alkmaar: The Seven Works of Charity, with a background of a late medieval town (1504); Jan Mostaert: Tree of Jesse, Adoration of the Magi, Portrait of a Lady (c 1535–40); South Holland Master: Allegory of the Vanity of Human Life; Anon: St Catherine. **Room 203**: J.C. van Oostsanen: Portrait of Jan van Egmond, Calvary. **Room 204**: Cornelis Engebrechtsz.: two scenes from the life of Christ; Lucas van Leyden: *Worship of the Golden Calf. **Room 205**: Jan van Scorel: Portrait of a man, Mary Magdalene, a Mona Lisa-like image set against a landscape; Maerten van Heemskerck (a pupil of Van Scorel): Portrait of Pieter Bicker Gerritsz. (c 1529, before the artist's visit to Italy), The Erythaean Sibyl (after the visit to Italy).

Room 206. This is a complicated room divided into several subsections: Anthonis Mor van Dashorst (Antonio Moro): Portraits of Sir Thomas Gresham and his wife; Jan van Scorel: Bathsheba; later 16C painting from the Netherlands south and north is represented by Joos de Momper in landscape and Adriaen Key in portraiture, amongst others; Pieter Aertsen (The Egg Dance) from Amsterdam and Joachim Bueckelaer (The Well-Stocked Kitchen), his follower from Antwerp where both had thriving careers, are recognised as having been important in combining daily life imagery with symbolic or narrative religious material. Here also are examples from the two principal Dutch Mannerist schools, Haarlem and Utrecht: from Haarlem the Flemish immigrant Karel van Mander (The Magnanimity of Scipio), who was also a distinguished poet and historian, and Cornelis Cornelisz. (Bathsheba, The Fall of Man); from Utrecht Abraham Bloemaert, a man as important in his role as a teacher as for his painting. Note also the full-length militia portrait by Cornelis Ketel: The Company of Captain Rosencrans and Lieutenant Pauw. Amsterdam militia companies preferred full-length portraits from the late 16C onward (there is a very good display at the Amsterdam Historical Museum, see above).

What came to be known as the Golden Age began properly during the stadholdership of Prince Frederick Hendrick (1625–47). Political and religious dissension eased, while trade and the arts flourished. Those elements of painting heralded in the previous room—individualised portraiture, daily life imagery, an exhibitionist approach to refined technique—came to the fore and Dutch painting can be said to have developed a national character. Artists also tended to specialise (as landscape, portrait, genre or still life painters) in the highly competitive market which succeeded the late-medieval aristocratic, ecclesiastical and municipal commissions. The noblest genre remained 'history' painting, the depiction of narratives taken from biblical, classical and historical sources.

Rooms 207, 208, 209 and **210** are hung with a variety of works—a wide range of subject matters and scales are represented. Smaller paintings, such as the minute pair of landscapes by Jan Breughel, are in the tiny, circular Room 207.

Room 208 is usually dominated by **Frans Hals**: *The Company of Captain Reynier Reael (the 'Lean Company', 1637, though see also Room 236, below). The figures on the right were finished by Pieter Codde—Hals did not feel inclined to travel all the way to Amsterdam (19km) to finish this most prestigious commission and an acrimonious correspondence over the matter remains. (Other Hals paintings in this and the following rooms include The Merry Toper and *The Marriage Portrait of Isaac Massa and Beatrix van der Laen.)

An important group portrait of the Regents and Regentesses of the Leper Asylum by Werner van den Valckert shows this peculiarly Dutch emphasis on group identity in another context. Superficially it is not so different from the Seven Works of Charity in Room 202 except, it may be noticed, those doing good in the Valckert painting are doing it for the good of the recipients rather than for the good of their own souls, a subtle distinction which indicates the Protestant nature of the commission.

There are also examples of still life painting, the portraiture of things, notably by Pieter Claesz. and Willem Heda; although the principal subject would seem to be the surfaces of things, still life painters invariably represent the material world to comment upon human vanity, the transience of life and the deception of appearance.

Vigorous figure paintings from this earlier period include works by Jan Lievens (Samson and Delilah) and Gerrit van Honthorst (The Merry Fiddler). Honthorst, a Utrecht artist, experienced at first hand the revolutionary painting of Caravaggio in Rome.

The landscapes of Hendrick Averkamp (Winter landscape with ice-skaters) and the earlier works of Esaias van de Velde are crammed with incidents like those of their 16C forebears, but already show that consideration for an overall and realistic atmosphere which characterised Dutch landscape painting. This could also be said for Adriaen van de Venne, whose work combines portrait, landscape and genre—*Fishing for Souls is a satire on the Reformation (from a Calvinist point of view, he was painter to the Princes of Orange and a native of the extremely Calvinist city of Middelburg where his family ran a printing works).

Off Room 209, straight ahead of you as you enter from 208, is Room 212, not part of the gallery space; off this is Room 212A which is used for special exhibitions.

Room 210. Also by Van de Venne are The Harbour at Middelburg and Princes Maurice and Frederick Hendrick at the Valkenburg Horse Fair, vivid images which combine truthful renderings of particular places (the polder to the right of the Harbour, the town in the background of the Horse Fair) and personalities (the eponymous Princes and the painter and his family who bow to them). Hendrick Averkamp's Winterscene shows a similar 'all human life is there' image of the town of Kampen.

The painting of social life, usually with a moral message, succeeded 16C representations of biblical and moral tales in contemporary costume: examples from Pieter Codde, Jan Miense Molenaer (the husband of Judith

Leyster whose Serenade hangs two rooms further on) and Willem Duyster which introduce the kinds of bourgeois interior we more readily associate with later masters such as Vermeer and De Hooch. More typical of the 1620s are the Buitenpartijen, outdoor parties, by Willem van Buytewech and Dirck Hals—exquisite and self-evidently fanciful scenes.

Room 211 is usually devoted to early **Rembrandt**—mainly influences: those upon him and his own upon others. Pieter Lastman's Dispute between Orestes and Pylades demonstrates the kind of archaeologically accurate narrative painting that held sway in Amsterdam during the 1620s and demonstrates why the young Rembrandt sought him out as a teacher. Lastman's precise use of gesture and emotional confrontation were very important for Rembrandt's own development.

Jan Lievens (Portrait of Constantijn Huygens, Portrait of Rembrandt, An old woman reading) was Rembrandt's fellow student at Lastman's; they set up a workshop together in Leiden. From Rembrandt's Leiden period: The Musical Company and Tobias accusing Anna of stealing the kid; these two works show Rembrandt's variety as a painter even when still a young man. The brilliant colour of the Musical Company is reminiscent of some of the works by the Utrecht Caravaggisti; the scrupulous finish of the Tobias picture reminds us that Rembrandt was the teacher of Gerrit Dou, the principal Leiden *fijnschilder* (lit. precise painter) who is represented in this room by his own version of Rembrandt's mother. The earliest *Self Portrait securely attributed to Rembrandt is worth close attention—the young man engages us directly, his face half-shadowed; notice how the hair is rendered by scratching through dark paint to the lighter underlayers.

Soon after his arrival in Amsterdam Rembrandt added to the moody chiaroscuro manner a looser application of paint apparent in *Jeremiah lamenting the Destruction of Jerusalem. Paint is rolled off the brush; opaque and translucent paints interlock to make the visionary substantial. A virtuoso treatment of paint is also apparent in the *grisaille* of Joseph telling his dreams.

Rooms 213 and **214**. Both of these rooms show a similar range of landscape, townscape and still life painting; paintings are hung in one or another room according to size. The whole range of landscape painting is displayed: highly finished mythological and biblical scenes by Cornelis van Poelenburgh, Cesar van Everdingen and Moyses van Uyttenbroeck were prized by contemporaries and fetched hundreds of guilders. The new school of 'realist' landscapes employing local scenery by artists such as Esaias van de Velde (especially *The Ferry), Jan van Goyen (see especially his early roundels of Summer and Winter and the huge *Landscape with Two Oaks), Salomon van Ruisdael (among others a typical *River Scene) and Aert van der Neer (who specialised in moonlit scenes) could be bought for a few guilders. Pieter Saenredam, the son of a celebrated engraver and an official in the Painters' Guild at Haarlem, made scrupulous church interiors which are well represented here. His painting of Amsterdam's town hall (which burned down in 1652) is inscribed with a message on the neighbouring shop front stating that it was painted in 1657 after a drawing made in 1641.

Unusual paintings include an early Aelbert Cuyp of a Mountainous Landscape and a view of a *River Valley by Hercules Seghers, an artist whose works in paint and print were avidly collected by Rembrandt. Still lifes by Pieter Claesz. and others, notably Claesz's simple *ontbijtje*, breakfast piece, showing wine and fish set casually on the corner of a table and his more elaborate *Vanitas on human learning which includes a striking statuette of a small boy removing a thorn from his foot. Note also the Still Life (Allegory of Temperance) by Torrentius, a Haarlem artist prosecuted for witchcraft and obscenity.

Room 215. Here there is a variety of portraits, some of important 17C characters—for example Andries Bicker (the Amsterdam burgomaster and merchant of whom it was said that with his brothers he ran the whole world's trade) by Bartholomeus van der Helst, who also painted the fat boy by his side, Andries' son Gerard, and the almost informal full-length image of Maria Henrietta Stuart, widow of Stadholder William II, holding an orange. Jan Verspronck: portraits of an old and a young man. Michiel van Miereveld was supposed to have painted 20,000 portraits. Of course, he did not, but his industrious studio certainly documented the faces of an entire generation of the ruling classes of The Hague and London—here two in his more relaxed late style. With the Bicker pictures and the brother and sister pastoral portraits of Martinus and Clara Alewijn by Dirck Santvoort (there is a later pair of portraits of Martinus and his wife Agatha Geelvinck, also by Santvoort), family portraits seem to be a minor theme in this room. Jacob van Loo's Family Group with a Horse and Carriage (note the handsome contemporary frame) completes the suite.

Family is surely a principal theme of **Room 216**, devoted pre-eminently to Jan Steen. Many of the pictures feature the artist and his family—we can imagine it as an extended family which includes the bogus doctors (out of the *Commedia dell' Arte*) and mocking *pickelharings* from Dutch rhetoricians' dramas. Works here include *The Dancing Lesson (children teasing a cat); *The Sick Lady (we see pregnancy tests taking place); The Feast of St Nicholas (Steen did for the Dutch feast what Dickens later did for the English Christmas); *The Parrot's Cage; *The Merry Family (the moral is written on the cartellino at the top right-hand corner—As the old sing, so do the young pipe); and a Self-portrait. Steen is the master of the comic/instructive commentary on daily life; English-speaking visitors should 'read' his works in the same way that they read the comedies of British playwrights of the period. His Adoration of the Shepherds reminds us that Steen had ambitions as a narrative painter, producing many scenes from the Bible and classical literature. Three small pictures by Paulus Potter: Orpheus charming the Animals, Landscape with Cattle and Herdsmen with Cattle—all of which seem to share similar settings. The animal theme continues with Willem van Aelst's Dead Birds.

Landscape is the dominant theme of **Room 217**. Jacob van Ruisdael: *Landscape with a waterfall (c 1670), Rocky landscape, *The mill at Wijk bij Duurstede (c 1665), a magnificent landscape which although a picture of a real place has been dramatised by Ruisdael on an heroic scale. Ruisdaels' interest in the dramatic is also evidenced in the Landscape with a waterfall; Scandinavian subject matter was introduced into the Netherlands by Allaert van Everdingen who had visited Sweden (see his picture of the cannon foundry at Julitabroeck in Södermanland in the Historical section in the north basement).

Ruisdael's pupil Meindert Hobbema is well represented with the Landscape with Fishermen and The Watermill—thanks to the history of English taste both Ruisdael and Hobbema are better represented in English collections. Landscape is the setting for Adriaen van der Velde's Hunting Party (departing from the gateway of a country house). A more intriguing picture is his Family in a Landscape where they promenade, the nurse too, while a shepherd pipes away like a hired extra to the right. One of the most popular postcards in the shop is of Jan Verspronck's *Girl Dressed in Blue;

his portraits of Edward Wallis and Maria Strijp are also worth some attention.

Rooms 218 and **219** show small paintings in various genres. In the first a group of genre scenes by the Haarlem artist Adriaen van Ostade including Company of peasants, The Fish Woman, Travellers Resting, Interior with Skaters (their skates lie on the floor—skates might imply slippery moral ground) and an intriguing view of a Painter's Studio; in the background you see the apprentice grinding colours on the stone. More landscapes by Jacob van Ruisdael: a View of Haarlem with the bleaching fields in the foreground. This view is taken from the dunes near Bloemendaal; there is also a view of these dunes. Ruisdael's visit as a young man to the German border is recorded in a romanticised view of Bentheim Castle and a Forest Scene. The Winter Scene is astonishing for the leaden sky characterising with a pitiless accuracy the bitter cold.

Thomas de Keyser's small-scale Equestrian Portrait of Pieter Schout, like Rembrandt's equestrian portrait in London, is a rare example of an aristocratic genre in Holland. Note the precise townscape by Gerrit Berckheyde of the Spaarne at Haarlem. A fascinating exhibit in this room is the painter's box decorated with landscapes, hunting scenes and battle scenes attributed to Anthonie van Croos and Jan Martszens II.

Room 219 continues with town views by Berckheyde (The Herengracht) and the master of the genre, Jan van der Heyden (who also invented a system of street lighting and a fire engine supplied by water from the canals): German Town View, Nijenrode Castle and the Martelaarsgracht in Amsterdam. The detail is such that visitors are frequently to be seen counting the bricks and the paving stones. All the paintings in this room demand scrupulous attention.

More paintings by Jan Steen include The Quack, The Prince's Birthday (a satire of ultra-Orangists?), The Village Wedding and After the Drinking Bout. In the last a print of an owl above the exhausted couple seems to ask: what use are a candle or spectacles if you will not see? The Toilet is a rare venture into soft porn and The Baker Oostwaard into portraiture. Do not miss Adriaen Coorte's trompe l'oeil of asparagus and Melchior d'Hondecoeter's Plants and Animals.

Room 220. There was a widespread interest in and fashion for Italianate landscapes during the 17C. This room has examples from second generation practitioners (the first generation were displayed in Room 213)—painters like Jan Asselijn, Adam Pijnacker, Nicolaes Berchem, Karel Dujardin and Jan Both produced seemingly artless views crowded with motifs drawn from the Roman Campagna, peopled by peasants, shepherds and their beasts; the evening sun is invariably gilding the western sky, creating interesting shadows and gorgeous colours across the entire scene, the distance is hazy.

The pure escapism of this art, rooted as it is in the poetry of Horace and Virgil, can be compared to the equally idyllic (though closer to home) elements in such paintings as Jacob Esselens' The Shore, where townspeople buy fish from the fishermen, or Lieve Vierschuier's Rippling Water (where we see a ship being tarred—not, admittedly, the stuff of elegiac verse but a labour of the day in the spirit of Virgil's Georgics).

The sea is the main subject of most of the painting of Jan van de Capelle and Willem van de Velde II both of whom can range from the dramatic (Van de Velde's The Squall) to the lyrical (Van de Capelle's State Barge saluted by the Home Fleet). The continuing popularity of maritime subjects throughout the 17C and later is evidence of a strong patriotic sentiment.

Room 221 includes some more Italianate landscapes but here they are set in the different context of the continuing 'classical' or 'academic' traditions within Dutch art represented by Michiel Sweerts, a painter who until recently has received scant attention (Portrait of Jeronimus Deutz, *The Painter's Studio, The Card Players, Visiting the Sick, Clothing the Naked). Here, too, is Frans Post's remarkable View of Olinda. Post visited Brazil in the 1640s with the Dutch expedition led by Prince Maurice of Nassau; on his return he made his living almost exclusively by producing landscapes of Brazilian subjects often, as here, crowding the foreground with detailed representations of the flora and fauna, including an anteater. The Threatened Swan by Jan Asselijn is a beast allegory in which the swan (*De raadpensionaris*, i.e. Jan de Wit, see History section) is shown defending its eggs (Holland) from the attacking hound. (The room to the right, 221a, is dealt with below.)

Room 222 is presently occupied with paintings by Rembrandt's pupils. These change from time to time. Rembrandt had many pupils who became important masters in their own right, such as Gerrit Dou (see Room 222a), Nicolaes Maes, Ferdinand Bol, Jacob Backer, Govert Flinck and Aert de Gelder. Their works are displayed here and in the Gallery of Honour (Rooms 229–236). Presently in this room is an example of Maes at his most Rembrandtesque in Girl at a window and Jan Victors' strange The Pork Butcher.

Backtrack a little and enter **Room 221a** and the difference could not be more striking. After the bombast, rhetoric and chiaroscuro of the Rembrandtists, the works of the Delft School of the 1650s and 1660s are so understated as to seem bland. Here are the four **Jan Vermeer** paintings: *The Milkmaid, *Woman reading a Letter, * The Love Letter and *The Little Street, all of them startlingly small. It is easy to understand how it was that Vermeer was 'rediscovered' by the generation that invented photography, the pictures seem so immediate and 'real'.

A comparison with Pieter de Hooch, who was so influential upon Vermeer's style and subject matter, immediately highlights Vermeer's extraordinary accomplishment. Even in one of De Hooch's most successful images, *The Linen Closet, there is a stiff, doll-like quality to the figures which gives the work a look of contrivance. There are three other paintings by De Hooch: an Interior where the child holds a whip (a motif which alludes to a contemporary emblem—the top will only spin for as long as it is whipped!), a Kitchen Interior with a mother and child, and The Country Cottage. Gerard ter Borch (also in Room 222a where you can see *Lady in front of a Mirror) was a painter who came close to Vermeer's artless realism, for example in the so-called *Parental Admonition (though in fact, it would seem, a whore and her client); powerful little portraits by Ter Borch are of François de Vicq and Aletta Pancras.

Emmanuel de Witte (not from Delft) specialised in church interiors which, unlike those of Saenredam, included telling incidents—thus his *Interior of a Gothic church, through the agency of the gravedigger who looks up from his work to speak to a burgher, might invite a meditation upon human mortality familiar from Hamlet. The mixture of attention and inattention in the Interior of the Oudekerk, Amsterdam, invites speculation on the various spiritual destinies of the people we see.

Room 222a. After Rembrandt left Leiden his pupil Gerrit Dou emerged as the most important artist in the city, influencing several generations of younger artists with his painstaking and precise technique and creating the *finjnschilder*, fine painter, style. His works frequently employ distancing devices such as curtains or a stone sill in the foreground which cut us off from the dim and magically lit interiors beyond. The *Self Portrait is a rare example of his artistry turned towards portraiture, more familiar are The Hermit, The Fisherman's wife (virtuously seated by the window) and *The Night School. If you pay very great attention you can determine individual brushmarks, but Dou's appeal lies in his submergence of all technique behind a transparent, glossy wall—the end result being a surface like a coloured photograph.

Gabriel Metsu, a follower, laid his paint on more freely but was more innovative in his treatment of the inner lives of his human subjects. One of the most sentimentally appealing images in the whole museum is his *Sick Child, equally compelling is the *Old Woman Meditating which derives ultimately from his master's versions, after Rembrandt, of Rembrandt's Mother. Note, too, his Old Drinker, Girl Feeding a Cat and The Huntsman's Gift, a sly and dirty joke. At a further remove still is the exquisite and classically informed manner of Adriaen van der Werff (A Painter, Two Lovers).

Presently in this room are more works by Rembrandt pupils, notably Samuel van Hoogstraaten (Sick Woman); Hoogstraaten went on to write an important treatise on art.

Rooms 223 and **224**, reached via 222 described above, are devoted to Rembrandt's *THE NIGHT WATCH, Room 223 contains background material and 224 the picture itself, handsomely restored after its slashing by a vandal (understandably, perhaps, an art student) in 1975. This is Rembrandt's largest and one of his greatest works.

The familiar name 'The Night Watch' is an 18C misnomer probably arising from the fact that the picture was long obscured by soot and that oil paint anyway has a natural tendency to darken. The correct title is 'The Company of Captain Frans Banning Cocq and Lieutenant Willem van Ruytenburch'. Painted in 1642, one of a suite of new pictures for the militia guild hall of the Kloveniers (arquebusiers), the picture shows the company emerging, in broad daylight, from the shadows beneath a triumphal arch upon which, in a large oval cartouche, the names of the officers are listed. The light falls strongly from the left, throwing the darkness of the deep archway into contrast, and there is again contrast between the tall Captain Cocq in his sombre garb and the shorter Lieutenant van Ruytenburch in his bright yellow buckskin (which, if you look closely, you will see is covered in embroidered detail).

The small girl, whose figure catches the sunlight, has a cockerel hanging from her belt, perhaps a play on the captain's name—the prominent claws of the bird are probably a play on the name of the company (Kloveniers); an astute eye will notice that a number of the characters in the picture, although doubtless portraits, are also symbolically dressed. No doubt the two children (there is a boy in 16C armour in the middle ground) are part of an allegorical scheme, but the exact plot of this allegory is now lost. It also seems likely the historical costumes celebrate the history of the militia guild and are probably drawn from its own collection: we know that they had a small museum in the building, as well as a series of group portraits of members going back a century.

Attention may be drawn to the difference between the treatment of the subject in this picture and in other group portraits and corporation pieces. In others the likeness of the sitters seems to have been the artists' principal aim, they are usually individuals posed in readily decipherable space. Rembrandt, though, asserts the dynamic of a whole picture over the demands of portraiture. It seems likely that this work was admired as a grand finishing touch to the militia hall and there is no reason to suppose that any of the sitters was dissatisfied with the picture when it was painted; this is part of the mythology around the 'romantic and misunderstood' Rembrandt.

A 17C copy of the picture by Gerrit Lundens (in Room 223, on permanent loan from the National Gallery in London) shows that the original has been cut down by some 60cm on the left and by some 30cm at the top. This is thought to have occurred in the 18C, but the reason remains uncertain, it may have been to enable the picture to be hung between two doors in the War Council Room in the Town Hall on the Dam.

Also in **Room 224** are, to the left of The Night Watch, Bartholomeus van der Helst's The Company of Captain Roelof Bicker (1639; in front of the tavern De Haen on the Geldersekade), and to the right his *Platoon of Cornelis Jansz Witsen and Lieutenant Johan Oetgens van Waveren cele-brating the signing of the Treaty of Münster in 1648. Opposite The Night Watch is Govert Flinck's The Company of Captain Albert Bas and Joachim von Sandrart's Corporalship of Captain Cornelis Bicker and Lieutenant Frederick van Banchem waiting to welcome Marie de Medici into Amster-dam in September 1638. These works, three of which originally hung in the same hall as The Night Watch, and two of which are by former pupils, provide an excellent context for Rembrandt's masterpiece, emphasising its uniqueness and yet retaining a sense of real historical place and time.

Behind The Night Watch, approached by a staircase on the left, are **Rooms 225–228** into which are crowded the rather small and undistinguished collection of Italian, Spanish and Flemish works. These include: Lorenzo Monaco, a Madonna and Child, a St Jerome in his Study and a St Francis receiving the Stigmata; School of Ferrara (15C), The Flood; Piero di Cosimo, portraits of Giuliano da Sangallo the architect and Francesco Giamberti; Filippino Lippi: portrait of a young man; Fra Angelico, a Madonna; Tin-toretto, an Annunciation (in two halves) and Christ and the woman taken in adultery; Ludovico Carracci, Vision of St Francis; Tiepolo, Telemachus and Mentor; Alessandro Magnasco, Landscape with St Bruno; Canaletto, two Venetian views; Murillo, an Annunciation and a Madonna; Rubens (and studio), Portraits of Helena Fourment, the artist's wife, and of Anne of Austria (a replica of the portrait in the Louvre), Christ bearing the Cross (a study for the painting now in the Musée d'Art Ancien in Brussels) and a Caritas Romana (Cimon and Pero); Van Dyck, portraits and a Penitent Magdalene; Jordaens, The Road to Calvary.

The wide parade of rooms leading directly from The Night Watch towards the shop and Information Desk is known as the Gallery of Honour (**Rooms 229–236**). The first rooms on either side (229–230) are usually dominated by Rembrandt's Jewish Bride and Syndics.

The *Jewish Bride* (usually in 229), also known as The Bridal Pair, was painted very late in Rembrandt's life, in about 1666. The picture is techni-cally interesting for the way in which the colour is laid on freely with brush and palette knife and then qualified with transparent glazes of paint. These glazes seem to have been poured onto a high-relief latticework of paint; from a distance there is the powerful illusion of fabrics and figures in real space, close too there is the pleasure of the apparently arbitrary run of paint and the abstract allure of the colours. It is also a riddle. On the one hand it looks like a history painting and has been likened to representations of Jacob and Rachel, on the other hand it is understood to be a portrait. The bride's costume has led to the traditional name being adopted.

'Character' portraits are by no means rare, Hals' portrait of Isaac Massa and Beatrix van der Laen is an example of another marriage portrait of this kind. The extraordinarily powerful St Paul Denying Christ, of the same date, is usually hung next to this picture.

The ***Syndics** (*De Staalmeesters*), painted in 1661–62, represents the sampling masters of the cloth hall; they are shown addressing a meeting ... they are frozen forever addressing a meeting. An arresting feature of the picture is that all the sitters seem to be interested in what we are doing or thinking, as if we were in the room with them, rather than performing their actions in that more or less unselfconscious manner typical of such corporation portraits. This is one of the rare pictures for which Rembrandt made sketches and each of the officials is highly individualised. This work proves that, although his reputation may be in decline towards the end of his career, Rembrandt could still obtain important commissions—even after the bankruptcy of 1656.

Other important works by Rembrandt that you might see here include the Portrait of Maria Trip, *The Anatomical Lesson of Doctor Deyman (badly damaged by fire; if you have seen Rembrandt's Anatomy of Dr Tulp in the Mauritshuis at The Hague you would do well to see this for comparison), Portrait of Titus as a monk and the compelling *Self portrait as the Apostle Paul.

The rooms are at the moment hung with paintings of the Rembrandt School. In **229**: Ferdinand Bol, Six Regents of the Board of the Nieuwezijds Institute for Outdoor Relief of the Poor; Govert Flinck, Rembrandt as a Shepherd; Roelant Roghman, Mountainous Landscape with Fishermen; Philips Koninck, Distant view, with Cottages lining a Road; Aert de Gelder (Rembrandt's last and most faithful follower), Hermanus Boerhaave, Professor of Medicine at Leiden, with his Family.

In **230**: Koninck, Entrance to a Wood; Bol, Peace negotiations between Claudius Civilis and Cerealis, a work associated with his commissions for the Town Hall decorations which has a spectacular *pentimento* where the ghostly figure of the protagonist, originally painted over, looms through the increasingly translucent oil paint in the middle of the picture, and a *Portrait of a Man in a splendid contemporary gilt frame, the man dressed in some kind of historical costume; Nicolaes Maes, Woman Saying Grace, and a very grand portrait of Vice Admiral Cornelis Evertsen; Carel Fabritius (an artist who died young in an explosion at Delft and whose works are consequently rare), The Beheading of John the Baptist.

Room 231 is presently dominated by Karel Dujardin's Regents of the Spinhuis and New Workhouse of 1669 (the date is on the letter held by the man in the front centre). This is flanked by two handsome seascapes by Allaert Bakhuysen. **Room 232** presently displays a suite of paintings by Ferdinand Bol: a Self Portrait, Aenius at the Court of Latinus (with a delightful mixture of Roman armour and 17C ships' rigging), Consul Titus Manlius Torquatus Beheading his Son (an emblem of disinterested Justice), Venus and Adonis, and a pendant pair of portraits of Roelof Meulenaer and his wife Maria Rey.

Room 233 shows examples of one of the more unusual sub-genres of 17C art, *penschilderij*, pen-painting. These are drawings in ink on a panel prepared for paint. All here are by Willem van de Velde I, two in their original frames, and they depict various sea battles—off Dunkirk in 1639, Terheide in 1654, Livorno in 1653 and on the Downs in 1639.

Rooms 234 and **235** have examples of Italianising and classicising painting. The first room has three *landscapes by Aelbert Cuyp. Cuyp is one of the few examples we can point to of a 'hard-line' Calvinist practising painting; we know that he married into the family of Gomarus, the leader of the Counter-Remonstrants (see History) and that he was a deacon in his local church in Dordrecht. Steen was a Catholic, like Vermeer; Rembrandt was nominally a member of the Reformed church as was Ruisdael; many painters were Mennonites (for example Flinck) and some seem to have had very little religion at all. It is not easy to relate a painter's religion and the style of painting—the idyllic, nostalgic and pseudo-classical world of many of Cuyp's pastorals seem as pagan as those of Claude (who was a devout Catholic, of course).

Also Cesar van Everdingen, Young Woman Warming her Hands, possibly an allegory of Winter; Jan de Bray, The Haarlem Printer Abraham Caste-leyn and his Wife (she is shown pulling him away from his books and into the garden, he is shown conceding with a play of reluctance); Jan Steen, *The Sacrifice of Iphigena, another example of Steen as a history painter, in which guise he received qualified praise from Joshua Reynolds. The second room has works by Gerard de Lairesse, now better known for his writings on art: Mars, Venus and Cupid, Ulysses urged on by Mercury to leave Calypso, and Diana and Endymion; Abraham van den Tempel, Group Portrait of the Family of David Leeuw; Jan Weenix, Dead Game; Melchior d'Hondecoeter The Floating Feather, a display of exotic birds.

Room 236 presently contains Frans Hals' Company of Captain Reinier Reael and Lieutenant Cornelis Michielsz. Blaeuw and the Marriage Portrait of Isaac Massa and Beatrix van der Laen, as well as still lifes by Floris van Dijck, Willem Claesz. Heda and Pieter Claesz. (discussed above, see Room 208). In addition to works by these Haarlem artists there are portraits by Michiel van Miereveld and Paulus Moreelse.

Later Dutch Painting (18C–19C) (Ground Floor. Rooms 135–137 and 141–149)

Having followed the patriotic trail from medieval art to the glories of the baroque, visitors have to find their way to the back of the museum in order to pick up the scent and continue with the story of painting in the Nether-lands. The best route is to leave through the door out of Room 224 in the wall to the right of The Night Watch and follow the signs which lead to **Room 135** (a corridor). Here you will find paintings by artists of c 1700, some of whose names will be familiar from the upper galleries: Godfried Schal-cken, The Smoker; Frans van Mieris the Elder, The lute player; Adriaen van der Werff, *Self portrait; Gerard de Lairesse, Antony and Cleopatra.

Rooms 136 and 137 are dominated by Cornelis Troost, a painter of portraits and genre scenes reminiscent of Hogarth's work. Most prominent is his large group of the Regents of the Almoners' Orphanage in Amster-dam, painted in 1729. To the right **Rooms 137** and **138** are laid out in period style. There are some excellent portraits too by George van der Mijn. **Room 139** is the 'Pastels Room' with very fine examples, especially by the 18C Swiss artist Jean-Etienne Liotard, and amongst others by the French anarchist painter (though it is hardly apparent in the works on show) Prud'hon. Later Dutch painting resumes beyond the small **Room 140** in which are displayed the collection of miniatures, some of which may be of particular interest to English visitors. This small room in fact takes you into the Drucker Wing of the Museum devoted to Dutch 19C painting (the Druckers donated the bulk of this collection) and Islamic art (in the base-ment reached via the stairs in Room 141).

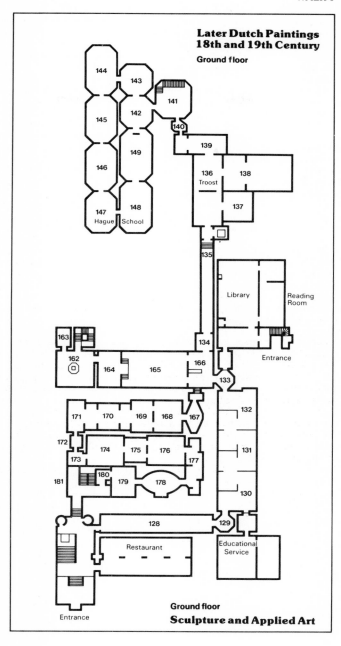

Later Dutch Paintings 18th and 19th Century

Ground floor

144

143

141

145

142

140

139

146

149

136 Troost

138

137

147
Hague School

148

135

Library

Reading Room

163

162

134

Entrance

164

165

166

133

171 170 169 168

167

132

172

174 175 176

131

173

177

181

180 179 178

130

128

129

Restaurant

Educational Service

Ground floor

Entrance

Sculpture and Applied Art

Room 141 is a landing above an 18C staircase with stucco ceiling decoration. The group portrait of the Hasselaer family (1763) is by George van der Mijn. Here too are cases of 18C Chinese porcelain and, at the foot of the stairs, two magnificent Kanghi vases. You, however, should remain on the same level and carry straight on.

Rooms 142 and **143** contain late 18C and early 19C works, portraits by Johann Tischbein and Wijbrand Hendriks, including Hendriks' Woman sewing, and Man writing at his desk by Jan Ekels the Younger—both strikingly 'Golden Age' images. By Adriaen de Lelie, Jan Gildemeester's Gallery, and the Sculpture Gallery of the Felix Meritus Institute; Pieter Kleyn, Park at St Cloud; Wouter van Troostwijk, Snow scene on the ramparts of Amsterdam; Pieter van Os, In the Graveland; J.L. Augustini, Regents of the Leper House; J. Jelgerhuis, The Bookshop. It is clear from all of these that many characteristics of earlier art survived and indeed developed.

Rooms 144 and **145** exhibit examples of Dutch Romantic painting in which painters not only come under the influence of other European Schools, but also explore varieties of earlier Dutch art admired abroad at that time. Wijnand Nuyen, Shipwreck on a rocky coast; Barend Koekkoek, Winter scene; Jan Kruseman, Regents and Regentesses of the Leper House; Jan Weissenbruch, Church of St Denis at Liège; C. Springer, View at Enkhuizen; Andreas Schelfhout, The Maas, frozen; D.J. Blès, Conversation; A. Allebé, Young girl, and Young Woman; Charles Hodges (a native of Portsmouth, England, who lived in the Netherlands, 1788–1837), a number of portraits, notably of Johan Fraser and his family.

Rooms 146–149 display paintings of the Hague School and the Amsterdam Impressionists, both belonging to the latter part of the 19C and the early 20C.

Room 146 provides an introduction, with a number of watercolours.

Rooms 147 and 148 are mainly Hague School works by the Maris brothers: Willem Maris whose speciality was animals, Jacob Maris, beaches and town views, and Matthijs Maris whose work was more varied and included mystical themes, more like scenes from fairytales. The Hague School painters sold well in England; they were the first painters for more than a hundred years to earn the Netherlands a reputation abroad. Together with Anton Mauve (see his Marshland, and the luminous *Morning Ride along the Beach), they have been seen as the first highpoint in the re-ascent of the Dutch national school and were tremendously influential on Van Gogh, Piet Mondriaan and many others.

This room and **Room 149** include works by contemporary Amsterdam painters, the so-called Amsterdam Impressionists, who include George Breitner, who has stylistic and personal links with the Hague painters and Jozef Israëls who, like Rembrandt (with whom he was often compared) and like Van Gogh (who admired him), used paint dramatically and expressively—the expression is sombre and the drama often ironic: Portrait of Louis Jacques Veltman, Maternal bliss. Note also the Landscape by Willem Roelofs.

Sculpture and Applied Art

The Sculpture and Applied Art Collections are in three sections. The first floor, Rooms 238–261, includes the Middle Ages, Italy, the Renaissance, Glass and Silver, Colonial art, Delftware, and Sculpture by Artus Quellin and Rombout Verhulst. On the ground floor, Rooms 162–181, are Doll's

Asiatic Art

Basement

Sculpture and Applied Art

Basement

Dutch History

Ground floor

Houses, Lace, Porcelain (German) and Silver. In the basement, Rooms 24–34 include Glass, Textiles, European and Dutch porcelain and work representative of the Empire and art nouveau periods.

FIRST FLOOR. **Rooms 238–248** are devoted to the Middle Ages and the 16C, a fine and varied collection of decorative art, mainly of ecclesiastical provenance. In **Room 238** a tympanum from the abbey church of Egmond (c 1125–35), representing St Peter with Count Dirk VI and his mother Petronella; also Statues of Apostles from the abbey of St Odilienberg (1250–75). *Enamels and bronzes (13C); ivory hunting horn (South Italy, 11C); a small Scandinavian reliquary (11C); a Catalonian crucifixion (13C). **Room 239** *Bronze statuettes from the tomb at Antwerp of Isabelle de Bourbon (died 1465), a macabre silver *head reliquary of a bishop (1362) by Elyas Scerpswert of Utrecht, a French 14C Madonna. **Room 240**. Late 15C Dutch silver, including guild chains. **Rooms 241** and **242**, Dutch sculpture of the late 15C and early 16C, including fragments of altars, notably Death of the Virgin and St Joseph and an Angel choir by Adriaen van Wesel (c 1475), and a Meeting of Joachim and Anna by an unknown master. Also in this room a Flemish tapestry (Orange Harvest) of c 1500.

Rooms 243–247 generally cover the 16C, a period during which the art of religious sculpture declined in the face of the iconoclasm of the Reformation. Noteworthy in **Room 243** are *a most original small carving showing riders (the Three Kings) descending through a rocky defile (Brussels, c 1500); three panels of knightly figures bearing shields, the panels being Rhenish workmanship from Naarden (1590) and part of an organ case; organ cases were one of the few forms of decoration allowed in post-Reformation churches and are often well worth close attention (look at the later examples at either end of the Entrance Hall, Room 237, as you leave). **Room 245** (principally German works) contains figures by the famous Tilman Riemanschneider; also a remarkably grouped Last Supper. **Room 246** (principally Netherlandish works) displays an Antwerp altar with scenes of the Passion, and also a balustrade with carved animals. In **Room 247** are ecclesiastical robes, silver and a tapestry (Brussels, c 1520) representing the Washing of the Feet, perhaps from a work by Bernard van Orley. **Room 248** contains objects in copper and bronze, notably a bronze candelabrum by Verrocchio; also a Gothic rood screen from Helvoirt, as well as a tapestry (Brussels, c 1510) depicting the Triumph of Fame. **Room 249** is the Acquisitions Room.

Room 250 illustrates the transition from Gothic to Renaissance, the emphasis being on tapestry, notably, in **Room 250A**, the Scenes from the Life of Diana woven in Delft and remarkable for their colouring; there are also examples of glass, sculpture and furniture. In **Room 251** the furniture and majolica represent the solid but stylish comforts of the 17C in that mix of showcase and room-setting display so loved by museum curators. **Room 251A** (the Treasure Room) displays jewellery, crystal, gold and silver, including guild silver, all part of the rich culture of the 16C and the Golden Age. **Room 252** is a panelled room from a house in Dordrecht, while **Room 253** shows Flemish baroque and **Room 253A** presents colonial life. **Room 254**, *Dutch silver of the 17C, the principal artists being Paulus van Vianen (died c 1618), Adam van Vianen the Elder, Christiaan van Vianen (son of Adam), all from Utrecht, and Johannes Lutma of Amsterdam, the friend of Rembrandt. Especially noteworthy, by Lutma, are the *Basin and Ewer, with tritons and nereids, presented to Admiral Tromp in 1647. There is a portrait of Lutma by Jacob Backer.

Rooms 255–257 contain the *Delftware Collection, both blue and polychrome; there are some remarkably unlikely household objects crafted in this material, note especially a bird cage of c 1700, a *violin (18C), with a musical occasion depicted on it, and an ingenious calendar.

Room 258, sculpture of the 17C, with many terracotta busts and reliefs. Rombout Verhulst, sketch for the tomb of Admiral Tromp; Bartholomeus Eggers, G. Munter, burgomaster of Amsterdam (1673); Artus Quellin, bust of the burgomaster Andries de Graef and reliefs of Cornelis de Graef and his wife. Also sketches for the sculptures now on Amsterdam's Town Hall, now the Royal Palace, on the Dam. Also (attributed to Quellin) Madness, a nude female figure, formerly in the garden of the old lunatic asylum at Amsterdam. **Room 258A**, Delft tapestries (1650). Also a mantelpiece and portico by Philip Vingboons (1639), the great architect of Golden Age Amsterdam and a group portrait of the Regentesses of the Leper House (c 1665) by Ferdinand Bol.

Room 259 has gilt leather wall hangings which came into fashion during the 17C, and some handsome furniture; also a case of ivory work (mostly 17C). **Room 260** shows the rather less ornamented furniture of the later 17C. **Room 261**, Chinese screens.

GROUND FLOOR. **Room 162**, two magnificent doll's houses, dating from c 1700 and illustrating in miniature typical patrician furnishing. A case of silver, mainly 17C German. **Room 163**, Dutch sculpture. **Rooms 164** and **165**, the latter a large tapestry and carpet hall, exhibit 18C furnishings. Note an elaborate barometer of 1709, and also two paintings (Farmyard, and Parrot, hen and chickens) by Melchior d' Hondecoeter. **Room 166**, *lace work. **Room 167**, an attractively diamond-shaped room, reached through a lobby, with Delft tiles of c 1690 (Daniel Marot), contains two large paintings by Gerard de Lairesse and Johannes Glauber, made as decorations for a room. In **Room 168**, with gilt leather wall hangings of four designs, there are Gobelins tapestries of c 1684 illustrating Ovid's Metamorphoses, and also tapestry (Brussels, 18C) illustrating Diana and her maidens. In **Room 169** are a corner hearth in the style of Daniel Marot, and a rare *apothecary cabinet. **Rooms 170** and **171** offer a *collection of Dresden china, while **Room 172** displays Japanese Kakiemon porcelain and derivative European ware.

Room 173, Louis XV French furniture and panelling; two portraits by Louis Tocqué. **Room 174**, Dutch furniture of the mid 18C, including a large bookcase of 1760. The murals and the fireplace grisaille are by Jacob de Wit. **Room 175** displays muffle-fired Delftware (ware fired in a special furnace allowing colours with low heat resistance to be used), and a doll's house (18C), furnished in Louis XV style. **Room 176**, Louis XV furniture. **Room 177**, Dutch silver (18C). **Room 178** is an attractive oval in plan, the gilded consoletables with mirrors are by Robert Adam. **Room 179**, Louis XVI French furniture. Portrait of a boy by J.-B. Greuze. **Room 180** displays precious trinkets (18C). **Room 181**, silver, a case of keys and sculpture. Pallas by Laurent Delvaux.

BASEMENT. **Room 24**, Dutch and other glassware, with examples of the 18C stippled technique. **Room 25**, Dutch Louis XVI furniture, c 1775. **Room 26**, a corridor, exhibits Dutch and Belgian silver. **Room 27** is a Dutch Louis XVI room of c 1790, all the furnishings of which came from the same house in Haarlem. **Room 28**, German and Austrian porcelain, with pieces from Höchst, Fulda, Fürstenberg, Berlin and Vienna. Note the amusing Höchst coiffeur group. **Room 29**, Dutch Louis XVI furnishing. **Room 30** is a gallery in which Dutch and French clothing and accessories are well presented in contemporary settings. **Room 31**, lace (18C and 19C). **Room 32** Dutch porcelain from Weesp, Loosdrecht, Amstel and The Hague. **Room 33**, Empire period furniture and silver. **Room 34**, art nouveau.

Dutch History (Ground Floor. Rooms 101–114)

The material derives from the collections of the stadholders, the Admiralty, the offices of the East and West Indies companies, as well as from private individuals—it therefore projects a particular cast onto Dutch history. The collections, arranged generally by subject rather than chronologically, although including some prehistoric material, essentially cover the Middle Ages to modern times.

Room 101. At the entrance, a clock from the tower of the Nicolaaskerk in Utrecht: dating from the 16C the clock strikes the hour and half hour. A case of prehistoric material, mostly ceramic. Altar panels illustrating the disastrous St Elisabeth Flood (near Dordrecht) of 1421 (late 15C copies of lost originals). Contemporary portraits of four lords of Montfoort, three of whom were killed in Count William IV's campaign against the Frisians (1345); these are the oldest known Dutch portraits. Among other portraits are Elizabeth I of England, by an unknown artist; William of Orange by Adriaen Key; the Duke of Alva, an old copy of an original by Willem Key; Maximilian I (studio of Joos van Cleve, c 1510). Other pictures include the Siege of Rhenen (Master of Rhenen); the Battle of Gibraltar, when the Dutch under Admiral Heemskerck defeated the Spanish, by Hendrick Vroom, c 1625. In the passage between Rooms 101 and 102 can be seen what claims to be the chest in which Hugo Grotius was smuggled out of Loevestein and also Jan van Oldenbarneveld's walking stick.

Room 102 (with the gallery 102A) is known as the Seventeenth Century Square. The gallery contains cases with material illustrating 17C everyday life. Not to be missed are examples of Chinese porcelain recently recovered from wrecks. The main floor covers a range of 17C themes, among the many exhibits being a case showing the weapons of a musketeer, a pikeman and a cuirassier; a model of Prince Frederick Hendrick's siege of s'Hertogenbosch (a little dusty at the last viewing, it works best if you crouch down and view from the side); a herald's doublet; *model ships, including a large one of a 17C warship and one of a galleon built for Peter the Great; relics of the expedition of Willem Barentsz. and Jacob van Heemskerck to Nova Zembla (1596–98) in an attempt to discover a north-east passage to the Indies. The many *pictures include several illustrating colonial life (Bengal, Amboina, East Indies, Surinam, with a map of 1737), a picture of the Hoogly river, Bengal, a fascinating if naive glimpse into everyday activities. There is also a series of twelve paintings by Otto van Veen (Rubens' teacher, a Hollander living in Antwerp) illustrating the revolt of the Batavian tribe against the Romans; these were well-known images during the 17C, they were engraved as the illustrations to Van Veen's own edition of a history of the Batavian Revolt.

Room 103. Sea battles, particularly against England, the main exhibit here being the *escutcheon of the 'Royal Charles', captured by Admiral de Ruyter. Also a captured Union Jack, the oldest in existence; two large, elaborately carved ships' lanterns; and paintings by the Van de Veldes, father and son. **Room 104** contains portraits of admirals and their families, a number by Bartholomeus van der Helst. In **Room 105** the main feature is the painted ceiling, originally in the bedroom of William and Mary in their palace at The Hague (before they came to England). **Room 106** is a chapel (normally no adm.). **Room 107**, Colonial history, with particular reference to Ceylon, Japan and China. Note a Japanese screen with a Dutch ship; a Sinhalese 'Kastane' weapon, an elaborately decorated cannon belonging to the King of Candy, and a portrait by Govert Flinck. **Room 108**, pastel portraits of members of the House of Orange by Johann Tischbein. **Room 109** covers the formation of the Batavian Republic (1795–1801): political ribbons and badges, silhouettes of the delegates who drew up the constitution; and a delightful family portrait of the Schimmelpennincks by P. Prud'hon. In **Room 110** there is a huge painting by Jan Pieneman of the Battle of Waterloo, with the Duke of Wellington occupying the central position; a key identifies the many well-known people included. Also by Pieneman, the Prince of Orange (later King William I) at Quatre Bras.

Rooms 111 and **112** cover the later 19C and the 20C, some of the early photographs being particularly interesting. **Rooms 113** and **114** are used for temporary exhibitions.

Oriental Art (Basement. Rooms 11–23)

The main sections are Hindu-Javanese, Japanese and Chinese. The **Hindu-Javanese Collection** includes stone statuary, fragments of buildings, and bronze and silver figures. In the **Japanese Collection** are sculpture, screens, lacquer and painting.

The interesting **Chinese Collection** includes prehistoric earthenware (c 2000 BC); a series of six tomb figures, with four horses and two camels (T'ang, 710C); a cave temple torso (T'ienlungshan, c 7C), showing Indian influence; the bronze head of a warrior (c 1000–1100); Buddha heads of the 7C, one with a gold cap; and, also showing Indian influence, a bronze Siva dancing within a ring of fire.

Other Departments

The NATIONAL PRINT ROOM (Ground Floor. Rooms 128–133) presents changing exhibitions, the material being either from the museum's permanent collection or on loan for special exhibitions. The permanent collection dates mainly from the 15C on, the 16C and 17C being well represented and including works by *Rembrandt* and his pupils and by *Hercules Seghers*. Also represented are works by the German 15C etcher known as the *Master of the Amsterdam Print Room*; French drawings of the 18C; and Dutch historical prints, portraits, and topographical illustrations.

The LIBRARY (entrance Jan Luykenstraat 1A) contains over 45,000 volumes on the history of art, and a large selection of current periodicals, catalogues etc. (Monday–Saturday, 10.00–12.30, 14.00–17.00).

The STUDY COLLECTIONS (Basement. Rooms 40–47) cover all the main departments of the museum.

One of the pleasant ways to return from the Rijksmuseum to the Centraal Station is to take the Museumboat. This can be reached directly opposite the museum from Singelgracht. Another is to take tram 1, 2 or 5 from the Leidsebrug, a short walk NW along the Stadhoudenkade.

2

The Heart of the City

The heart of medieval and Renaissance Amsterdam, and most mythical Amsterdams since, is the dense network of alleys and waterways which lie between the Damrak and the Rokin to the W, the Oudeschans to the E and the Amstel to the S. The northern part is this district is called the 'Wallen'. This is the Oude Zijd; it was the first area settled when the city was originally founded, and it retained a certain distinction until the 19C; it has now long been a centre of Amsterdam working-class and immigrant life. North of the Damstraat, at night, it is the 'red light' district. The Duke of Alva lodged in the Warmoesstraat when he came to subdue the Northern Netherlands for King Philip; Rembrandt lived on the Jodenbreestraat and his Night Watch first hung at the nearby Kloveniersdoelen (now the site of a hotel), the Tripps built their city palace on the Kloveniersburgwal.

Nowadays you are as likely to hear a Chinese dialect spoken as Dutch. It is also an area where drugs are openly traded (despite regular police clean-ups) and marijuana is legally on offer in some cafés. The southern part of the district is the University quarter where the railings are encrusted two or three bicycles deep. Art galleries open and close; yuppies have bought up older properties and the council has torn down many more; medieval almshouses stand side by side with some innovatory public housing. To the SE of this area lies the Waterlooplein, heart of what was once Jewish Amsterdam. This was called the Lastage in the late Middle Ages, it was then a district of carpenters and shipbuilders. They were moved a short distance north to the islands, some street names still recording their presence. Jewish Amsterdam is the part of the inner city which has seen most redevelopment mainly because during the German occupation the spiritual and material heart was ripped out of it.

The best route into the Wallen is down the Zeedijk from the Prins Hendrikkade. The wooden-fronted house on your left at Zeedijk 1, 'Int Aepjen', dates from c 1550. The structure is substantially rebuilt in brick at the back and sides and the lower part of façade was altered in the 19C, but this a rare example of a timber-framed medieval house. It was built as a seamen's hostel and apparently got its nickname because an early owner accepted monkeys (aapjes) as payment for accommodation. It is now a 'rariteitencafé' (opens at 12.00), full of antiques and curiosities including wall panels from a 1920s travelling dance hall.

Take the first turning right along the Zeedijk and walk down towards the Oudezijds Voorburgwal along the Nieuwebrugsteeg. At Nieuwebrugsteeg 13 ('In de Lompen') note the distinctive step-gable and arcaded façade with witty carvings in the keystones and plenty of folksy shutters; although the building dates from 1618 it is rather old-fashioned even for then.

Once on the Oudezijds Voorburgwal there is the much grander 'Burcht van Leiden' at 14—note how the upper storeys overhang the lower and note too the primitive note given by the tiny windows. The lions on the frieze give it its other name of 'Leeuwenburg'. The stone coat of arms are those of the city of Riga, the original home of the builder. 'Int Slodt Egmont' at 22 is attributed to Hendrick de Keyser (1565–1621), the name deriving from the stone relief representing Egmond Castle which is set above the handsome carved wooden beam in the façade; only the upper ground and first floors are original.

The ambition of builders only a generation later is apparent at Oudezijds Voorburgwal 40, the 'Schuilkerk het Haentje', topped with its original 'spout gable'. This building houses the **Museum Amstelkring** (open weekdays 10.00–17.00; Sunday and holidays 13.00–17.00). It was built as a merchant's house in 1661–63 by Jan Hartman; at that time Roman Catholic worship, although officially banned, was tolerated if practised inconspicuously and Hartman, a Catholic, incorporated a church (dedicated to Amsterdam's patron saint St Nicolaas) in his attic. The church extended over his canal-side house and the two smaller ones he built behind. This original attic was three storeys tall, the church's altar was on the lowest and the other storeys had openings so that worshippers could participate in the services. Later the church was enlarged and the church and furnishings as you see them today date from c 1735. The church served as parish church for the Catholic community until the opening in 1887 of the large St Nicolaaskerk to the N on Prins Hendrikkade, after this being taken over by a foundation and turned into a museum. Services, notably weddings, are still held in the church, now known as Onze Lieve Heer op Zolder (Our Lord in the Attic).

The most notable furnishings are the altarpiece The Baptism of Christ (1736) by Jacob de Wit and a revolving pulpit (late 18C). The church apart, the museum is worth visiting for its 17C and 18C rooms with contemporary furnishings. Among the many pictures are the Four Evangelists by Jacob de Wit (in the 17C back room), a Virgin and a St John by Thomas de Keyser, Italian Landscape by Jan Wynants, and portraits by Jan van Bijlert and Abraham de Vries.

You are now approaching the heart of the Wallen and Amsterdam's oldest parish church, the **Oude Kerk** (open weekdays 10.00–16.00) set back from the waterside in an oval-plan churchyard. The church, dedicated to St Nicolaas in 1306, was founded at the end of the 13C (there are Romanesque traces from this period); most of the present Gothic building dates from the 14C. The building was subsequently enlarged, principally during the two following centuries as it was transformed from a single-aisled church to a hall-church and then a basilica. The spire (1566) is by Joost Bilhamer (1541–90) and contains a carillon of 1658 by François Hemony—it is well worth finding an angle from which to view it.

Features of the interior include 15C paintings on the vaults revealed during restoration in 1955; the pulpit of 1642; in the choir ambulatory a memorial window to the Treaty of Münster, designed in 1655 and installed in 1911(!); the choir screen of 1681; and the two organs, the smaller in the N aisle dating from 1658 and the larger one from 1724. In the N choir aisle (the Mariakapel) there are three fine windows (1555). Two of these, illustrating the Annunciation and the Adoration of the Shepherds, were carried out by Digman Meynaertsz. to designs by Lambert van Noort; the third, the Death of Mary, is ascribed to Dirk Crabeth. A view of the interior as it was in the 17C can be seen in a picture by Emmanuel de Witte in the Mauritshuis in The Hague.

All around the interior there are memorials to admirals, all killed in action. These include, in the N choir aisle, Jacob van Heemskerk (1567–1607), who fell at the victorious battle of Gibraltar against the Spanish; at the crossing, Cornelis de Haan, killed in 1633 fighting Dunkirk privateers; at the W end of the N aisle, Willem van der Zaan, killed in 1669, this memorial being by Rombout Verhulst; and, in the SW chapel, Abraham van der Hulst (1619–

66), Gillis Schey (1644–1703) and Isaac Sweers, killed off Kijkduin in 1673, this monument also by Verhulst. A plaque on a pillar by the pulpit commemorates Kiliaen van Rensselaer (1595–1643), founder of the colony of Rensselaerwijk (now Albany, Rensselaer and Columbia counties, New York). Although he was born at Hasselt in Belgium, he spent much of his life in Amsterdam and was buried here in 1643.

The Oude Kerk—a medieval church with a Renaissance tower

Across the canal from the Oude Kerk at Oudezijds Voorburgwal 57 stands the 'Gecroonde Raep', a building of 1615 by Hendrick de Keyser. Once again you can see the stepped gables with arcading 'supported' by double pilasters and additional drama provided by volutes. The whole looks like a frontispiece to a contemporary book, not least because the cartouches and masks crisply picked out in white seem to invite a reader's rather than an architect's eye. Indeed, these busy wedding-cake houses owe a great deal to designs in the books of Hans Vredeman de Vries, a much travelled authority on Renaissance architecture who published in the last quarter of the 16C; a Gothic tradition of decorative ebullience combined with a fastidious interest in authentic Renaissance forms to create the fantastical mannerism of early 17C Netherlandish building.

This area was built in several growth spurts over the centuries. This growth is reflected in the street and canal names, of course, but it is also marked by the remnants of defensive works.

Walk a little way N along the E bank of the Oudeezijds Voorburgwal and pass through the Korte Niezel and Stormstraat which brings you to the Geldersekade. At the N end of the Geldersekade stands the **Schreierstoren** of c 1487, a rampart tower with a handsome original round-arched frieze above which there is now an enclosed attic—a later addition as are the doors and windows. There is a relief of 1560 and a weathervane recalling the departure of Henry Hudson from Amsterdam in 1609 on the voyage, on behalf of the Dutch East India Company, to find the North West Passage which led to the discovery of the Hudson River; the association between the tower's name (Weepers' Tower) and Hudson's departure seems to be more legend than fact. The tower bears plaques from the Greenwich Village Historical Society (1927) and from the Port of New York Authority (1959).

Other remnants of the old defences include the **St Antoniespoort** (i.e. St Anthony's Gate), also known as the Waag, on the NIEUWMARKT (follow the Geldersekade directly southwards; the far side of this waterway was a most infamous area during the 17C; Van Gogh's uncle lived in a house on the site of 77). There had been a gate here at the end of the 14C but the present structure dates from 1488. By the end of the 16C, with the city expanding, there was no longer a requirement for a gate and in 1617 the ground floor was converted to a **Waag**, a weigh-house for the cannon and anchors being made nearby, while the rest of the building was taken over by the militia and by the various guilds (smiths, painters, surgeons and masons, the room of these last still being preserved here with fancy brickwork to show for it).

In the early 19C the weigh-house ceased to function, the guilds moved out, and the building served as furniture store, fencing academy, fire station, and (1891) archives. From 1926 until 1975 this was the home of the city's historical museum (now in Kalverstraat, see Walk 1), then until 1986 the building housed the Joods Historisch Museum (now on Jonas Daniel Meijerplein, see below). There are plans afoot to convert the building into a television studio.

From the NE corner of the Nieuwmarkt, Rechtboomssloot leads SE along a canal to reach the broad Oude Schans waterway. Walk along the N bank of the Rechtboomssloot and take the first turning left into Lastageweg continuing as far as the bridge over the Waalseilandsgracht. Directly across the water from you is the eccentric profile of the **Scheepvaarthuis**. As the name suggests this was originally office accommodation for shipping companies; it now houses the Municipal Transport Authority.

This has been called the first example of Amsterdam School architecture; it is certainly a very striking example of 'expressionist' decoration. A British visitor might be reminded of the restless invention of Arts and Crafts—perhaps in one of its more 'decadent' manifestations, as at Cardiff Castle. But this is also a conscientiously modernist building; it is an office block. Built between 1911 and 1916, it was designed by J.M. van der Mey (1878–1949), P.L. Kramer (1881–1961) and M. de Klerk (1884–1923), all very young architects, all trained in P.J. Cuypers' studio. The repeated vertical motifs are essentially decorative; if you half close your eyes you can see the four-storey plus attic office block beneath—in other words, this is not a revolutionary building from the structural point of view.

However, the decoration is relentless: every doorknob, every windowpane, every inch of wall is shaped or patterned with nautical imagery; you could believe that Jules Verne's Captain Nemo passed through here approvingly. Even the furniture was designed along similar lines, although unfortunately it does not all survive. This is an example of Total Art, more Wagnerian than Bauhaus. It is one of the architectural gems of the 20C. Normally visitors are not permitted to enter but Archivisie (tel. 625 8908, or ask at the VVV) may be able to help you.

A short walk SE along the Waalseilandsgracht, take the S side of the water along the Oude Waal, brings you to the **Montelbaanstoren** which overlooks the Oude Schans. This is another rampart tower and dates back to 1512. The upper storeys, octagonal in plan and reminiscent of the tower of the Oude Kerk, are by Hendrick de Keyser. This building presently houses the offices of the City Water Authority. Across the water at Oude Schans 3 is a recent exercise in canal-house building by H. Zeinstra (b. 1937). The façade is made of two screens set one in front of the other, one white and one grey, linked by the oriel windows. This is an architect-designed house in which the architect lives.

Follow the waterside route SW to the junction of the St Antoniesbreestraat and the Jodenbreestraat at the bridge at the St Antoniessluis; the St Antoniesbreestraat runs NW back up to the Nieuwmarkt. To either side of this road there has been recent redevelopment but the whole area around the Zuiderkerk (on the left-hand side as you look up the street; see below, p 102) was fundamentally reshaped at the same time that the Metro was laid down in the early 1980s. This is the **Zuiderkerkhof**, designed by Theo Bosch (b. 1940) laid out on a five-sided plan (it is also known as The Pentagon) in uncompromising glass, steel and concrete; the whole is good of its kind but there is a perceptible change of atmosphere as you move into it—suddenly the litter and graffiti are no longer picturesque but carry the same threat they do in other cities.

A little way along on the other side at St Antoniesbreestraat 69 stands the **Pintohuis** of 1671, designed by Elias Bouman (1635–1686) the architect of the great Synagogue (see below). The façade is dominated entirely by the giant order of pilasters and overshadowed by a deep cornice which steps in and out across the pilasters. This makes for a very distinctive building though one wonders how much light was forgone in the desire for architectural impact. Isaac de Pinto, who commissioned the building, was a Portuguese Jewish banker whose wealth was legendary. The building now houses a number of organisations associated with the preservation of historic buildings as well as a library; visitors are allowed to look inside.

We, however, are going to cross the St Antoniessluis to the SE and cross the road. There, looking rather undistinguished as it is at a lower level than the present road, stands the *****Rembrandthuis** (open weekdays 10.00–17.00;

New housing; the Pentagon near the Zuiderkerk

Sunday and holidays 13.00–17.00. Closed 1 January). The building dates from 1606, it was Rembrandt's home between 1639 and 1660. The lower floor was the domestic quarters, the upper floor the studio, and the attic (there was no third storey at this time) a studio for the pupils, who during those years included Govert Flinck, Jacob Backer and Ferdinand Bol. Rembrandt's son Titus was born here in 1641, and the following year his wife Saskia died here.

Owing to Rembrandt's decline into bankruptcy, partly caused by the purchase and running of a house such as this, he was forced to sell in 1658, although he was allowed to stay on in the house until 1660. Soon after he left, the house was given a third storey, the earlier step gable being replaced by a classical pediment. Purchased by the city in 1906, the house was restored and opened as a museum in 1911. Its general interest apart, the house is visited for its collection of Rembrandt's etchings of which 250 out of a possible total of 280 are held here.

The etchings in the Sydelcaemer, to the left of the entrance, include Christ presented to the people (1655), Death of the Virgin (1639) and The Three Crosses (1653–60). There are also portraits of the patrician patron Jan Six (1647), the physician Ephraim Bueno (1647) and the landscape artist Jan Asselyn (1647). Beyond there is a room in which the technique of etching is explained. In the Achterkamer, at the rear of the house, are a self portrait with Saskia (1636), a self portrait (1648) and portraits of the artist's parents, a costume portrait (as a good governor) of the receiver-general Jan Uytenbogaert (1639) and portraits of the publisher Clement de Jonghe (1651) and the goldsmith Johannes Lutma.

The Tussenkamer, on the entresol, has many interesting works on display, notably the series of Beggars and Vagabonds (c 1630) with a depiction of Rembrandt himself as a beggar, too. It also has the Ratcatcher (1632), Beggars at the door (1648), prints on mythological themes, several self portraits and portraits of the artist's parents.

On the upper floor, the Schilderkamer exhibits two themes: landscapes and biblical subjects. Among the former the View of Amsterdam (c 1640), with its line of windmills, shows Rembrandt as a 'realist' artist; Rembrandt was notably more 'realist' in landscape drawing and etching than in landscape painting. The many biblical subjects include the Presentation in the Temple (c 1639), the Triumph of Mordecai (c 1641) and Christ preaching (c 1652). The De Kunst Kamer is used for temporary exhibitions.

The WATERLOOPLEIN is just behind the Rembrandthuis. The area around the Waterlooplein is at the heart of Jewish Amsterdam, or was. The Jews (see below) settled here on a polderised sandbank called the Vlooyenburg, until as late as the 19C (from which time one can date the site of the market) an unpleasant and frequently flooded area. The Waterlooplein is now dominated by the **Stadhuis and Opera House** (nicknamed the Stopera) completed in 1986, a building which ought really to be viewed at night from the S, across the Amstel (pick a warm evening, the wind can be bitter when it blows off the water).

Amsterdam's first opera house was opened in 1680 by the son of a former Dutch Consul in Venice, Dirck Strijker, and closed a little more than a year later. Although a tremendous success it faced intense opposition from the Calvinist authorities and suffered from the sheer expense of staging musical drama as do all opera houses without subsidy. Further opera houses flourished from time to time outside the city boundaries, but it was not until after the last war that the city council decided to build a proper opera house of their own. Various sites were discussed and this one was agreed upon in 1969 but in 1972 funding was denied by the provincial authorities.

The stalemate was broken in 1979 when the architect, the Austrian Wilhelm Holzbauer (b. 1930), came up with the idea of combining his design for an opera house with a Stadhuis (a Town Hall) and the Stopera was born. Money was immediately made available by the government but just as quickly objections were raised by burghers who felt that such a plan was inappropriate for this particular area, only recently predominantly Jewish and the victim of a vicious German pogrom during the Second World War. Furthermore, the properties cleared for the original plan were now filled with well-organised and belligerent squatters who had no intention of moving for such élitist nonsense as opera. Dispute raged throughout the building of the Stopera and at the opening the Queen and Prince Claus had to be diverted through a side door to avoid the ugly scenes at the main entrance. The complex seems to be working happily enough now and resentments have apparently died down.

The **Mozes en Aaron Kerk**, marking the E corner of the Waterlooplein, is a ponderous neo-classical work of 1837–41 by T. Suys the Elder. The church (the two towers are wooden, painted to resemble sandstone) replaced a clandestine Catholic church of 1649 on the same site which took its name from two gable stones, depicting Moses and Aaron, which decorated the houses in which it was hidden. The house next door had been the birthplace of the philosopher Baruch Spinoza (1632–77). After years of being moved about the **Waterlooplein Flea Market** (in operation on weekdays 10.00–16.00) now has a permanent home here.

The Jodenbreestraat runs into the MR VISSERPLEIN (named after the Jewish President of the Supreme Court dismissed in 1940), now reduced, or expanded, into an unfriendly traffic system. On the far side stands the **Portugees-Israelitische Synagoge**, built by *Elias Bouman* (1635–86) between 1671 and 1675 and restored after the atrocities of German occupation in 1953–69. The synagogue has an impressive, rich interior. Bouman believed himself to be recreating Solomon's Temple with this design, although no one who was familiar with contemporary church architecture— say a Wren church in London—would feel out of place here.

The *Joods Historisch Museum** (daily 11.00–17.00; closed Yom Kippur) is next door, facing onto the nearby Jonas Daniel Meijerplein and built on the site of a group of late 17C Ashkenazi synagogues. (Jonas Daniel Meijer, 1780–1834, a child prodigy, was the first Jew to be admitted to the Dutch Bar and fought for and obtained Dutch citizenship, paving the way for full liberties for Jews under the French Law introduced after the Batavian Revolution.) The museum, opened in the 1980s, combines the job of explaining Jewish history, mainly that in the Netherlands, with displaying Jewish artefacts and art from all periods, including the present. Jewish life and culture are illustrated through temporary exhibitions and a permanent collection, the latter covering both life at home and ceremony in the synagogue, and showing also works by Jewish artists and an important collection of Second World War documents. For the foot-weary or hungry there is a good kosher café.

The Jews played an important part in the life of Amsterdam from the time when the Union of Utrecht (1578) opposed persecution, then at its height throughout much of Europe and especially in Spanish territory. The Sephardic, or Spanish Jews, many of whom had been leading a precarious existence as Maranos, or crypto-Jews, flocked north following their expulsion in 1592 and soon took a leading part in the banking and exchange activities of a country rapidly growing wealthier. The Ashkenazi or German Jews who arrived a little later, during the mid 17C, tended to occupy an inferior position in Amsterdam Jewish society. The museum also documents the rivalry between the two groups. Although classified as foreigners and strictly controlled as commercial competitors, the Jews were allowed a generous measure of self-government, until they were granted full civic status in 1796.

The resistance of the majority of the population of Amsterdam to the German occupation, notably the General Strike of February 1941 which followed upon the first abductions of Jews, is marked by Mari Andriessen's bronze *De Dokwerker* (1952) which stands in the middle of the Jonas Daniel Meijerplein.

Walk back through the Turfsteeg, an alley which runs from the museum towards the Waterlooplein (the Stopera is in front of you across the road as you emerge). On your immediate right are a group of handsome 17C buildings at Waterlooplein 211–219. The Architectural Academy now occupies the pedimented, classical-looking building to the left, built in 1654 as the Huiszittenaalmoezeniershuis (Almshouse for those living at home). This is where the poor would come to queue, at the back door of course, for bread, cheese and peat (the Dutch word for peat is *turf*, thus the nearby street name). Many of the interior features survive including, in the governors' room, a handsome fireplace and original decorative scheme. The peat was stored next door in the Stadsturfhuizen, originally the Arsenal of 1610, which has an appealing symmetry with the two spout-gabled 'wings' flanking the trapezium-shaped central block. This now accommodates the Amsterdam Architectural Centre.

Cross the road and follow the route around the Stopera. Looking S down the broad course of the Amstel you see immediately in front of you one of the city's grander bridges, the Blauwbrug of 1884, and beyond that the picturesque Magerebrug (Skinny bridge) which dates from the 17C, although it was entirely rebuilt 50 years ago. Our route follows the pavement around the Stopera to the Zwanenburgwal. The Zwanenburgwal is substantially and attractively rebuilt, proving, perhaps, that scale and rhythm are more important than ersatz and repro even at the heart of an historic city. Cross the first bridge to the left and cut through to the next canal, the Groenburgwal. From the bridge you have one of the most attractive and atmospheric views in Amsterdam, trees, water and ever-modulating light.

Further along and across the bridge at Staalstraat 7a is the distinctive trapezoidal gable of the **Saaihal**, designed by Peter de Keyser (1595–1676) and completed in 1641. If you did not know what the Saaihal was, then there would be a clue in the decoration of the gable which is carved to appear as if draped with sheets—this is the Cloth, or Drapers' Hall. Above the attic windows is a large cartouche containing the city's coat of arms, on the top is the imperial crown. The Amsterdammers continued to use the symbolism of dead affiliations for many years, the national anthem still loyally refers to the King of Spain! In the Groenburgwal itself, at 42, is the **English Episcopal Church**. The façade is a truly appealing piece of Georgian Gothic by an unknown, it is thought British, architect. Walk N along the Groenburgwal and take a loop, left or right, to cross the Raamgracht and continue along the Zanddwarstraat to reach the Zandstraat.

You may already have noticed how complex Dutch street names can be. The compounding of elements into a single word is confusing enough to an English speaker, but the elements themselves can at first seem incomprehensible. Frequently you will come across the word *'dwars'* built into one of these compounds, meaning 'cross' in the sense of 'cross-street'. The Zanddwarsstraat crosses the Zandstraat. Rather than inventing a new name, the Dutch will often identify a street by telling you its location relative to another street, probably one that you do know, in this case the Zandstraat.

Turn right and at Zandstraat 17 stands the **Zuiderkerk**. This is the first Protestant church built in the city. It was designed by Hendrick de Keyser and begun in 1603. The building is a purely Renaissance church displaying De Keyser's sophisticated knowledge of Italian building—a basilica (i.e. an aisled building with a central nave) tunnel vaulted in timber and with handsomely proportioned Tuscan columns. The tower, as can be well seen approaching from the Groenburgwal, is a complex assembly of octagonal elements, stone at the base and wood further up. Christopher Wren was much impressed by this tower and it has been influential in the design of many English churches. The Zuiderkerk is no longer a place of worship and presently houses an information centre for urban renewal.

Retrace your steps along the Zandstraat until you reach the Kloveniersburgwal. The distinguished pedimented building opposite is now the headquarters of the Military Police. It was built in 1792–93 as a Lutheran church. Turn right and walk past the Nieuwe Hoogestraat to Kloveniersburgwal 29, the **Trippenhuis**. The building is in fact better seen from across the water. The façade is one of the grandest in the city, a giant order of Corinthian pilasters, a rich frieze above and a pediment on the attic level.

It was built in 1660–62 after designs by Philip Vingboons (1608–78) for the brothers Louis and Hendrik Trip and their in-laws, the De Geers. Both families were armaments manufacturers, the De Geers having control of the Swedish iron and steel industry. The chimneys are designed to look like mortars and the gun motif is also included on the pediment (carved by Jan Gijselingh de Oude). The interior was richly furnished, notably with family portraits and a series of overdoor landscape paintings of Scandinavian scenery by Allaert van Everdingen. Between 1815 and 1885 this was the home of the Rijksmuseum. It now houses the Dutch Academy.

There is a story that their coachman grumbled that he would be happy if he had a house as big as their front door. Across the canal a little further N the two and a half metre wide 'Klein Trippenhuis' at Kloveniersburgwal 26 is said to be the result. The sphinx on this tiny façade does not answer the riddle.

The Kloveniersburgwal runs as far as the Nieuwmarkt; at the junction there are some curiously decorated benches often occupied by down and outs. Take a sharp turn here and return down the other side of the Kloveniersburgwal. As you turn, at Nieuwemarkt 20–22, there are a pair of step-gabled houses of 1605 with attractive patterning created in projecting bricks. The buildings originally had windows at street level similar to those on the first floor; the present shop-fronts are not original. Further along at Kloveniersburgwal 6–8 (called 'Isaac and Abraham') is a very elegant and beautifully restored neck-gabled façade in dark brick and white stucco, two of three original buildings from 1722. The gable cartouches originally had Isaac and Jacob looking towards Abraham, but house 4 (Jacob) has been pulled down.

There are fascinating façades, gateways and gables to be seen down every side street; for example, turn right into Koestraat and at 20 the Vergulde Leeuwhooft of 1611 has the oldest known neck-gable, seemingly a stretched step-gable with stone scrolls. This was once the wine-merchants' guildhouse and their patron, St Urbanus, is set into the broken pediment of the gateway.

Further down the Kloveniersburgwal and right along the Oude Hoogstraat stands the **Oostindisch Huis**, formerly the headquarters of the East India Company and designed in 1605 (it is said by Hendrick de Keyser). The severity of the outside is ameliorated by the rich decoration within the courtyard which even has a gable set eccentrically and against a roof-line running right to left.

Continue to the end of the Oude Hoogstraat and turn left down the Oudezijds Achterburgwal. Turn left into Spinhuissteeg where, on the left, is the entrance to the **Spinhuis**. As the name implies, the Spinhuis was where spinning was done—by women prisoners, usually prostitutes but with a fair number of wilful daughters sent here by their families. Above the door there is a relief showing women being whipped. The verse below translates: Do not weep, I do not seek revenge but urge you to virtue/Severe is my hand but my heart is kind. This is the sister institution to the Rasphuis (Walk 1). The idea of corrective rather than vengeful imprisonment was a much admired feature of Dutch society during the 17C and later. The Spinhuis especially was frequently visited by tourists who would pay to peep at the women at work. Sadly, given its noble purpose, the Spinhuis also provided, at a small fee, access to the 'incorrigible and lewd' women.

Continue down Oudezijds Achterburgwal to the junction of streets at the S end where on your left there is a handsome gateway with modern glass doors marking the entrance to what was once the **Oudemanhuis** (the old men's house, or hospice). The buildings, rebuilt in 1754, now house a part of the university. The passageway to the courtyard is known for its second-hand bookstalls and visitors are welcome.

Cross the complex of bridges heading directly W to arrive at the S end of the Oudezijds Voorburgwal. On the S tip of the junction to the Achter- and Voorburgwals stands the aptly named Huis op de Drie Grachten (The House on Three Canals). Take the right-hand side N up the Oudezijds Voorburgwal to pass the **Agnietenkapel** (open Monday–Friday 09.00–17.00; admission by appointment only, tel. 55 3341; there is a fee payable). This 15C convent church was adapted in 1631–32 to house the Athenaeum

Illustre, the forerunner of the university. It now contains a museum of the university's history.

A little further on at 215–217 is one of the most elaborate stuccoed cornices in the city, this from the late 18C; the frieze contains two windows which is thoroughly incorrect and very attractive. Just before you reach the Oude Doelenstraat do not fail to look up at the raised neck-gable of 187; along with the usual architectural dressing, there are carvings of Africans and Indians reclining on bales of tobacco.

Cross the bridge and return S along the same canal. There is the Oude Vleeshuis (Old Meat Hall) at 274, with cattle heads on the gable; alongside is a shop claiming to be the oldest butcher in Amsterdam. At 300 is the **Bank van Lening** of which the oldest part dates from 1584 and has been the municipal pawnbrokers for the last 300 years, known as *Ome Jan* (Uncle John's) to Amsterdammers. Interest rates are set at rates related to the lender's ability to pay. Joost van den Vondel (1582–1674; see Walk 5), the poet, worked here as a clerk in his old age. At 316 there is a pedimented façade of 1655 by Philip Vingboons with correctly arranged Doric and Ionic pilasters, festoons and swags. The windows are set with striking elegance and economy; note the stone tablet with the resting pilgrim and angels.

Turn right into Grimburgwal at the S end of the Oudezijds Voorburgwal and walk on past cafés, art galleries and a souvenir shop with a windmill outside to the Langebrugstraat which leads to the Rokin. Around the corner to the left is Oude Turfmarkt 127, the **Allard Pierson Museum** (Tuesday–Friday 10.00–17.00. Saturday, Sunday, holidays 13.00–17.00; admission charge). The building was put up 1865–69 as the Nederlandse Bank, designed by W.A. Froger (1812–83), and is in itself a very handsome and restrained exercise in Victorian classicism, the structure adapting itself very well to the curving building line of the front of the site. The colour contrast in the façade is achieved by using Bremer and Bentheimer stone. The museum took over in 1934 and is named in honour of the scholar and humanist Allard Pierson. It houses the University of Amsterdam's archaeological collections, the emphasis being on Egypt, the Near East and the Mediterranean. The museum is rather old-fashioned in its presentation which is not such a bad thing for a change nowadays when slickness is all.

In the HALL there is a shaft-grave of c 2000 BC. On the FIRST FLOOR, the first four rooms display Egyptian material, including a papyrus Book of the Dead, a model boat complete with oarsmen, and many everyday articles— bronze statuettes, jewellery, combs, etc.—the majority of these intended for the owner's use in the Nether World. The next three rooms are devoted in turn to the Near East (tablets with cuneiform writing, cylinder seals and some notable Iranian pottery); Crete, Mycenaean Greece and Cyprus, notable here being a Mycenaean bowl of 1300 BC; and finally, in Room 7 across a passage, Coptic material including some interesting clothing with a child's shoes and jerkin, the latter still well retaining its colour of the 5–9C.

On the SECOND FLOOR the progression (roughly anti-clockwise) is through Greece and southern Italy (Rooms 814), through Etruria (Room 15) to the Romans (Rooms 1618). Vases are the main theme of the Grecian rooms, these ranging from the 7C BC in Room 8; to (in Room 9) black-figured pottery of the Archaic period; on to red-figured vases of the 5C BC in Room 11; and finally, in Room 12, small black Attic pottery contrasting with some large vases from the Greek colonies in southern Italy. Beyond, the Etruscans are represented by votive offerings and bronzes; the Romans by a huge sarcophagus, jewellery (displayed on a special platform), small bronze gods, oil lamps and a variety of other homely articles.

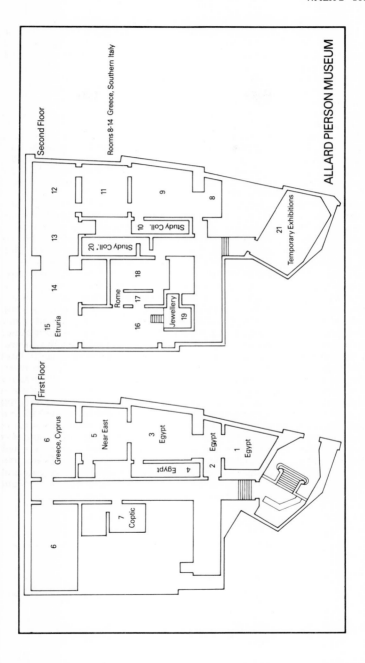

ALLARD PIERSON MUSEUM

Second Floor

Rooms 8-14 Greece, Southern Italy

12
11
9
8
13
14
15 Etruria
10 Study Coll.
20 Study Coll.
18
17 Rome
16
19 Jewellery
21 Temporary Exhibitions

First Floor

6 Greece, Cyprus
5 Near East
3 Egypt
4 Egypt
2
1 Egypt
Egypt
7 Coptic
6

Further along at Oude Turfmarkt 145 is the 'House of P.J. Sweelinck' of 1642 by Philip Vingboons. Sweelinck was a distinguished musician and composer whose works are still included in repertoires having become popular since the rise of interest in baroque music over the last decades. The building is now part of the university. At the far end of the Oude Turfmarkt, between the Nieuwe Doelenstraat and the Amstel and best viewed from across the water, is the **Hotel d'Europe**, an exercise in picturesque Northern Renaissance by W. Hamer (1843–1913) who designed many attractive Amsterdam buildings in a number of styles, including the pavilion in the Vondelpark, now the Film Museum.

Cross to the Rokin, a major thoroughfare, once a canal (the inner reach of the dammed Amstel) filled-in during the 19C. On the far side of the road is the Muntplein with **Munttoren**, a tower of 1490, and part of the ancient Regulierspoort, an early city gate, with a steeple of 1620 by Hendrick de Keyser, which housed the mint briefly between 1672–73; it now houses a Delftware shop.

Rokin is a broad street, which is not surprising when you consider that it is made up of both the streets one usually gets alongside a canal, plus the breadth of the canal itself. The Rokin is a mixture of styles, perhaps best summed up in the façade of Rokin 99, a stockbrokers' office designed by M. van Schijndel (b. 1943) which is a witty and extremely well crafted Po-Mo reworking of a canal house. All the quotations are there—the banding of red and white brick (here done in exotic red, white and green granites), the triangular gable and even, with the first and second floor window which is made up of one huge, bowed oriel, the 17C fascination with giant orders linking two or more storeys. The Rokin is gradually rising in tone, it was very much more run-down 20 years ago. The antiques' shops are, as always, very pricey and seem more like private clubs than shops. Sotheby's Amsterdam is at 102. The hotels are being replaced by offices.

The Rokin leads into the Dam square. You should cleave to the right-hand side and pass in front of the Hotel Krasnapolsky, entering the Warmoes-straat at its S end. The Warmoesstraat is the oldest street in the city; at times it has been a very distinguished address and names as various as the Duke of Alva, Mozart and Karl Marx have been associated with it. There is little of great architectural interest to show for its long history (except for the backs of the houses which you see from the Damrak) and it is a sunless, shabby thoroughfare. For the visitor, it is an 'interesting' walk and if you can avoid the instinctive desire to shuffle through with your eyes to the ground you will see the underside of life. At the S end there is a condom shop and art gallery, further up there are some sex bars, a gay cinema and sex shops and Geels at 67, a tea and coffee shop. Follow it to the end and you arrive at Zeedijk, where you started.

3

The new side, the islands and the Jordaan

This walk takes you through docklands, out to the Western Islands and down into the Jordaan. These parts have a reputation similar to London's East End. There is the same long history of riches, poverty and exploitation, the same frisson of gangsterism and riot and the same sentimental mythology of warm-heartedness and 'real people', much of it entirely justified.

The 17C suburbs of the Jordaan, or the Nieuw Werk (New Project) as it was called, was the response of the city authorities to massive immigration, mainly Huguenot and Walloon refugees driven by the persecution and war of the late 16C. In 1570, before the start of the Rebellion against Spain, the population of Amsterdam had been approximately 30,000. In 1640, just before the end of the wars, the population had risen to 140,000 and was still rising. During the Twelve Year Truce in 1609 the authorities decided to expand the city. A new wall was built with 26 bastions; this survived until the 19C. The old city towers were given spires. Massive gateways were put across the major roads. The concentric system of canals was devised by Frans Hendriksz. Oetgens and Hendrick Staets—the familiar pattern of the Herengracht, Keizersgracht and Prinsengracht. This development was for the wealthy and for the existing Amsterdam 'poorters' (i.e. registered citizens). It paid no attention to existing property lines or drainage patterns and was an expensive investment; a joint-stock Versailles. Jewish immigration was rapidly transforming areas in the SE of the city, and piecemeal development was continuing in the islands to the NE and NW as well as across the IJ at Zaandam where the heavy shipbuilding trades were prospering. A new area to the W of the city was proposed for the huddled masses. It would not involve the expense of laying out new canals and building sites, it would simply need the deepening of watercourses and the widening of tracks for roads. What resulted was an area consisting of 11 canals and 14 streets linked by dozens of cross-streets. The streets and canals were named after the trades carried out there and, most frequently, names of plants and flowers.

Thus it was that the area got the nick-name the 'Jordaan', a corruption of the French word '*jardin*', or garden. It is possible that the word has always been used ironically. Hendrick Staets devised rules for the siting of domestic and industrial premises in order to keep the district habitable but these were soon ignored and within a few decades the Jordaan was a vital, thriving, unhealthy riot of activity. During the 18C the area declined and became the famous slum it remained until recent times.

We start the walk at the Centraal Station, crossing Prins Hendrikkade to arrive at the top of the Damrak. Turn to the right and go along Prins Hendrikkade as far as the Martelaarsgracht, following the road around to the left until you reach the crossing which will lead you into the NW extreme of the Nieuwendijk, a pedestrianised street which you follow to its end. The broad road running away to your left as you cross is the Nieuwezijds Voorburgwal; at 20 is De Klompenboer where you can see clogs being made in a chaotic carpenters' workshop (see Shopping).

Entering Nieuwendijk look out for 30, a house of 1630 with a stepped gable, now part of a hotel complex; note the use of niches, ledges and 'pilasters' to organise the façade. At Nieuwendijk 16 the Oude Ambachten (weekdays 10.00–17.00; closed Wednesday in February and March, and Monday in November and December; there is an entrance charge) is a Dutch arts and crafts centre with demonstrations of traditional trades and their techniques; the products are on sale. At the far end of the Nieuwendijk you emerge onto the Stromarkt, overlooking the Singel, the innermost of the concentric canals.

The Singel has some of the most picturesque canal houses in Amsterdam. Follow the Stromarkt to the left and at 7 is what the boat trip commentators call the 'smallest house in Amsterdam', barely wide enough for a door. It is not in fact a house at all, but the rear entrance to a house on the Jeroensteeg. Next door at 7a–9 is an early 20C reworking of the canal house with attractive windows. The whole prospect on this bank is dominated by the dome of the **Lutheran Church** beyond, designed by Adriaan Dortsman (1625–82) and built 1668–71. The church gives its name to the area—the Koepelkwartier, the Dome Quarter. The severe classical exterior is breached only on Sundays when the church is opened for a Koffieconcert; enter via the green doors on the Kattegat side of the church (doors open at 10.30, concert begins 11.00; entry f7 which includes coffee. Tickets available from VVV).

Once inside, the building's severity manifests itself as a clear-headed simplicity. The church was burned down in 1822 and rebuilt in the following year but with a coffered vault replacing the dome's original ribbed interior. The plan of a central church with a semicircular ambulatory was retained. After de-commissioning as a church it was bought to be developed as a conference and banqueting hall by the Sonesta Hotel (the hotel is reached via a tunnel); the work was carried out in 1975.

As you come out, note the pair of step-gable houses next door to the church on the Kattengat known as De Goude Spiegel and De Silveren Spiegel (the gold and silver mirrors) commissioned by the businessman and poet Laurens Spiegel in 1614.

Continue along the Singel. At No. 17 a peculiar half-timbered fantasy from the 19C; next door a 17C house unusual in that it is wider than it is deep—houses were taxed on their width, not their depth. The eccentrically placed bell-gable dates from the mid 18C. Next door, at 23 and 25, is a pair of houses with very attractive cornices containing attic windows. The *stoep* of the house on the right still has its original bench. The façade of No. 29, beyond the Koggestraat, looks shorn of its cornice—in fact it is a straight cornice, typical of 19C 'renovations' many of which, like this, were rebuilt from the first floor leaving the 17C entrance level original. Houses 33 to 37 are all handsome 20C contributions to the canal-house theme and all were rebuilt from the ground up. The tiles over the door of No. 33 should not stop you looking up at the variety of windows ascending above. No. 35, with its projecting frontage, looks squeezed-in. No. 37 has a very elegant and understated commercial façade.

Cross at the bridge and walk back down the Singel. Over the next hundred metres or so you can see all the varieties of canal façade. No. 76 is a big, fat 19C house with a straight cornice with openings for dormers. Next door is a tall, skinny 18C façade with a neck-gable dripping with decoration and looking not unlike a turkey's neck; at the ground level the façade of 74 has been attractively reworked in an art nouveau style (c 1912). Nos 70 and 72 share a hipped roof. Nos 66 and 68, one of the many sets of twins (like 23 and 25 opposite, see above), have Louis XV elevated cornices, corner vases and attic windows in the cornice frieze. Neither building has been much altered since it was built; note the handsome doors and over-door glazing (in fact, look out for this everywhere). No. 64 dates from 1638 above the first floor, with a bland Georgian lower façade. No. 62 is Renaissance only up to the stoep, the rest is late 19C. Nos 60 and 56, flanking 58, have fine sandstone elevated cornices incorporating attic windows; the cornice of 58 is a later straight cornice which slips elegantly between its neighbours. Nos 52 and 54 are both 19C adaptations with straight cornices and, most unusually, balconies. No. 50 is a pair of houses united behind one 19C frontage.

Just before Roomolenstraat at 46–48 is an Amsterdam School façade. Note the clever use of brick, triangular elements and ironwork. (Look down to the canal, in front of No. 40 is the *Poezenboot*, the cat boat, open 13.00–14.00 daily, a boatel for stray felines.) The rest of the houses are predominantly 18C with every variety of roof line—a neck-gable at No. 44, a flat cornice at No. 42 (note the window over the door); the cornice of No. 40 has Louis XIV ornaments and two vases at each corner; No. 38 has a 19C reworking of the neck-gable which is allowed to protrude through a 'broken' cornice; No. 36 has the elaborate cornice punctured by an attic window (note the matching over-door); No. 34, as well as a fine fanlight over the door, has a hipped roof, a later modification, as is the straight cornice next door. The handsome cornice at No. 32 remains but the front door has gone to be replaced by a pair of doors set within. There are neck-gables at Nos 26 and 28, and No. 24 has a straight cornice with a ship motif on a large cartouche. No. 22 has been much altered since it was built in 1712. Nos 18 and 20 both have early 19C 'Empire' cornices and No. 20 has a later 'straight up' stoep. No. 16 is a double-width building.

Return a few steps and walk up the right-hand side of the Brouwersgracht, the Brewers' Canal. This canal connects all of the concentric canals at their starting points as well as taking you into the Jordaan's northernmost end. It is an excellent place to set off on rambles S into the 17C city. Quiet and full of character the canal offers quintessential Amsterdam views. Many of the houses are evidently traders' warehouses, this is an old commercial district intimately associated with the 17C and 18C port.

Just beyond the Herengracht is a small open space, the Herenmarkt, the main feature of which is the **Westindische Huis**. This building was put up in 1615 as a meat hall. In 1623 it was adopted as the headquarters of the West Indies Company, and although the Company was not there long the name has stuck. It has been substantially remodelled; during the 19C it served as the Lutheran orphanage and now it is a municipal building. Only in the courtyard are the original 17C elevations intact. Here there is a memorial to Pieter Stuyvesant, Governor of the then New Amsterdam.

Follow the Brouwersgracht W; you will need to take a short detour to the right in order to cross the Korte Prinsengracht. At 188–194 there are four identical warehouses of 1636, each with a spout gable, which have been converted, like so much else here, into apartments. Continue all the way to the end of the canal and you emerge onto the noisy Haarlemmerplein. On the far side, the squat, neo-classical gatehouse is the **Willemspoort**, designed for the triumphal entry of King Willem II into the city in 1840 by C. Alewijn (1788–1839) and C.W.M. Klijn (c 1800–60). The building straddled the old road though it is now marooned on a traffic island. Neither architect was a great specialist in this kind of work (De Klijn's other landmark in the city is his contribution to the design of the Kadijksplein in the Entrepotdok on the far side of the city, a handsome row of warehouses) and nor, it seems, were the masons—the columns taper too dramatically at the top in a botched attempt at entasis.

This building originally functioned as a tax office but in 1986 it was restored and is now converted into homes. An interesting feature are the marks of where the *stokmaat* used to be on the inside of the second pillar on the left-hand side. This was used to judge whether a horse was large enough to be used for military service and was apparently still in use at the beginning of this century.

Take the Planciusstraat under the railway bridge, N out of the Harlemmerplein, and you are in the WESTELIJKE EILANDEN (Western Islands). The arches under the railway, which has marked the boundary between the Islands and the mainland since the first line was build in 1839 (the year before the Willemspoort was built), were decorated during the 1980s with half a mile of mural, commissioned by the city from Fabrice Hünd. They do not look their best in dull wet weather and have since been embellished with amateur efforts.

The Western Islands were the creation of Amsterdam's early capitalists. The name of one of the great 17C mercantile families, Bicker, is preserved in the name of Bickerseiland and that of Jacob Real in Realeneiland. They are man-made incursions into the shallow waters of the IJ. As you emerge from under the railway you will see, a short distance away on the left, though better viewed from Houtmanstaat which runs parallel to Planciusstraat, some 19C philanthropic working-class dwellings, the Modelwoningblok Vereenining ten behoeve der Arbeidersklasse. We, however, turn right into the Sloterdijkstraat which takes us past the painter George Breitner's studio across a narrow white bridge to **Prinseneiland**. This is a delightful jumble of buildings, some restored and some in charming decay.

Once across the bridge, the Sloterdijkstraat becomes the Galgenstraat (Gallows Street), reminding us that we are near the site of the old place of execution (not all executions, the Town Hall on the Dam had the glamorous ones). The street which runs around the inner perimeter is called, confusingly, Prinseneiland. At Prinseneiland 7 is one of the artistic institutions of contemporary Amsterdam, **De Appel**, founded in 1975 (open Tuesday–Saturday, 13.00–17.00). As well as being an exhibition space, it is a place where lectures and films are presented on topics relating to theoretical issues in contemporary art practice. If you have time to return you might check the programme to see if there is anything in English which might be of interest.

Prinseneiland is worth a complete circumambulation; finish up, however, at the N end of the island and cross the bridge leading to **Realeneiland**. From here you can look back at the Walvis boatyard and down onto the Realengracht, on the right, against Realeneiland, is the floating police station. This is not the place for great and noble buildings but there are a number of attractive houses here—Vierwindenstraat 1, to the left, with its distinctive chimneys and steeply-pitched tile roof is a handsomely restored building of 1781. There is a small estate of recent housing by L. Lafour (b. 1942) and R. Wijk (b. 1948) to the right lying between the Vierwindenstraat and the Realengracht where it adjoins with the warehouse you see at the waterside. The new building is in no way a compromise; it is cleanly designed modern accommodation, but it does not soar above the surrounding properties. The courtyard inside is very attractive. This won the Merkelbach Prize in 1991.

Walk through to the Vierwindenstraat and turn right. At the end of the street you are on the Zandhoek. On the immediate right is a very pretty group of late 17C houses with a variety of gables, though all share the peculiar double storey lower front. The Westerdok and Realengracht are well viewed from the bridge which leads S back towards **Bickerseiland**; the water is full of houseboats—boats of all shapes and sizes. Umbilicals providing electricity and water dangle in webs which defeat the conventional laws of physics. The boats have been here for more than 20 years now. After the first increase in numbers during the late 1960s and early 1970s the council was obliged to limit them; existing owners, however, were allowed to remain legally. Life is very slow on the boats. There is great diversity in the kind of owner: tidy boats which look fit for a sea-journey have hale-looking types in white ducks touching up the varnish; corporate lawyers slouch around on prodigiously equipped houseboats; and urban gypsies scratch their heads over piles of rusting scrap.

We turn from this improbable nautical scene and walk down Groot Bickersstraat, taking the first right for a detour through Bickersgracht and pick our way past a city farm—goats, chickens and the rest. After the war Bickerseiland was to have become a business zone; however, protests from local residents ensured that at least some of the space was reserved for domestic use. Not all the redevelopments are attractive. Bickersgracht 210–218 by P. de Ley (b. 1943) and J. van den Bout (b. 1943) is one of the better inner-city developments of the 1970s, the crisp lines of the brickwork overlain with oriel windows and balconies.

Take a left and return to Groot Bickersstraat and then turn into Zeilmakerstraat (Sailmakers' Street). At Zeilmakerstraat 15, one building not redeveloped, there is the **Amsterdams Beeldhouwers Kollektief**, known as the ABK. This is a Sculptors' Collective, a subsidised exhibition and selling space, interesting especially for figurative sculptural work (Wednesday–Friday 10.00–17.00; weekends 13.00–17.00). Follow Zeilmakerstraat to the waterfront and pass along the narrow walkway above the boats under the railway and out onto the Harlemmer Houtuinen, a busy road. Cross the street and take the first road to your right, the aptly named Oranjestraat, which leads you across the Brouwersgracht and into the Jordaan.

The immediate impression you get when entering the **JORDAAN** from any of the grander parts of town is of a sudden reduction in scale. It is a miniature Amsterdam. This northern half of the Jordaan is the locals' equivalent of being within earshot of Bow Bells. The houses are small, many have only recently been equipped with modern conveniences. Until the advent of gas and electricity they were pitifully dark and damp. This was not helped by the putrid air pumped out by the dirty industries, such as tanning. Now the area is full of very desirable inner-city dwellings, sought after by the professional classes and served by cafés, late-night shops and restaurants that range from the trendy to the luxurious. This is also one of the whiter parts of the city. Local landlords resisted the immigration of Surinamese and East Indians despite the council's plans for the even distribution of ethnic minorities, who have congregated in the SE suburbs, the Wallen and elsewhere.

The greatest pleasure of the area is wandering the streets finding delightful prospects at every turn—one is loathe to assert any one route but simply recommend that you enjoy the pavement gardens, eccentric shops and inviting cafés. With the narrowness of the streets and the large picture windows favoured by the inhabitants you get a very intimate view into the daily lives of Jordaaners. Front rooms, however, are decently tidy and often furnished with imposing amounts of lace and heavy mahogany furniture.

There are a number of interesting sights which should be seen. Turn left on the S bank of the Brouwersgracht and walk as far as the Palmgracht, a filled-in canal. On the right-hand side at Palmgracht 28–38 is the Rapenhofje, a group of almshouses founded by Pieter Adriaensz. Raep for elderly women and orphans (a very sensible combination of inmates). Built in 1648, the year of the Netherlands' transformation into true statehood, this is a most characteristic little courtyard complex. There are a number of these charitable institutions in the district—for example the Nieuwezijds Huiszittenweduwenhof at Karthuizerstraat 21–127, designed by Daniel Stalpaert in 1650 (note the clever drying frames outside the windows), and the St Andrieshofje at Egelantiersgracht 107–114 built in 1616 (with a Delfttiled entrance into the courtyard).

Make your way S cutting through the Palmdwarsstraat and the Goudsbloemdwarstraat; crossing the filled-in Lindengracht into the Lindendwarstraat, turn left into the Lindenstraat (you must be becoming aware of the system behind the street and canal names now, '-*dwarstraat*' means crossstreet). The Lindenstraat leads into the **Noordermarkt**, an open area around the Noorderkerk. Several times during the week this is the site of markets (see Shopping). The most interesting market is the Monday morning flea market.

The **Noorderkerk** of 1620–22 was the last great work by Hendrick de Keyser (1565–1621) and it is the most distinctive of Amsterdam's great Renaissance churches. Unlike the contemporary Westerkerk and Zuiderkerk, it was not designed on the traditional plan of aisle and nave, but laid out as a Greek cross. It was the church of the poor and the focus upon the pulpit, emphasised by the overall design, and the concentric rows of pews, makes it seem something of a missionary church. The whole is very austere—four rather plain gables topped with pinnacles, balustrades and a tall, hipped roof above. The clock tower with its cute little angled flagpole is positively understated. In between the arms of the cross there are triangular penthouses with attractive windows. It is a shame that the structure has for so long been so badly neglected.

The next destination is the Westerkerk, the church of the rich on the other side of the water. You can see the tower away to the south.

An interesting diversion might be to follow the Westerstraat back into the Jordaan and take a left turn, wandering the streets southwards to the attractive Egelantiersgracht and Bloemgracht. If you take this route be sure to see Bloemgracht 87–91 (position half-way along the canal on the S side). This is a trio of modestly embellished step-gabled houses dating from 1642, built in timber and brick, each decorated with a tablet representing either a townsman, a countryman or a seaman. Then you emerge, blinking and dazzled, onto the busy Rozengracht (another filled-in canal). Rozengracht 184 was Rembrandt's modest home from 1660, when he had to leave the Rembrandthuis, until his death in 1669. Hendrickje Stoffels, his model and mistress, also died here in 1663, as did his son Titus in 1668.

The Jordaan continues away to the S, increasingly a commercial district with the antique and art trades much in evidence. Turning left and following the Rozengracht towards the bridge over the Prinsengracht leads to the Westermarkt and the Raadhuisstraat, the Westerkerk at the E bridgehead.

An alternative route is to follow the Prinsengracht. There are a number of attractive buildings along this stretch of the canal, and this is one of the quieter sections to walk down. Directly opposite the Westerstraat, on the other side of the canal, at Nos 89–113, stands the tripartite form of the rear of the Starhofje, built in 1804, a Roman Catholic chapel and almshouses.

Few buildings have had no alteration over the centuries—which is no bad thing from the point of view of the architectural detective. For example, No. 24 is 17C up to its eccentric bell-gable of c 1765; likewise the shopfront of No. 32 is 17C to roof height. No. 26, however, was built in 1969 whereas No. 36 is an authentic building of 1650. Side by side you are likely to come across similar structures of very different dates and contemporary buildings in markedly different styles.

Across the canal at No. 151 is a double-width 19C façade with a straight cornice (note the height of the doorway; there was originally a stoep here, the door being lowered to street level when it was removed). Next door to it on your right, the stuccoed house front is in traditional Amsterdam style and is of more or less exactly the same date. That the buildings remain standing at all when you consider that many have stood on the same wooden foundations for several centuries, or have been rebuilt on old foundations, is remarkable. What can happen can be seen at No. 52, half-way between Anjelierstraat and Tuinstraat on the Jordaan side. This house must surely have been upright when the 18C neck-gable was added.

A suite of attractive 17C and 18C warehouses lies across the canal as you walk S; on the Jordaan side the buildings are more retail or domestic types. All the way along (on the far side at No. 181, worth crossing over for a closer look, and No. 207, at No. 56 on the Jordaan side) examples of art nouveau are interspersed among the old and new. Then suddenly the far bank is dominated by massive blocks of 19C and 20C commercial and municipal buildings. So the variety continues as far as the Rozengracht where you cross to the Westerkerk.

The **Westerkerk** (open May–mid September, Monday–Saturday 10.00–16.00) was built in 1620–38 after designs by Hendrick de Keyser who died in 1621 just before his Noorderkerk was completed. It is the largest Reformed church, that is, church built *for* reformed worship, in the Netherlands. The 85m tower, the last part to be completed, is the highest in Amsterdam (access June–mid September, except Monday, Thursday and Sunday 14.00–17.00). It is composed of diminishing cubes (admirers of Christopher Wren take note) and topped by a small decorated and coloured cupola. The bells are a fine peal; the largest bell in the Netherlands (weighing 7500kg) hangs in the tower.

Inside the church there is an organ of 1687 with an allegorical decoration showing King David dancing and the Queen of Sheba bringing gifts for Solomon, by Gerard de Lairesse. De Lairesse, the 'Dutch Raphael', knew Rembrandt and admired him in his own way. Rembrandt was buried in the church (though no one knows quite where) as was the landscape painter Claes Berchem.

The church stands in the Westermarkt. The philosopher Descartes lived at Westermarkt 6 during the early 1630s, just at the time that the young Leidener Rembrandt was making a name for himself in the city. Also in the Westermarkt is the understated and affecting pink triangle of the **Homomonument** commemorating persecuted and misrepresented homosexuals.

Beside the S side of the church stands a small statue of Anne Frank (by Mari Andriessen) and just NW, at Prinsengracht 263, is the **Anne Frank Huis** (Monday–Saturday 09.00–17.00; Sunday and holidays 10.00–17.00; open until 19.00 between June and August; closed Yom Kippur) in a building dating back to 1635.

This was the home of the Frank family, Jewish refugees from Germany who fled to the Netherlands in 1933. We know their story thanks to a diary given to Anne Frank as a birthday present in June 1942, just days before they went 'under' at this house, and kept faithfully until 1944 when they were betrayed to the German authorities. They shared the hiding-place with the Van Daan family and a dentist called Dussel. The diary is a record of a young woman growing up in this bizarre environment, about the tensions in the marriage of the Van Daans, about Anne's own dreams of a life. The house extends well back, and it was in the back-house (the *'achterhuis'*, a rebuilding of 1740) that the families lived. After their capture in August 1944 they were all deported and died in concentration camps, only Anne's father survived. The diary was found later. Visitors see the whole of the back-house, including the concealed bookcase-door and such pathetic items as a map with the Allied advance hopefully indicated, pencil marks recording the growth of the children and magazine pictures pasted on the walls by Anne. The building is maintained by the Anne Frank Foundation, an organisation dedicated to the fight against prejudice and discrimination. The rest of the house is filled with an exhibition recording wartime German persecution as well as present-day information on persecution in all parts of the world.

Away to the S of the Westermarkt, on the far side of the Keizersgracht, stretches the Raadhuisstraat, a commercial and retail street cut through older buildings behind the Royal Palace (formerly the Town Hall, i.e. *Raadhuis*, from which it took its name). As you cross the Keizersgracht note the Coymanshuizen at Keizersgracht 177, one of the most severe examples of 'classical' canal-house design in the city. Designed in 1624 by the young Jacob van Campen (1595–1675), the absence of anything but the minimum of decoration, and that consisting only a few architectural motifs, is reminiscent of his Amsterdam masterpiece, the Royal Palace on the Dam. Meanwhile, on the Raadhuistraat the Winkelgalerij Utrecht (Utrecht Shopping Arcade) is on your right-hand side as you face S. This was built in 1899 and designed by the prolific A.L. van Gendt (1835–1901) for an insurance company. The façade is an apparently organic clustering of buildings apparently in a number of historic styles which on closer inspection are revealed to be expressive reworkings of traditional forms. Wrought iron and carved stone keep the surface lively, as do the crocodiles which snap at the passers-by and encourage them to purchase insurance.

Turn left into the Herengracht. The short stretch along the left-hand side has a group of buildings as interesting as any in the city. At the corner a clever adaptation of the 'corner house' theme of 1897 built in sandstone after original designs by Berlage. Next door at No. 182 is the massive sandstone frontage of the 'Zonnewijzer' (sundial) of 1772, a building which replaced a house of the same name on the site, inheriting the sundial in question; note the very grand double-sided stoep. Next a nicely restored late 18C house, next door to that a house of about the same age with a hipped roof hidden behind the flat cornice. This row continues with a 'baby' house, 17C in origin but with a much restored 19C façade and another flat-corniced 18C house. Then comes a splendid step-gabled wedding cake of a building, the Bartolotti House, a double house of 1617 designed by Hendrick de Keyser. The front follows the bend of the canal. The Bartolotti House now shares the **Theatre Museum** (Tuesday–Sunday, 11.00–17.00) with the 'Witte Huis' next door at 168, built in 1638 by Philip Vingboons (1608–78). The name of this latter comes from the white sandstone façade which stands out so prominently against the red brick of the Bartolotti House. It is difficult to believe that such abrupt transformation could come about merely in one generation. However, if you look closely, you will observe that the 'language' of the architecture is essentially the same—a

Huis Bartolotti and Witte Huis, home of the Theatre Museum

mixing and matching of copy-book architectural figures for gable, windows and the like. The Witte Huis has been rendered more austere by the removal of window surrounds during the 18C. It is the white trim of the detailing stark against the brickwork on the De Keyser building, with the traditional elements such as shutters, which give it the extra fussiness (and charm). Vingboons' house sports the first neck-gable in Amsterdam. After some modernisation in c 1730 the Witte Huis was given rich interior decoration, and later, ceiling and wall paintings by Isaac de Moucheron and Jacob de Wit. The right half of the Bartolotti House was substantially rebuilt at the same time. The elegant 18C houses, mansions really, continue as far as No. 160. If you are interested in seeing more in this vein, continue down the canal beyond Leliegracht, at least as far as Herengracht 120 (the 'Coningh van Denemarken'), the upper part of this step-gabled façade is authentic, the frontal stoep gives away the c 1800 reworking of the lower parts. Return along the E bank of the canal to the Raadhuisstraat.

Turn left to follow the Raadhuisstraat toward the Dam. At Raadhuisstraat 12 is the **Spaarpotten Museum** (Monday–Friday 13.00–16.00) which displays over 2000 money boxes, the earliest dating to 500 BC, in space no larger than a small apartment—there are another 10,000 in storage below. The walk continues as far as the Dam from where you have a view down the Damrak to the starting point at the Centraal Station.

4

Victorian Amsterdam: zoos and music

In 1848 Amsterdam at last broke through the barrier of the line of its 17C fortifications and the suburbs were built. One of the first areas for expansion was the Plantage, a district to the SE of the main city. The concentric rings of the 17C city went little further E than the river Amstel. The Weesp, the district bordering the E side of the river, had a number of almshouses for the elderly which remain to this day, and the Jewish community formed a large part of the population in the streets further north, but it was not until 1682 that the council decided to do something about the more or less derelict area between the Weesp and the docks on the IJ.

A project was conceived of laying out gardens to be rented to citizens in need of fresh air and peace of mind. For more than a century the Plantage served this purpose, the high walls required by law protecting not only discreet bourgeois retreats but also, increasingly, gambling dens and brothels.

In 1838 a group of wealthy citizens formed the Artis Natura Magistra society (meaning: Nature, Mistress of the Arts) in order to 'promote the knowledge of Natural History in a pleasing and appealing way', in due course they decided to build a zoo and sought land to do so. The reputation of the Plantage was then at an all time low and they managed to persuade the city authorities to allow them a large portion of land between the Plantage Middenlaan and the Entrepotdok. At the same time the suburb developed and 'improved'—elegant villas were built, the natural science departments of the University were grouped beside the Plantage Muidergracht.

The Plantage became, especially, a middle-class Jewish suburb. Immediately to the S the Tropenmuseum was opened in the 1920s; more recently the Nederlands Scheepvaartsmuseum was opened to the N. In recent decades the docklands became home to many squatters who have made their own contribution to this little-known (to visitors) corner of the city.

The district to the S of the concentric canals, bordering the W bank of the Amstel, was hurriedly built for working-class occupancy during the Victorian period; it forms the eastern part of the district known as the '*Oud Zuid*', Old South. Tall houses were crowded together to maximise returns on investment producing characteristically narrow and cavernous streets and this is might be why the area is called the '*Pijp*'—in the old days a long, narrow house was called a *pijpenla*, a pipe drawer.

Running through the heart of the district is Albert Cuypstraat, home of the famous market; just to the S of the Albert Cuypstraat is the Sarphatipark. On the E edge is the NINT museum of science and technology and to the S some remarkable examples of Amsterdam School architecture and town planning as the district runs into the '*Nieuw Zuid*', New South. The Pijp is now a multi-racial district, full of interesting shops and worth visiting for the experience of the market alone.

Cross the Boerenwetering canal and you move into rather posher suburbs grouped around the De Lairessestraat and extending N as far as the Overtoom on the far side of the Vondelpark. This includes the Museum and Concertgebouw districts, the elegant shops of P.C. Hooftstraat and the very desirable residences, often mansions to match the finest on the inner-city canals, scattered around the Vondelpark.

N of the Overtoom is the '*Oud West*', the Old West, which has an overall character something between the two parts of the Oud Zuid. Close to the heart of the city it houses office and shop workers.

As you move out of the city along any of the radial routes you progress through all the styles of architecture of the last 150 years, decade by decade. Right across the S of the city lies the Nieuw Zuid, the equivalent districts to the E and W are the Watergraafsmeer and Bos en Lommer. Amsterdam was not bombed during the War and a culture of conservation has ensured that replacement of collapsed or obsolete buildings is usually 'in keeping', thus each band of expansion has retained its own architectural character. The two walks described here take you through the various districts and present you with different Amsterdams from the conventional one.

Take Bus 22 (or the Museum Boat, see p 52) from the Centraal Station to the **Nederlands Scheepvaart Museum** (Dutch Maritime Museum; Tuesday–Saturday 10.00–17.00; Sunday and holidays 13.00–17.00), this museum opened in 1979 in a building which had been a marine warehouse built in 1657 to a design by Daniel Stalpaert. Carved pediments on the front and rear of the building depict the Maid of Amsterdam, a crown of ships, sea gods on one side, and on the other Neptune and Amphitrite.

The museum is arranged chronologically by themes and provides a thorough survey of the Dutch maritime story. Themes include fishing, navigation and cartography, war, trade, the East India Company (VOC), clipper ships, polar expeditions and the arrival of steam, among others. Exhibits include astonishing ship models, enormous charts, navigational instruments and the rest, and everywhere there are many fine paintings, with the Golden Age especially well represented. Most memorable are the ships, both inside and outside the museum, including the Royal Barge and two towing barges, a sailing lugger, a steam ice-breaker and a lifeboat. The star exhibit is the full-sized replica of the East Indiaman *De Amsterdam*.

Cross the Kattenburgerplein and follow the bend of the Prins Hendrikkade turning left into the Schippersgracht (note the fine view of 19C warehouses in the Entrepotdok) and then left again into Anne Frankstraat which leads to Plantage Parklaan. The district is immediately distinguishable by its large, elegant houses. You will find all styles here—medieval, neo-Renaissance, neo-classical and the rest. A number are what they call 'carpenter's classicism' or 'plasterer's style', generalised and often meretricious stucco façades concealing poorly designed structures and provide nothing but worry for their owners. The first turn on the left is the Henri Polaklaan where, at Henri Polaklaan 9, you will find the **Nationaal Vakbondsmuseum** (Tuesday–Friday 11.00–17.00; Sunday 13.00–17.00). This is a museum devoted to the history of Trades Unions in the Netherlands. The stunning Italian Renaissance building was designed by H.P. Berlage in 1900 for the diamond workers, the first Dutch Trade Union, as their headquarters.

At the end of Plantage Parklaan you reach the busy Plantage Middenlaan. Across the road is the **Hortus Botanicus** (April–October: weekdays 09.00–17.00; Sunday and holidays, 11.00–17.00). This was originally an apothecary's garden; it was later stocked with exotic plants brought back from the Indies (seeds from a coffee plant from here were presented to Louis XIV and were used to found the South American coffee business) and served as the botanical garden of Amsterdam University from 1682. There was a menagerie on this site before the Artis opened up the road, and Louis Bonaparte wished to turn the Hortus into a proper zoo. The greatest attraction here was the huge water lily plant whose leaves could support whole families; this, however, died when its greenhouse was demolished in the 1960s. The Hortus remains one of the more interesting and nontouristy attractions in the city.

The Wertheimpark opposite is a tiny reminder of what the original Plantage gardens must have been like with its fancy entrance. It is named in memory of A.C. Wertheim, a 19C philanthropic Jewish banker, whose motto was 'Be a Jew in the synagogue and a human being in society'.

Plantage Middenlaan runs SE towards the Oosterpark. The complex of buildings lying on the left is the **Artis Zoo** (daily 09.00–17.00). Entrance to the zoo and **Zoological Museum** is via Plantage Kerklaan 38–40 (the first turn on the left). As was said above, the Artis dates back to 1838. The idea was initiated by G.F. Westerman (1807–90) and the original conception was for more than a mere display of animals. Today the Artis includes a zoo with some 6000 animals, beautiful gardens, a very good aquarium, a planetarium (last show 16.00) and a museum and library. It is not cheap, but is ideal for children who do not seem to notice the language difference! They will be especially taken by the children's farm. The whole ethos is appropriately ecological.

Across the main road at Plantage Middenlaan 36 stands the Hollandse Schouwburg, opened in 1897, originally as an opera house. Later, as the home of the Nederlansche Toneelvereeniging (Dutch Theatre Union), it was the centre for new theatre in the city. The theatre was intimately connected with Jewish life and for that reason, with a piece of ugly German irony, it was chosen as the place where Jews were brought prior to deportation and death. On Remembrance Day (4 May) each year it is a place of pilgrimage, a national memorial to the murdered thousands.

The Plantage Middenlaan continues SE towards the **Muiderpoort**, a gate rebuilt in 1770, beyond again, through the Alexanderplein and across the bridge over the Singelgracht, towards the large Royal Tropical Institute which includes, at Linnaeusstraat 2, the **Tropenmuseum** (Monday–Friday 10.00–17.00; Saturday and Sunday 12.00–17.00). This is a most comprehensive introduction to the life-styles and problems of tropical and sub-tropical peoples, all housed in a handsome building of 1926. In the huge central hall and on three levels of galleries surrounding and overlooking the main hall you can see imaginatively presented displays, sometimes, as in a memorable recent exhibition on the Yemen, you find actual reconstructions of houses, villages and enviroments. Originally a monument to Dutch Imperial pride, the Tropenmuseum (set as it is in an area full of new immigrants) is now an important anthropological and ethnological institute. The **Soeterijn Theatre**, part of the Tropenmuseum complex, is one venue for World Music in the city. Events are listed in *Uitkrant* and elsewhere.

Cross back over the bridge to the Alexanderplein and walk (or take Tram 10) W along the Sarphatistraat, past the science departments of the University, across the Weesperstraat and the Professor Tulpplein, over the Hogebrug, across the Frederiksplein to the stop just before the Vijzel-gracht/Weteringschans/Weteringlaan roundabout from where it is a short walk S down the Ferdinand Bolstraat to the Albert Cuypstraat.

This takes you through Dr Samuel Sarphati's Amsterdam. Dr Sarphati (1813–66) has been called the father of modern Amsterdam. He was a financier and philanthropist who sought to restore Amsterdam's fortunes, and provide employment for the poor, by a series of large works. The Amstel Hotel between Professor Tulpplein and the Amstel was one such development; it was the city's first modern hotel (see Hotels).

Built in 1867 it commanded a view across to the Frederiksplein where his greatest achievement stood, the Paleis voor Volksvlijt, the Palace of National Industry, built between 1857–64 (burned down in 1929), an enormous glass and iron structure along the lines of the Crystal Palace, London or the Grand Palais in Paris. The site is now occupied by the Nederlandse Bank, a glass, concrete and steel edifice of 1968.

The whole, rather grand, Victorian tone of the area, the elegant villas of the Weteringschans and the pompous commercial spread of the Frederiks-plein, reflect his vision for the city. Of course, much of this land was newly released for building after 1848 when the town walls were systematically removed. The spaciousness is in stark contrast to the jostling, crowded Pijp.

If you linger in this area it is worth a short walk to look at the **Theater Carré** which stands at Amstel 115–25, 100 or so metres N of the Hogebrug. Built for Oscar Carré in only a few months in 1887 this one time circus still dominates the river front, the roof appearing to float above the crisply detailed, apparently under-scale façade. If you approach you will see the decorative details of clowns, jesters and dancers. The architects, J.P.F. van Rossem and W.J. Vuyk, based their design on an example in Cologne. If you are here during the Christmas season be sure to try to get a ticket for the annual circus.

Another Amsterdam marvel lies in the river in front of the Carré, the **Amstelsluizen**, great gates that control the flow of the river through the city. Each day at about 21.30 they are closed, by hand, and a distant hydraulic station starts pumping hundreds of thousands of cubic metres of water through the city's canals, thereby keeping Amsterdam sweet.

As you enter the Pijp the first building on the right at Stadhouderskade 78 is the former **Heineken Brewery**, now a museum of beer and brewing (guided tours only, tel. 523 9239; allow two hours for the tour). In 1864 G.A. Heineken bought 'The Haystack', a brewery which dated from 1592. The modern, model factory, which for a generation was one of the most popular sights in the city, ceased production in 1988. Rather than bulldoze it the Heineken company decided to maintain the factory for visitors who can still file wonderingly past huge copper vats standing in an enormous white-tiled room big enough to accommodate a power station. Heineken still provides a free beer at the end of the tour.

Continue S along the Ferdinand Bolstraat as far as the Albert Cuypstraat. The line of the Albert Cuypstraat follows that of the old *Zaagmolensloot*, the Saw Mill Canal, a stretch of industrial waterway dating back many years. When building began in the Pijp in the late 1860s the windmill owners objected to losing their canal and it was not until 1889 that it was filled in. This is the reason why the Albert Cuypstraat is so broad in comparison to neighbouring streets.

Construction of the Pijp had started in the area around the Frans Halsstraat (which runs parallel to the Ferdinand Bolstraat to the W) and by the end of the century the whole quarter was complete. At an early stage the district had been considered as a potential site for the new Centraal Station but, obviously, this did not occur and it remains one of the few areas in Amsterdam without architecture, that is to say, without monuments of interest 'in themselves'. Some elements of the earlier Amsterdam suburb remain, notably around the Gerrit Douplein where a few smaller houses are witness to individual citizens' resistance to property speculators.

The Sarphatipark, a few streets to the S, has a memorial to Dr Samuel Sarphati erected in 1886. Sarphati had wanted a much larger park, something the size of the bourgeoisie's Vondelpark. Today his image smiles down upon a most heterogeneous population: Asian, Middle Eastern, North African and South American immigrants; third and fourth generation working-class Amsterdammers; a transient population of students and, as everywhere else, colonising yuppies. The Albert Cuypstraat market itself (open Monday–Saturday 09.30–16.30) is a fascinating place through which to wander—it is especially good for fish and vegetables, notably exotic vegetables, clothes, shoes and jewellery (new and second-hand). In recent years the street itself, and the surrounding streets, have filled with excellent small shops, bars and cafés.

When you have seen enough follow Albert Cuypstraat to its western extremity and cross the bridge to the Ruysdaelstraat taking the second on the right which leads up to the J. Vermeerplein. Here is an early building of 1911–12 by M. de Klerk (1884–1923), the **Hillehuis**, an important precursor of Amsterdam School architecture by the movement's working-class child prodigy. From here the G. Metsustraat leads to the Concertgebouw.

The **Concertgebouw** is a sprawling neo-classical pile facing N over the Museumplein. It was designed by A.L. van Gendt (1835–1901) and built between 1886 and 1888; it was recently (controversially) remodelled, exactly in time for its 100th birthday, with a new basement and a glazed gallery on the S side, by P. de Bruijn (b. 1942). The Concertgebouw was the first outpost of what was to become a middle-class invasion of the Oud Zuid. The architect, who had worked on the Centraal Station with Cuypers, was famous rather for his building to a price than for any artistic excellence.

It is, frankly, a rather boring building; however, the acoustics are reckoned to be the best in the world. The building was financed by private capital and soon became a most fashionable destination. The Royal Concertgebouw Orchestra is world famous. It was conducted for the first 50 years by Mengelberg (who was sacked for his anti-Nazi views in 1942 despite his being a close friend of Mahler and Richard Strauss); Haitink is the most celebrated recent conductor; the present conductor is Riccardo Chailly.

On Wednesdays at 12.30 there is a free concert (arrive early) which may be the full orchestra in rehearsal—not to be missed, for unless you buy tickets well in advance (tel. 671 8345) you will not get to a concert.

The large green(ish) area to the N of the Concertgebouw is the Museum-plein. At the far end, straddling the Museumstraat, is the Rijksmuseum and hidden by trees and buildings to the left include the Van Goghmuseum.

The Museumplein is not the most amenable public space in the city. For a start, traffic roars through it at depressingly high speed. At the N end there are some basketball pitches and a skateboard ramp which provide amusement for spectators as well as the (often talented) kids playing there. Not far away on the corner of the Hobbemastraat and the Hobbemakade is the Zuiderbad, bathing pool. On the E side is the American Embassy. There are a number of memorials dotted around (all molested by grafittists), to female and gypsy concentration camp victims, among others.

Follow the Van Baerlestraat N and you will see, on your right, the **Stedelijkmuseum** (daily 11.00–17.00). The Van Baerlestraat side is glazed like a shopfront, most unusual in a museum. The museum owes its existence to the bequest to the city in 1890 of the collections of Sophia de Bruyn-Suasso. Her house, which she had also bequeathed, was far too small, and it was therefore decided to build a new museum to house both the De Bruyn-Suasso collections and also the works of contemporary artists for which there was no space in the Rijksmuseum. The present building is based around the neo-Renaissance block of 1895 which faces onto the Paulus Potterstraat and was designed by A.W. Weissmann (1858–1923). A new S wing (including that glazed portion) was added in 1954, and further extensions and alterations have followed.

The first floor of the Stedelijkmuseum

The Stedelijk is Amsterdam's museum for modern art, the period covered being roughly 1850 to the present day; the permanent collection includes paintings, sculpture, graphic art, applied art, industrial design, posters, pop art, video, photography and installations. The Stedelijk's strengths are Malevich (a forgotten collection buried under rubble in Germany, sought out and snapped up by the director Willem Sandberg), the De Stijl group (Mondriaan and Doesburg) and post-war art generally. The collection of Gerrit Rietveld furniture is worth seeing. Karel Appel's 1956 mural in the former café was controversial at one time; he was awarded the commission after another of his murals, at the Town Hall, was covered up. Although some of the permanent collection is always on view it is best seen between May and September (the show is changed at intervals). During the rest of the year the ground floor at least may be given over to special exhibitions.

A short way up from the Stedelijk at Paulus Potterstraat 7 is the **Rijks-museum Vincent van Gogh** (Tuesday–Saturday 10.00–17.00, Sunday and holidays 13.00–17.00) in a beautiful building of 1963–73, designed by Gerrit Rietveld (1888–1964). The museum owns some 200 paintings, 500 drawings and 700 letters. When Vincent's brother Theo died in 1891 his widow, Jo van Gogh-Bonger, inherited her husband's collection which included the bulk of Vincent's works. She devoted her life to promoting Vincent's work, publishing his letters to Theo and arranging exhibitions around the world. Her son, Vincent Willem van Gogh, continued his mother's work creating the Vincent van Gogh Foundation in 1962 which engineered the opening of this museum in 1974.

You enter the museum via broad steps set at right angles to the glass doors of the main entrance; you may have to queue for tickets, but unless you are behind a badly organised coach party you will not have to wait long. You pass into a low, dark foyer with a cloakroom to the right. A second set of glass doors lead straight into the central hall of the museum, brightly lit from the glass roof and offering a view up to all the floors of the display area. The effect of light and air is impressive. The museum shop is to your right, lifts to all floors directly ahead and the restaurant/café ahead and to the left. (The restaurant has a glazed open-air section for fine weather, mind the step if you go outside with a tray.) The museum has an enterprising exhibition policy and the displays are frequently changed—though the core collection of Van Gogh's work is always on show.

The GROUND FLOOR has a display drawn from the museum's large collection of late 19C paintings. These are on the whole dark and serious-looking works chosen to represent the varieties of contemporary art known to Vincent. Artists represented include Honoré Daumier, Thomas Couture, Puvis de Chavannes, Maurice Denis and Fantin Latour from France and Jan Toorop and Jozef Israëls from the Netherlands.

The FIRST FLOOR has a representative selection of Vincent's paintings set out in chronological order. The exhibition starts at the N end with brooding images from his time at his parents' home in Nuenen. Peasant heads, landscapes and landmarks (for example the Old Church at Nuenen) frame the celebrated Potato Eaters of April 1885. Vincent was 32 years old and after a number of false starts (as an art dealer, missionary and teacher) he had turned to painting. As we walk around even the early exhibits we note how many have been given very precise dates; one gets the impression that time is important, that time is being measured out in tiny parts, we know that Vincent did not live long and this is the essence of the Vincent myth.

In striking contrast to Vincent's dour images The Haymakers by Leon Augustin Lhermitte is big and bright, celebrating a much more lyrical idea of rural work and community. Brighter colour was Vincent's first borrowing from the art he saw in France when he arrived in 1886. Initially, with the Hill of Montmartre with a Quarry it is simply brighter, but by the spring of 1887 with The View from Vincent's Room, Rue Lepic and Japonaiserie: The flowering Plum Tree (after Hiroshige) we can observe a pleasure in dabbing, disjointed brushstrokes quite different from the oppressively ploughed brushwork in the earlier pictures. The influence was, of course, from Impressionism and its stylised off-shoots, such as Neo-Impressionism.

But although the colour is brighter, it retains a peculiar intensity—as, for example, in the Self Portrait with a grey felt hat where orange-yellow is used to halo the head. In Red Cabbages and Onions he uses coloured outline to mark a structure on the canvas, and in Still life with Lemons, Pears, Apples, Grapes and an Orange he paints over the frame as well, colour bursts out into our own space.

If he found his characteristic technique in Paris, he found his characteristic subject matter upon his return to the countryside. He left Paris for Arles in Southern France. His dream was to set up a community of artists, the actuality was a period of corrosive isolation although he managed to persuade Gauguin to join him for a while (the famous Sunflower paintings were painted to decorate Gauguin's room). He was isolated, but he was remarkably productive. He used so much paint and canvas that he had to write begging letters to his brother. Pictures piled up, one can often detect the impression left by the canvas of one picture in the paint surface of another. His fascination with people and places continued in works such as The Yellow House, Vincent's Room, Gauguin's Armchair and The Zouave. He depicted the surrounding countryside with vivid colours. We can trace the seasons of 1888—from the Orchard in Blossom to The Harvest. The horizon lines push farther and farther up the picture surface, crowding into the sky like those of Brueghel. Gauguin's acrimonious departure and Vincent's despair led, as everybody knows, to a breakdown and his celebrated mutilation of his ear. Despite that there are many records of lyrical moments—for example, Boats on the beach at Saintes-Maries-de-la-Mer. Committed to an asylum at St Rémy, Vincent ceased painting for a while but in the summer of 1889 he began once more and his abiding interest in older art is witnessed by his free copies after Delacroix (the Pietà), Rembrandt (The Raising of Lazarus) and Millet (a series after the Labours of the Field).

Vincent's madness has become the subject matter of his paintings for many people. This is a pity, because if we are to believe his own estimation of his work we should interpret him more as a realist painter searching not principally for expression of his feelings but for the representation of appearances. For example Undergrowth, a contorted pattern of shrubs, can all too easily be read as an allegory of paranoia when it is, in truth, an exercise in realism. It should be set beside the bland prettiness of the Vase with Irises. The dramatic Roots and Tree Trunks, painted only a short time before he died, is balanced by the neutral ordinariness (for Van Gogh!) of Daubigny's Garden.

The chronological display returns one to the staircase. Upstairs on the SECOND FLOOR there are specially darkened galleries displaying water-colours and drawings by Van Gogh, Gauguin, Odilon Redon, Pissarro and Toulouse-Lautrec and many others. The Study Collection hangs floor to ceiling behind a glass wall. Special exhibitions complete this floor and the THIRD FLOOR; recent shows have included an exhibition of Japanese prints (Vincent was an enthusiastic collector) and works from the H.W. Mesdag Museum in The Hague.

This is probably far enough for one walk. Depending on how thoroughly you took up the options it might have taken a morning or a whole day. Trams 2, 3, 12, 15 and 16 will take you back to the Centraal Station, our usual point of departure and arrival.

Ideal cities: the Vondelpark and the New South

Trams 2, 3, 12, 15 and 16 from the Centraal Station will set you down near to the Stedelijk Museum from where we take up the walk. Heading N up the Van Baerlestraat you cross first the Jan Luykenstraat (at the E end of which is the 'Residence Ed. Cuypers', a house built in 1899 by and for the architect to which it owes its name, much influenced by Norman Shaw's architecture and itself influential on the Amsterdam School of architects) and then the P.C. Hooftstraat, a fashionable shopping street.

The Van Baerlestraat then crosses a handsome bridge affording good views over the Vondelpark at which point it becomes the Constantijn Huygensstraat. Continue as far as the Roemer Visscherstraat and turn right to see the curious suite of houses, Nos 20–30a, in a variety of 'national styles': Dutch, English, French, German, Italian, Russian and Spanish. This kind of gimmickry reminds us that the Vondelpark area was largely built by speculators who had to woo potential purchasers; no doubt the selling point here was that the houses would one day be mentioned in guide books.

Continue as far as Tesselschadestraat, turn left and left again into Vondelstraat. Cross the Constantijn Huygensstraat and at the bottom of a low slope, marooned in the middle of the road, is P.J.H. Cuypers' Amsterdam masterpiece, now known as the **Vondelkerk**, previously the Heilige Hartkerk, Church of the Sacred Heart. This was built in 1872–80 to serve the wealthy families who had moved into the district. It remained in use until 1979 but by 1985, when it was adapted for use as offices, the richly furnished interior had been stripped. The church is designed after German Gothic models and its clustered spires have a most appealingly romantic look.

Cuypers also designed the setting, the oval 'square', and a number of houses nearby at Vondelstraat 73–79. The façade of No. 77, which was Cuypers' own home, has a tiled decoration filling three 'window' bays showing the architect, the mason and the (jealous) critic; the motto means something like: Jan thinks it up, Piet puts it up, Claes rips it down. Oh, who cares?

You should not leave the Vondelstraat without seeing the **Hollandse Manege** (daily 10.00–24.00). At Vondelstraat 140, through an arch and along a passage, is an indoor riding school designed in 1881 by A.L. van Gendt, the architect of the Concertgebouw. Follow the broad stairway to the left and pass either through the door marked 'Tribune' or the one marked 'Foyer'. The first takes you to a balcony from which you can watch horses and riders exercising. The smell and the damped acoustics are extraordinary. The other door leads to a café. All the spaces are decorated with equinabilia. The model for the Manege was, of course, the Spanische Reitschule in Vienna, but this was done in the age of steam. The prefabricated iron roof is by the St Pancras Iron Works of London, as were the horse stalls, some of which remain. The huge brackets along the walls do not support the roof; it rests on top of the walls which are held in place with tie-rods. The horses' heads which intersperse the lights along the frieze at balcony level are cast in zinc.

Walk back up to the Vondelkerk and turn right into the **Vondelpark**. All of the streets in this section are named after poets, just as the streets in the Pijp were named after painters. **Joost van den Vondel** (1582–1674) has been compared to Shakespeare (because he wrote plays) and Milton (because of the self-conscious classicism of his work). In truth, comparisons of this kind do little good as Vondel's works have a temper of their own, a result of his distinctive personality and, of course, of his Dutchness. Little has been translated, though a hunt through your local library might unearth the translation of his *Lucifer*, a play which takes place in heaven and thought-fully and wittily examines the struggle between God and his favourite angel as they squabble over newly-created man. His most celebrated play is *Gijsbrecht van Amstel*, an historical drama which deals, like Shakespeare's history plays, with the origins of Amsterdam's right to rule and the means of applying that right. Unlike Shakespeare's plays, Vondel's work is static, action is described in speeches rather than mimed on the stage. There was no rabble to please in performances in Vondel's Amsterdam. *Macbeth's* high action, most of it off-stage and conveyed to the seated, courtly viewer in rich verse, is the nearest Shakespearean equivalent. A more telling comparison might be with the work of Dryden who was also a poet with a strong sense of decorum in poetry.

Vondel's career, in a city without a court, was notably different from the careers available to his London contemporaries. He rose from tradesman's rank through talent and learning, early in life he was a Calvinist, by middle age he had become a Catholic. The small fortune he accumulated through writing and trade was lost by his son and at the age of 70 he was forced to return to work, in the city's pawnbrokers (see Walk 2, Bank van Lening) from which he was sacked at the age of 80 for writing during work-time. He died at the age of 92 from hypothermia.

That the city's principal park should be named after him, rather than after Rembrandt or any of the more famous painters, is an interesting choice. One might speculate that it had to do with his special Dutchness in that he was a literary figure (all Dutch literature is the private property of Dutch speakers thanks to the arrogance of European neighbours who have shown no curiosity about it); it might have to do with his broad religious appeal, having written as a Calvinist as well as a Catholic. Whatever it was, the Vondelpark was conceived and laid out between 1865 and 1877 by a group of private citizens rather than by the authorities. It was landscaped in the 'English' style by J.D. Zocher (1791–1870) and L.P. Zocher (1820–1915) and makes the most of its limited space with wandering paths, open and closed vistas over lawns and water and a great variety of trees, shrubs and flowers. The park is a regular venue for outdoor theatre and musical events during the summer months (details in *Uitkrant* or enquire at the VVV). The park is more like Central Park than Hyde Park, even moderately good weather brings out jugglers, buskers and posers, especially around the cafés.

Immediately on your left as you enter the park is the **Netherlands Film Museum** (museum open Tuesday–Sunday 13.00–20.30; cinema box office open Monday–Friday from 08.30, Saturday from 13.00, Sunday from 11.00) set in a gracious pavilion designed by P.J. Hamer (1812–87) and W. Hamer (1843–1913) in 1881. Since the arrival of directors Hoos Blotkamp and Eric de Kuyper, the Film Museum has become an important and lively centre for film both in the city and in the nation as a whole. The interior has been re-assembled from the remains of the Cinema Parisien, Amsterdam's first purpose-built cinema dating back to 1910, which was rescued in 1987; by early 1993 the whole should have been revamped.

There are three screenings daily, all in the original languages. The museum holds remarkable stocks of film, technical equipment, stills and posters. At weekends in summer there are outdoor screenings on the (highly trendy) bar-terrace. There is a library full of reference books. There are a variety of prices for the cinema with reduced 10 and 60 visit rates, reductions for students and senior citizens and a membership scheme.

The Vondelpark district is full of interesting buildings. Across the pond from the Film Museum is **'t Rond Blauwe Theehuis** by H.J. Baanders. This is a rigorous modernist building in a functionalist style and a very pleasant space in which to eat cake. Families may prefer the atmosphere at the café further to the SW where there is a playground. The park itself is surrounded by beautiful houses. Near the entrance on the Stadhouderskade there are some striking terraced houses in a Parisian style by I. Gosschalk (1838–1907) who is probably better known for his reconstruction of half-timbered Old Dutch at Reguliersgracht 57–59 and 63. For the rest, you should wander the streets lining the S of the park—the Van Eeghensstraat, Koningslaan and especially around the Emmaplein. Some of these houses have a faintly decaying grandeur at its most melancholic and powerful on a damp afternoon.

Leave the district by the Jacob Obrechtstraat which leads to the Jacob Obrechtplein. Just along the Heinzestraat to the right is a synagogue of 1928 by H. Elte (1880–1944), a strikingly rationalist treatment of Amsterdam School features, rather in the manner of Frank Lloyd Wright. To the right of the Jacob Obrechtplein in B. Ruloffsstraat is a housing block by J.F. Staal (1879–1940) from 1922–24. Although plainly an Amsterdam School building, the regularity of the geometry and decoration show some compromise here. Staal went on to work in a more technologically modernist style as can be seen in his 'Skyscraper' (see below). At the end of the B. Ruloffsstraat you cross the bridge S to reach the Beethovenstraat.

You are now on an island bounded by the Stadiongracht and the Noorder and Zuider Amstelkanaals. At the far W end is the **Olympisch Stadion** by J. Wils (1891–1972); it has not yet, at the time of writing, been demolished. Its clean lines and science-fiction tower are excellent examples of early Deco optimism and it is a shame that the whole thing is soon to go. From in front of the the the stadium, Stadionweg stretches the whole width of this island, the Minervalaan slices it in two from N–S (the Minervalaan was originally intended to lead to a local railway station, this was never realised and the Amsterdam Zuid Station is lost away to the S off the Beethovenstraat).

That the whole area is a treasure trove of fine 20C architecture is no surprise when you consider that it was conceived as a direct result of the authorities turning to an architect of world stature, Hendrik Petrus Berlage (1856–1934), in 1900. The last time that something of this kind had happened, several centuries before, the Town Hall had allowed Frans Hendriksz. Oetgens and Hendrick Jacobsz. Staets to initiate the concentric canal system, and with some success.

In 1917 Berlage produced his second *Plan Zuid*. He hoped to achieve a similar mixture of monumentality and the picturesque to that of the city centre. Public buildings were to be mixed in with the peoples' housing, neighbourhoods were to be linked by broad avenues, demarkations between areas for the rich and the poor were to be reduced. Three-quarters of the housing was to be blocks of workers' flats, though the area has since become rather posh. The continuous street façades and enclosed courts give the blocks a communal look. They are uniformly of brick, with tiled roofs and wooden windows (Berlage and his followers preferred these 'honest' materials) and there are plenty of fine details. Doors and windows are often treated with startling novelty; the concrete frameworks which supported the structure allowed the walls to be played with like fabrics.

Architects sympathetic to Berlage (generally speaking, Amsterdam School architects) came of age and took a dominant role in the design of the Nieuw Zuid as well as in planning generally, both national and local. For example, P.L. Kramer (1881–1961), who had trained with Cuypers, joined the Dienst Publiek Werken (Public Works Service) at the time of the Plan Zuid; to him we owe many fine and often fantastical bridges in the city (for example, the Leidsebrug near the American Hotel). However, the ascendancy of this group during the period 1917–40 while the Nieuw Zuid was being constructed meant that other kinds of modernist architects did not get quite so many opportunities.

Follow the Beethovenstraat S as far as Cliostraat, one right turn before the Stadionweg. You have to peer into a secluded square to see the **Openluchtschool**, Open Air School, at Cliostraat 36–40, designed in 1929 by J. Duiker (1890–1935). This is a monument not only to early concrete and glass architecture, it is also a monument to educational principles in an age of optimism. The structure faces south and the classrooms extend onto open balconies giving the city children the benefit of fresh air and sun.

Just around the corner in Albrecht Dürerstraat is the equally handsome and directly influenced **Montessori School** of 1936 by W. van Tijen (1894–1974) which has removable glazing on the S and W sides. Just behind the Montessori School at Anthonie van Dijckstraat 4–12 are a group of 'drive-in' houses (also by Van Tijen) where access is via the ground floor garage, a concept now so commonplace that it demands an effort of will to realise that these were built as early as 1937 as housing for modern middle-managers. Follow the A. van Dijkstraat to the W, take a right and a left turn to reach the Minervalaan.

At the top of Minervalaan, on the right-hand side at Apollolaan 141, is a house of 1961 by H. Salmonson. The upper (living) floor appears to float above the shrubs; it in fact rests on circular posts in a proper Le Corbusierian manner. Diagonally across the traffic island at the junction of Apollolaan with the Willem Witsenstraat is another schools complex (one beneath the other plus a third). The block combining the Willemspark School and a second Montessori School was designed by H. Herzberger and was completed as recently as 1983. Opposite the end of the Minervalaan is the Lennon-Ono Bed Peace Hilton (you can count four large hotels on this stretch of road).

Follow the Apollolaan E to the junction with Stadionweg. On the right, raised up on a circular understructure, is the **Rijksversekeringbank** of 1937–39 by D. Roosenburg. A compact and attractive office block, it features dividable office spaces with movable wall fittings, and a bright office canteen on the top floor.

Across the road, where the Apollolaan crosses the Amstelkanaal, is the Apollohal, an exhibition space most often used for five indoor tennis courts. This building, by A. Boecken and W. Zweedijk and dating from 1935, is sometimes used to illustrate the principles of 'Groep '32', being thoroughly functional, even though it has some decoratively adapted architectural forms, such as circular windows. It is not in the best of condition at present.

Leave the Olympic island and follow the linear forest of the Churchill-laan E. This is another of Berlage's grand avenues; to the right you can get glimpses of the sprawling RAI Congress Centre (1977–81) but what makes the prospect different is that from time to time through the trees you might glimpse the 12 storey building at the far end, the so-called '**Wolkenkrabber**', or Skyscraper. For a good view turn right into the Waalstraat and approach from the Merwedeplein. This was the Netherlands' first high-rise housing block, designed by J.F. Staal and built between 1927 and 1930. It had rubbish chutes, a lift, central heating and hot water supply, speaking tubes and bells from the start, but then it was not to be a warren for the unemployed, each floor had two six-roomed flats.

Follow the Waalstraat S, across the Rooseveltlaan, and turn left into the the Lekstraat. At Lekstraat 61–63 stands a former synagogue, designed by A. Elzas in 1934–37. The Nieuw Zuid was a popular destination for Jews fleeing persecution during the 1930s and there are a number of interesting synagogues. The Frank family lived on the Merwedeplein before they went into hiding. The Lekstraat synagogue now houses the **Verzetsmuseum** (Tuesday–Friday 10.00–17.00; Saturday and Sunday 13.00–17.00), the museum of the Dutch Resistance. The museum gives a compelling account of life under the Occupation, using displays, sounds and reconstructions. One ingenious invention is a bicycle-powered printing press. The synagogue itself is an austere, stone-faced building, combining a synagogue with a meeting hall and above, a flat.

Return up the Waalstraat and cross the footbridge over Amstelkanaal to enter the P.L. Takstraat. You are now in what is possibly the most famous Amsterdam School housing complex of them all. It was designed by M. de Klerk and P.L. Kramer for the socialist housing association **De Dageraad** (The Dawn) and was built between 1919 and 1922. De Klerk and Kramer designed De Dageraad from top to bottom. The estate has three- and four-roomed flats spread through a variety of terraces and squares. It was built under the protection of the socialist councillor Wibaut and therefore had plenty of funding which accounts for the high standard of the exteriors. The estates on the Olympic island were built in later, more stringent times, the decorative brickwork being applied to structures devised by engineering rather than aesthetic criteria. It has often been said that Amsterdam School architecture is more pleasant to look at than to live in. Windows are small, rooms are sometimes eccentrically planned. The folksy materials and craftsmanlike details are probably more pleasing to art historians than they were to the original inhabitants, though there was much community pride in the achievements of the housing associations; fully two generations passed before there was a widespread revival of interest in these buildings.

Away to the NW of the city, N of the Westerpark, De Klerk's Hembrugstraat complex built between 1917 and 1922 (take Bus 22 from the Centraal Station to see it) squats beneath the Amsterdam School's most famous icon, the brick spire of the '**Eigen Haard**'. Here the flamboyance seems not only a declamatory gesture to assert the self-reliance of the poor, but also a means of reassuring well-meaning liberals on passing trains (or enraging reactionaries who thought the buildings too luxurious!). Amsterdam School buildings have recently become increasingly gentrified and the city's underclass has been banished to the bleak estates of the Bijlmer, away to the SE.

Leave the De Dageraad via the Burgemeester Tellegenstraat and take the Tolstraat (running S) from the H. de Keijserplein. At the far end at Tolstraat 129, is the **NINT/Nederlands Institute voor Nijverheid en Techniek** (Monday–Friday, 10.00–16.00; weekends and holidays 13.00–17.00), located in a former diamond-cutting factory. The building is by H. van Arkel and dates from 1907, the style is ostensibly art nouveau, though the severity and

By clever grouping of forms and attention to detail, the Amsterdam School architects brought a new kind of dignity to public housing as here in De Dageraad

rectilinearity make this an unusual example. The museum's permanent collections cover all aspects of science and technology such as physics, metals, transport, construction, chemistry, energy, telecommunications and computers. There are a lot of 'hands on' exhibits which will entertain both adults and children, and there is a special children's room containing all manner of instructive apparatus including a giant soap-bubble maker which allows you to put yourself *inside* a bubble. The museum is due to be rehoused in the centre of town. In the new display there will be a much greater emphasis on chemistry.

Across the way the curious round-shaped building at Tolstraat 154 is the former Meeting-House (of 1929, by J.A. Brinkman) of the Theosophists, with next door the Adminstrative Building (of 1926, by L.C. van der Vlugt). The Meeting-House, with its apparently floating roof, was restored in the early 1980s and is now a public library.

Tram 4 from the Van Woustraat will take you back to the Centraal Station.

HISTORICAL INTRODUCTION

The maritime region of the Netherlands stretching from the Rhine/Maas delta to the Frisian Isles is known as Holland; it is nowadays divided into two provinces, North and South Holland. The Netherlands as a whole is made up of twelve such provinces or regions, the twelfth, Flevoland, consisting of the reclaimed land retrieved from the waters of the IJsselmeer since the last war. Although to the English-speaking world the whole country is Holland, to the Dutch their homeland is the Netherlands—Holland is the name of two provinces.

Throughout the Middle Ages this damp corner of Europe had developed from being a collection of feudal fiefs, isolated fishing and farming communities and trading towns into a broad alliance of peoples. The alliance was a pragmatic one brought about by common interest. For example, the economy of each town relied upon specific privileges or control of particular trades and industries—these privileges were wrested from the succession of nominal rulers, the last of whom was King Philip. The interest of the towns, which relied upon a degree of economic independence, was not always in the interests of the local nobility which sought to tax a revenue out of the towns, though both gained in periods of prosperity for the towns. Towns like Amsterdam relied upon playing off various local rulers the one against the other. There was a great deal of local rivalry sometimes escalating to minor warfare.

In the first place the simple business of survival had demanded co-operation; nearly the whole of the present-day province of Holland was under water all or some of the time during the Middle Ages. From time to time there were massive floods—such as the St Elisabeth's Day Flood of 18 November 1421 which made Dordrecht into the island it remains to this day. Many towns still have at their heart a prehistoric 'terp' or artificial mound, built originally to provide refuge above high tide. The amphibian life style of the region's bog-communities was commented upon by Pliny at the time of Julius Caesar; he observed that the people lived between the sea and the earth and even made their fires from burning mud (he obviously did not understand the uses of peat). He omitted, however, to mention their remarkable engineering achievements in holding back the sea with dykes and living above the water on these terps. It has been calculated that all the Netherlands' 1260 prehistoric terps combined make a volume some thirty times greater than the largest of the Egyptian pyramids. These mounds are no longer an immediately visible feature of the landscape having been built over for more than a thousand years; they are most frequently to be observed in Friesland. Communities combined to throw up sea walls and drain the low-lying lands behind, these lands were the polders. A typical polder landscape, characteristically adapted to dairy farming, can be found in the area to the north of the IJ—the fields here date back to the 16C and 17C.

During the Middle Ages the windmill became a principal means of pumping the polders dry. Windmills have all but disappeared from the landscape, but an attractive set (or *gang*) can be seen at Kinderdijk. It was not until the 19C and the advent of the steam-pump that the huge inland lake, known as the Haarlemmermeer, which lay between the towns of Amsterdam, Haarlem and Leiden, was at last drained. Schiphol airport lies in the middle of this drained lake. There are several fascinating museums devoted to the industrial archaeology of hydraulic engineering near enough to Amsterdam to make a good day out.

Another not to be underestimated unifying element was the Dutch language which had descended from the Germanic Frankish dialect of the region, taken into itself much Saxon, and become established as an important European tongue with its own literature. (Dutch is not the only official language of the modern Netherlands, in the north-east of the country Frisian is spoken daily by 300,000 people.) There is no Dutch race any more than there is an Irish, Scottish or English race and language is the identifying feature of nationhood and community. Dutch is today one of the European Community languages, spoken by some twenty million people in the Netherlands and Belgium—more widely spoken, therefore, than all the Scandinavian languages put together. Had history progressed differently, had New York remained New Amsterdam, had India remained Dutch rather than falling to the English East India Company, then it might be that all the world would draw their analogies from Joost van den Vondel rather than Shakespeare and aspire to a large house on Lang Eiland rather than Long Island. One of the principal reasons that we think of the Dutch as painters rather than poets is probably because so few of us speak a word of the language—whereas we feel we can instantly recognise the worlds of Jacob van Ruisdael and Vincent van Gogh.

The first high point of this civilisation was during the 15C when much of the Netherlands, together with present-day Belgium, Luxembourg and large parts of the Rhinelands, came under the control of the Dukes of Burgundy. The Burgundians were enlightened rulers on the whole and under their protection the region prospered. During the previous century Holland itself had been nearly ruined by a long-running civil war between bourgeois and aristocratic factions, known respectively as Kabbeljauws and Hoeks (Cods and Hooks—the fat fish of the towns and the means by which they were to be landed). Despite this the towns prospered, the citizens made their pilgrimages (to Rome and even Jerusalem) and through the efforts of guilds and religious organisations the basics of a welfare system took shape.

The Burgundian age of gold continued under the regency of Maximilian, the first Habsburg ruler, who was regent on behalf of his son Philip the Handsome. Philip died young and was succeeded by his son, later Emperor Charles V—a Netherlander who took a special interest in his richest province. Charles abdicated in 1555 and divided his empire (to which he had added by purchase or conquest Drenthe, Groningen, Gelderland and Utrecht) leaving to Philip the kingdom of Spain, the Italian possessions, the Americas and the Low Countries.

These were, as they say, turbulent times. The Reformation had long flourished in the Netherlands and could look back to the tradition of the reformed Catholicism of the Devotia Moderna, Thomas à Kempis was a Dutchman. Erasmus of Rotterdam was the leading Latinist and Greek scholar of his day and his critical re-appraisal of the medieval church's Latin version of the Bible did much to undermine confidence in the Roman church. A popular form of 'heresy', especially and lastingly in North Holland and Friesland, was Anabaptism (see also below).

At the time of Philip's accession, in the cities of Flanders and Brabant (in the north of present-day Belgium), the teachings of John Calvin took hold. Philip's war against Protestantism turned into a war against his people; one by one he alienated the aristocracy, the city governments and the common folk, whatever their religion. His persecution was perceived to be an invasion of local privilege. Sporadic warfare broke out. Under the leadership of Prince William of Orange (the title came from possessions in the south of France; William is commonly known as The Silent so reluctant was he to express his true religious convictions) the Protestant forces, first by sea and then by land, occupied and held the country to the north of the great rivers.

After a terrible war of independence, the 'Revolt of the Netherlands', that ravaged the countryside for some twenty years and rumbled on in the border regions for sixty more the Netherlands, as the United Provinces, gained true independence at the Treaty of Münster in 1648. By this time the United Provinces were a major European power and Amsterdam was its leading city.

The period between the expulsion of the Spanish forces from the United Provinces (effectively signalled by a Truce in 1609) and a second great invasion by the French in 1672 has become known as the Golden Age in Dutch histories. The cities that had suffered badly in the war, such as Haarlem and Leiden, enjoyed a revival brought about by the opportunities afforded an independent and relatively settled nation in a continent wracked by war. The countryside also benefited; relieved from basic food production by the import of Baltic grain into Amsterdam (Amsterdam merchants controlled the trade in grain throughout Europe—four out of five of Amsterdam's warehouses held grain stocks), farmers turned to producing cash crops, cheese and butter making and even horticulture.

In the towns the opportunities were enhanced by a massive influx of wealthy and skilled immigrants from the southern provinces. The powerful navy created during the early years of the war of independence jealously protected the trade routes and closed off rivals to the south, such as Antwerp, from any real economic life. The founding of the East India Company in 1602 (in truth, a form of licenced piracy in the early years) and the founding of the Bank of Amsterdam in 1609 transformed the economic life of the country and the world.

Modern capitalism was born in Amsterdam. All the towns prospered: Leiden became a centre for cloth production and Haarlem for linen bleaching; Amsterdam was an industrial and mercantile city controlling the East Indies trade, the Baltic trade and the North Sea fisheries. It was not only the scale of Amsterdam's trade but also its diversity that distinguished it as truly great. The city's industries included such diverse things as shipbuilding, sugar refining and, with the arrival of skilled Jewish workers from Spain and Portugal, the diamond industry. Luxury trades such as goldsmithery, painting and the rest thrived in all the towns of Holland; the names of the Dutch artists are universally known—Rembrandt, Vermeer, Frans Hals.

But for all this, life was by no means easy. Plague was a regular visitor, the population of Amsterdam was decimated (reduced by one in ten) on several occasions during the 17C. For those who were not recognised *poorters* (i.e. citizens) of any town life was unimaginably hard. They were whipped to the parish boundaries and driven from place to place if they were unable to get a begging licence. But Holland was still a better place than any other in which to be poor and the dispossessed of war-torn Europe sought their opportunities here.

The Hague had been the meeting place of the States of Holland (a form of parliament) during the Middle Ages, following the Revolt it became the meeting place of the States General, the national convention of the rebel United Provinces and still the name given to the Parliament of the Netherlands. The Hague was therefore the seat of government of the United Provinces. Here the representatives of local interests vied for position. Amsterdam as the wealthiest city became the voice of the city party and the voice of Holland itself. Because of its political importance, The Hague had been adopted by the Princes of Orange as the site of their court. The Princes of Orange were not monarchs, their constitutional role since the revolt was as Stadholders. The Stadholdership was an ad hoc appointment, traditionally more honorific than effective, and meant generalship of the provincial forces.

Prince William was assassinated in 1584 and was succeeded by his son Maurice, then a child. Maurice grew up to become a formidable general and 'inherited' the title of Stadholder. Maurice's view of the political agenda was that of a soldier. The cities generally favoured peace over war, religious tolerance over religious absolutism and low tax over high tax. When the States General negotiated peace terms in 1609, against Maurice's instincts (he felt the war was winnable), he became drawn into the broader disputes of the time, especially that between the two wings of the Calvinist Church (the Arminians or moderates and the Gomarists or hard-liners). The affair escalated so far that by 1618 Maurice effectively initiated a coup d'état, touring the Holland cities with an army and imposing his own selection of Gomarist town councillors. The matter was legally settled in the Gomarists' favour at the Synod of Dort in the following year.

After Maurice's death in 1625 his brother Frederick Hendrick found a more amicable means of co-habiting with the city interest and the hard-line Calvinists' grip on power loosened—but the seed was sown for trouble that was never to be entirely resolved until the advent of the constitutional monarchy in the 19C (and some would say not even then). Frederick Hendrick did, however, hold the Spanish at bay, winning lands in a series of victorious campaigns and within a year of his death (he died in 1647) the Treaty of Münster, a general settlement of a widespread plague of wars which had by then raged for thirty years throughout Europe, recognised the independent state of the United Provinces covering an area very similar to that of the present-day Netherlands.

Frederick Hendrick was succeeded by his son Prince William II who, now that the wars were over, turned to establishing his own authority within the new nation. He died from a sudden illness having settled an army at the gates of Amsterdam. The city faction decided to avert such an occurrence happening again and the 'Stadholderless Period' of 1650–72 ensued. This was during the infancy of William III (later, also, King William III of England) when the government was managed by the remarkable De Wit brothers. Their rule was dramatically ended in 1672 with a joint invasion by sea and land of English and French forces. Prince William stepped in and 'rescued' the situation, though he was unable or unwilling to prevent the disgusting massacre of the De Wits (a picture of their humiliating torture and death can be seen in the Historical section of the Rijksmuseum). From this time on the position of the hereditary Orange Stadholder was no longer in doubt. It was, if anything, secured by a more adventurous foreign policy during the reign of Prince/King William III when the United Provinces became embroiled in the War of Spanish Succession (1701–14).

The 18C has long been referred to as a 'period of decline'. Certainly, when one considers the achievements of the Dutch Golden Age, not only in art but in philosophy and the sciences, then the 18C appears to be non-eventful. In art, commentators complained, contemporary painters suffered from the strength of the market in Golden Age masters; there was a buoyant trade in pastiches of 17C styles. Britain, France and the German states produced the interesting philosophers, writers, composers and statesmen. The Industrial Revolution was setting a new agenda for the material sciences and this as yet unacknowledged transformation was taking place in small towns in England's Midlands.

The United Provinces were simply unimportant. The economies of the cities relied upon the tried and tested trades and manufactures of the previous century; the proverbial wealth of the Bank of Amsterdam (equal in mythic power to the idea of the Gnomes of Zurich today) was the sole distinguishing feature of an otherwise featureless, relatively degraded economic environment. Further to this there was corruption and complacency in the ruling class, not only in their running of the cities but also in their management of public corporations such as the East India Company and (crucially for public order, as with the Tax Farmers Riot of 1748) in the collection of taxes.

These last abuses were hardly distinguishing features of Dutch culture, they are typical of many parts of Europe in the 18C. It was corruption combined with the decline of Dutch commercial power relative to that of the other colonial powers which led to the liquidation of the East India Company in 1791. Meanwhile, in the United Provinces as elsewhere, the rhetoric of the rights of man and the notion of democracy became the intellectual justification of social critics. A new party had emerged who called themselves 'The Patriots'. By the spring of 1787 the Patriots had taken control of a number of smaller towns and had advanced upon Amsterdam where they staged a coup. This first, home-made revolution was suppressed by the Stadholder but revolutionary ideals were to return in 1795 with the Revolutionary armies of France.

Owing to the particular circumstances of the Patriot rebellion the French Revolution was widely welcomed in the United Provinces, especially in Amsterdam. The Revolution (called the 'Velvet Revolution') and the subsequent founding of the 'Batavian Republic' (Batavian from the name of one of the Germanic tribes who had occupied the region in Roman times) were, compared to events in France, bloodless. Events in France were to sour it, however. The French pursued a policy of blockade against Britain but their Dutch allies, true to form, did not wish to forsake profit for politics.

In 1806, the Revolution long dead in France, the Emperor Napoleon installed his brother Louis as King of the Netherlands with the express purpose of bringing the Dutch into line with imperial policy. Louis could not, or would not, deliver and in 1810 he was deposed and the Netherlands was brought into the French Empire. The only party not compromised by the Revolutionary episode were the Orangists and in 1813 the Kingdom of the Netherlands was proclaimed with the Prince of Orange, as King of the Netherlands, at its head.

The new Kingdom of the Netherlands created in the settlement of 1815 included present day Belgium. Belgium was Catholic and had a large French-speaking minority, the population was half as large again as that of the northern provinces. King William I insisted upon religious toleration which was anathema to the Catholic authorities. He insisted on Dutch (Flemish) as the official language and refused the southern provinces equal representation at the States General, also refusing any measure of regional autonomy. His policies were enforced with rigorous censorship of the press. Whereas the cities of the North sought to re-discover their former glory through trade, Belgium was close behind Britain in industrialisation, a development which William himself sought to foster through protectionism.

In 1830, one of the years of revolutionary activity throughout Europe, the Belgians seized power and, after a brief and ineffectual attempt to impose his sovereignty by armed force, William was compelled to concede independence to the new Kingdom of Belgium (Leopold of Saxe-Coburg had been invited to be King) at the London Conference of 1831. He again invaded and was driven back, holding on to Maastricht and Antwerp. Antwerp was handed over to the Belgians in 1832, the province of Limburg remained Dutch. William I ruled until 1840 when, ironically, he abdicated in order to marry a Belgian Catholic. His son, William II, also a conservative by nature, was forced to be the first properly constitutional monarch.

After widespread rioting in 1848 (another year of revolutions throughout Europe) Rudolph Thorbecke, the leading liberal statesman, was invited to chair a constitutional commission at which freedom of association, a system of direct elections (enjoyed under the Batavian Republic), provision of public elementary education and ministerial responsibility to the States General were recommended—the States General was to control public finance. William II was succeeded in 1849 by William III whose first government, led by Thorbecke, instituted the liberal reforms of the 1848 commission. In essence the constitution of the modern Netherlands can be dated back to this administration. The transformation of the nation as a whole from one of Europe's industrial and commercial backwaters is a longer and more complicated story and will be addressed in the following section covering the history of Amsterdam itself.

In 1890 William III's ten-year-old daughter Wilhelmina came to the throne. Constitutionally her reign saw the continuance of the liberal reforms which had been initiated in her father's time, politically the period was one in which the Netherlands progressively assumed the character and roles which distinguish it today. In 1899 (against the background of the Boer War) the International Conference for the Suppression of War was founded at the Peace Palace at The Hague; The Hague too became the home of the International Court of Arbitration. As a small nation the Dutch were painfully aware of the dangers of war.

Neutrality kept the Dutch out of the First World War, although the economic consequences of submarine blockade for a seafaring nation were severe and there was a failed socialist Revolution in 1918. In 1940, however, neutrality was no protection from the German war machine and the country was occupied and suffered appallingly, especially during the 'Hunger Winter' of 1944–45 when the whole nation became a concentration camp and many thousands died as a direct result of malnutrition. Worst hit by the occupation was the large Jewish community which had enjoyed remarkable toleration since the arrival of the first Jews from Spain and Portugal three and a half centuries before.

The compromises of an occupied nation have left a profound impression upon Dutch life. One can only marvel at the courage of most Dutch people confronted with the daily oppression, their phlegmatic contempt for the racist decrees of the Nazification (many non-Jews sported the yellow Star of David) and their unfailing moral resistance. But most Dutch people realise that Nazi rule was administered and connived at by Dutch Nazis; the effective civil war of the Nazi years has provided settings and themes for poetry, novels and drama for two generations.

Queen Wilhemina returned from exile in 1945 to a country stripped of everything by the retreating invaders. Before her abdication in 1949 the processes toward de-colonisation, European co-operation (Benelux was conceived of in 1944 by the exiled governments in London) and the end of any idea of neutrality (the Netherlands was a founding member of NATO) were in train.

Wilhemina abdicated in favour of her daughter Juliana during whose reign the Netherlands was rebuilt within the broader framework of the European Community. She, in turn, was succeeded by her daughter Beatrix. The nation has become the definitive European liberal democracy, tolerant and (football apart) internationalist. De-colonialisation brought about a huge influx of black immigrants from the East Indies and the Caribbean and, although their assimilation has not been without problems, it has been without major problems; Islam is one of the larger minority faiths in contemporary Netherlands. The elemental Dutch struggle with the sea has, for the moment, been fought to a truce. The huge (and boring) polders of the IJselmeer are, since 1986, a province of their own and in the same year the immense Delta Plan was completed. Until global warming alters the balance of forces back in the favour of the sea the Netherlands are safe from innundation.

History of Amsterdam

Amsterdam, with some three-quarters of a million inhabitants, is the Netherlands' largest city and the national capital. It is not however the seat of government which is at The Hague. It stands on the south side of the river IJ, on a chain of lagoons, now almost entirely docks, which form a long inlet at the south western corner of the IJsselmeer.

Amsterdam has the largest freshwater harbour in Europe. It is connected to the North Sea by the Noordzee Kanaal, constructed in 1865–76. Much of the old city rests on huge wooden piles driven down 20 metres through the marshy surface soil to reach firmer ground below. From the point of view of physical geography the site does not have much to recommend it; but Amsterdam, like the Netherlands as a whole, is not so much a creation of physical geography as of human geography.

The name 'Amsterdam' refers to the origin of the city: the dam on the Amstel. The dam is, of course, the Dam, the large square in front of the Royal Palace (not commonly called the Dam until the mid 17C, previously it was referred to as the *Plaetse*). The heart of many Dutch towns consists of a dam thrown across the mouth of a river and a pair of encircling canals running on either side just beyond the town wall (*burgwal*); the extent of the medieval city can be seen on present day maps as the Oudezijds and Nieuwezijds Voorburgwals (the 'new' side is to the west, the 'old' to the east). The heart of the oldest part of Amsterdam, therefore, is the Warmoesstraat. The original line of the Amstel was along the Rokin (the *in*ward reach), through the Dam and out via the Damrak (the Dam reach).

Amsterdam remained a small fishing village on the 'old' side of the un-dammed Amstel until the 13C, administered by the Bishops of Utrecht through the Lords of Amstel who lived at Oudekerk, today a suburb to the south of the city. In 1204 Gijsbrecht II of Amstel built a castle in the village and some sixty years later the dam was built. This was evidently completed by 1275 when *Aemstelle Dam* was granted toll privileges by Count Floris V of Holland. This was part of a general attempt to appropriate church lands by secular rulers as well as being an attempt by Floris to supersede the Lord of Amstel (now Gijsbrecht IV) who subsequently murdered Floris. Twenty-five years later *Aemstelledamme* was granted full municipal rights by the Bishop of Utrecht who left the town and lands to Count William III of Holland in 1313. In 1323 Amsterdam was granted the privilege of importing beer from Hamburg into the Count's lands confirming Amsterdam's orientation toward the Baltic trade.

The other important trade was fishing; it was the invention of a method of salting herrings by the Hollander Willem Beukels, in 1384, which did much to precipitate Amsterdam's extraordinary growth over the ensuing century. The herring trade demanded the importation of salt (from Portugal and France) and of wood (for barrels, from the Baltic ports). In order to exploit this invention the Amsterdammers were obliged to develop long-distance trade routes. Amsterdam merchants took on the might of the Hanseatic League and won, cornering the market in Baltic grain which was to be the real foundation of the city's wealth from the mid 15C.

Until 1452 when a second great fire swept through the town, Amsterdam was built of wood. From this date wooden houses were prohibited, although more must have been built as several of a later date remain (for example, Zeedijk 1, built in 1550, has a wooden façade; Begijnhof 34, of 1470, is constructed substantially of wood). Meanwhile the city had extended itself outward to another ring of canals, the present Singel to the west (the new side) and the Kloveniersburgwal and Geldersekade to the east (the old side). There were now two large churches, the Nieuwe Kerk (this on the scale of a cathedral) and the Oude Kerk serving respectively the old and new sides.

Amsterdam was the focus of a popular religious cult still celebrated each year in mid-March with the Stille Omgang (the Silent Procession). This dates back to the Amsterdam Miracle of 1345 when a dying man vomited up the host following his last communion. Thrown onto a fire the host refused to burn and was soon observed to possess miraculous powers of healing. Maximilian, the first Habsburg ruler of the Netherlands, was one of those cured by it. Maximilian's approval of Amsterdam extended to granting the city the right to place his own royal insignia in its coat of arms.

By about 1500 Amsterdam had some 9000 inhabitants; it was built substantially of brick; its merchants now had as large a fleet as the merchants of any rival city. It had chosen the right side in the long-running war between the Kabeljauwen and the Hoeks and basked in the affection of Maximilian, now the Holy Roman Emperor. The government of the city was administered through a council consisting of up to five burgomasters, a *schout*, who was the effective police chief, magistrates and councillors. The citizens were organised into guilds for trade and manufacture. The guilds were societies committed to establishing standards of workmanship and merchandise, they also provided basic insurance for members and protected local workmen against cheap, immigrant labour.

Medieval Catholicism demanded of good Christians that they should do good works. The members of numerous religious societies—male and female, lay and in orders—all sought redemption through following the example of Christ (healing the sick, feeding the hungry, supporting orphans and widows), meanwhile laying the foundations of a welfare system. Pilgrimage was another method of earning merit. Amsterdam had its own pilgrim attraction, of course. Many of its citizens combined a journey to Rome or Jerusalem with business; those who had made the journey would qualify to join, for example, the Romists. In Haarlem there was a society of Jerusalem Pilgrims, one of whom was the painter Jan van Scorel; the earliest known Dutch group portrait, painted in 1529 (one now in the Frans

Halsmuseum, Haarlem, one in the Centraal Museum, Utrecht), are by Scorel of members of this society standing in processional order, presumably designed to adorn their octagonal chapel. On a more obviously practical level male citizens might expect to be conscripted to serve in one of the militia companies and maintain and practice upon a hand-bow or a cross-bow. This they did at the *Doelen* (target ranges). Members of the patriciate formed the officer corps of these Civic Guards. The earliest group portrait of a Civic Guard officer group was painted in 1534. Whether or not the portrait is associated with the 'rise of the individual' in human history, one thing is clear, the rise of the group portrait is closely associated with the idea of community, fellowship and shared experience in the history of Amsterdam and the Netherlands. The most celebrated militia group portrait is Rembrandt's Night Watch.

Although Lutheranism had, since the very earliest days, been tolerated in Amsterdam it was not until 1534 that the first significant Reformation event occurred in the city. Melchior Hoffman of Münster, believing his home town to be the site of the New Jerusalem, proclaimed himself 'King of Münster'. Prophets were sent out to other cities proclaiming the end of the world and the message was enthusiastically taken up by many ordinary folk in Amsterdam. The movement has been characterised by its most distinctive tenet—that infants should not be baptised but that baptism should be reserved for adults convinced of their own redemption. They were known as Anabaptists.

This first Anabaptist movement was apocalyptic; speakers drew upon the Book of Revelations for their themes and their 'enthusiasm' (in the literal sense of possession by God) was immediately seen to be a threat to order. When, in March 1534, the Anabaptists drew hundreds from the surrounding countryside to Amsterdam for a march to Münster the authorities stepped in and had the leaders executed. The followers were scattered. In the next month a cache of weapons was found and the Anabaptists were proscribed, there was a round-up and further executions followed. The most astonishing incident occurred in the following February when during a religious meeting a small group of devotees, seven men and five women, stripped naked and ran through the Dam, proclaiming the wrath of God. The men were executed and the women chastised. Persecution fed the sect and in May the Anabaptists pulled off their most outrageous act when forty of them captured the town hall intending to rouse their co-religionists by ringing the bell—the bellrope had been cut, the conspiracy had been anticipated and the rebels were trapped. In the ensuing battles twenty-one citizens (including a burgomaster) and twenty-eight Anabaptists lost their lives. The Anabaptist's leader, 'Bishop' Jan van Campen, who had advised against the use of arms, was seized and put to death in a degrading and vicious series of tortures. The heresy was punished as an act of treachery.

The subsequent persecution drove Anabaptism, which subsequently, under the leadership of Simon Menno, developed into a gentle and appealing religion, deep into the countryside. Paintings were commissioned to hang in the town hall to record the episode and warn others of the fate of those who, blinded by religious mania, offended against the dignity of the city fathers. On the whole the successive waves of heresies were accepted by the burgomasters with an astonishing degree of toleration, but no direct threat to order could ever be countenanced, certainly not one perpetrated by mere artisans. The sects multiplied over the next fifteen years and in 1550 the Emperor Charles V instituted the Edict of Blood. The proscription of Protestantism was only sporadically enforced by the magistrates of

Holland, it was principally reserved for persecuting Anabaptists.

When Philip, Charles V's son, sought to drive out heresy in the Low Countries he did so by introducing the Inquisition (which interfered with the towns' traditions of policing themselves) and by seeking to re-organise the church's own institutions (for instance, by introducing four new bishoprics into the region). The fact that he tried to do it through agents while remaining in Spain was no great help to his cause. The result was a rebellion, as has already been described. But Amsterdam, perhaps because of the enduring shock to its system brought about by the Anabaptist outrages, remained, at least on the surface and in its dealings with the rest of the world, a good Catholic city through all the crises and revolts.

Amsterdam's policy during the revolt was to remain loyal to Philip, to appear to be (at least moderately) Catholic, to send up a few burnt offerings of heretics from time to time and to concentrate on business as usual. Protestant services were permitted outside the jurisdiction of the city itself, which ended at the city walls. This state of affairs continued until the arrival of Calvinism, a far greater political threat to established order than any so far. Calvinism's political potency, like that of Anabaptism, lay in the fact that it called upon its followers to establish the Kingdom of God not by wishing for it but by taking direct action to achieve it. But where Anabaptism had appealed to the emotions and to superstitious impulses Calvinism was intellectually rigorous, it appealed to aristocrats, patricians and ordinary working people alike. Personal salvation was assured the Elect—though how one was to be certain of election few non-Calvinists have ever been able to discover.

Once the leap of faith was established its emphasis upon the shortened line of authority from God, through the local church authorities and then directly into the homes of the Elect, provided a relentless logic of salvation. To be saved one had to be in the Church, to be in the Church was to be saved. In most ways Calvinism was conscientiously anti-superstitious and rational. Calvin, like many humanist reformers, had criticised the use of images in churches; the relic and image culture of the medieval Catholic Church was widely recognised to be corrupt even within the Catholic hierarchy. In areas where the Calvinists were strong open attacks were made on church furnishings and churches were stripped of ornament.

This led to a general iconoclastic movement (the *beeldenstorm*, the image-storm) in the southern provinces. When in the summer of 1566 some sailors arrived in Amsterdam with fragments of church sculptures from Flanders, Amsterdam's own iconoclastic frenzy was unleashed and the profoundly revolutionary tendencies of Calvinism became apparent.

Amsterdam was at that time a city with a population of more than 30,000, the expansion of the previous fifty years had been through immigration, especially of persecuted Protestants. The numbers had been swelled by the famine of 1565. It would be difficult to judge to what degree the disorders of 1566 were religiously inspired and how far they were simply opportunist riot. The miraculous host was saved by some intrepid womenfolk and the crowd turned to sacking churches and convents elsewhere in the city.

Peace was eventually achieved when the city fathers offered the Franciscan church for Protestant worship. This was a mistake. Philip sent the Duke of Alva to the city in the following year. Those Protestants who could afford to leave did so. The Duke helped himself to as much gold as he could lay his hands on. The vindictiveness of the Council of Blood convened by him to investigate heresy earned the city the nickname 'Murderdam'.

Alva held Amsterdam until 1573 when his financial mismanagement and greed, for example the 'tenth penny tax', eventually exasperated the populace. Even after Alva's departure the city remained loyal to Philip for as long as the Spanish King seemed to be the power in the land, but now they found that the tide of events was turning and they were besieged by the forces of the rebel William of Orange. On 26 May 1578 in a coup (more symbolic than anything else and referred to as 'The Alteration') the Catholic burgomasters and officials were replaced, overnight, with Protestants.

Throughout the whole of the Golden Age of the 17C Amsterdam's trimming to the winds of the Revolt made the city suspect to hard-line Calvinists; the city's famous religious toleration was frequently viewed as being Catholicism under another flag and Amsterdam's prudent mercantile opposition to continued war with Spain was seen as a form of treachery.

Within a decade Amsterdam was not only the most important city in the region, but also the leading city of a new Republic. The depredations of Alva, bad as they were, were not as bad as the sacking and siege which had brought about the decline of Antwerp. In Amsterdam business had continued and the city had survived; toleration (of tyrants as well as heretics), although it was an expensive policy, had proved to be the best policy.

Following the fall of Antwerp in 1585 immigrants flooded northward—not only Protestants seeking to escape persecution, but Catholics seeking peace enough to make a living. Amsterdam was a principal destination for these people. The southerners brought skills, capital and business contacts. The Protestants who had spent their war years in England, Scotland and Germany returned. Persecuted minorities from anywhere in Europe, if they had the means of getting there and the wit to survive there, could escape to the Netherlands and to Amsterdam.

The only problem was that the city was too small and the population was growing at a phenomenal rate (reaching 200,000 by 1650). From the beginning of the 17C new building transformed the medieval town encircling it with a Renaissance city. Three encircling canals were dug: the first was the Herengracht (Gentlemen's or Lords' canal, town councillors were referred to as 'Heren'), then the Keizersgracht (Emperor's canal) and lastly the Prinsengracht (Prince's canal).

When it was all finished (and it took most of the century) the city centre was surrounded by some of the finest townscape in the world—during the Golden Age itself, however, the larger part of Amsterdam was a building site. This was housing for the wealthy. One could compare it, in terms of scale, to Versailles—a joint-stock Versailles built by a corporation of merchants. To the west of the city an area was laid out for artisan housing, the 'Jordaan' (the name comes from a corruption of the French word 'jardin', meaning garden: all the street names are taken from flowers). Here houses and workshops were laid out according to a plan by Hendrick Staets with minimum distances between buildings and controls on the use of industrial and commercial sites.

Transformations at the heart of the city were just as impressive. The Town Hall burned down in 1646; it was an event important enough to bring out Rembrandt with his sketchbook. In 1649, a year after the Treaty of Münster, work began on a new building designed by Jacob van Campen. This is still the most impressive building in the city. It is constructed in stone in a city of brick; the exterior displays remarkable restraint in its decoration. One might get the impression that it is something of a citadel—no grand entrance welcomes the visitor and at the ground floor level there are slits cut in the wall for defensive fire.

Van Campen's austere Town Hall on the Dam, now the Royal Palace, was dismissed as 'a big little thing' by the 17C diplomat, Sir William Temple

The explanation is simple, the new Town Hall, like its predecessor, was to house the great Bank of Amsterdam. It also housed the law courts. In keeping with a long tradition of civic pride which has already been noted, the Town Hall was the symbolic heart of the city and it was to be protected at all costs.

Amsterdam was visited and commented upon by numerous foreigners during the Golden Age. The greatest expression of astonishment was reserved for the diversity of religions and their toleration by the citizenry; the Jewish community was an object of fascination, they even inspired an illustrated book by the engraver Romijn de Hoog. The Portugese Synagogue, a major attraction still for any visitor, was built between 1671 and 1675 at the heart of what was, until 1941, one of the great world centres of Jewish life.

Catholics were allowed to worship, although they were expected to do so in private, and there are a number of clandestine churches preserved, for example Onze Lieve Heer op Zolder ('Our Dear Lord of the Attic') at Oudezijds Voorburgwal 40. All the medieval churches in the city were given over to the Dutch Reformed Church or its friends (one such is the English Church in the Begijnhof). The large Lutheran community built their extraordinary circular-plan church on the Singel in 1668–71. This is now part of a hotel.

Next to its diverse godliness visitors were impressed by the city's cleanliness. Sir William Temple records an astonished caller being whisked into the air and carried over a newly cleaned floor and then deposited at the foot of the stairs by a strapping Friesland maid. Temple mused upon the cleanliness of the streets and the pride that the Dutch took in scouring and repainting their homes. It was, he concluded, a racial characteristic derived from necessity—coping with the unhealthy and corrupting airs of the bogs. The Dutch were also famously avaricious—it is still said that to hold a census in the Netherlands you need only roll a coin down the street.

To enter the mind of the 17C middle-class Amsterdammer one could look at the painting of the period. Portraits by Thomas de Keyser, Nicholas Elias, Govert Flinck and others present us with a deeply conservative class of patricians, indistinguishable in their unsmiling majesty from grandees in any other European country. After the Calvinist Reformation large-scale paintings for churches were not permitted and religious art took to the small scale, such pictures were hung in private houses. One could say that the transformation of art ownership from being a collective enterprise to being a private enterprise took place in the Netherlands during the Reformation. Paintings remained a privately owned pleasure until the 19C when the first galleries and museums were opened.

Paintings of Bible subjects remained popular throughout the century, they are on the whole straightforwardly narrative with a noticeable emphasis on Old Testament subject matter. Like the painting of classical subjects, they provide exemplars of wisdom, faithfulness and civic virtue—large-scale paintings played a role in the decoration of both the old and the new Town Halls. Landscape paintings of local scenery have been described as evidencing a sense of national pride.

It should be remembered that throughout the period urban growth was brought about by immigration from the countryside and that few Amsterdammers did not originate from somewhere else, most probably one of the Holland villages or farmhouses we see in the paintings of Jan van Goyen or Jacob van Ruisdael. Still life paintings often celebrated the riches of the earth with banquets of food strewn over valuable serving dishes, or modest beer and herring breakfasts at the corner of a rustic table. 'Genre' paintings present the quotidian drama of kitchens, drawing rooms and grocers' shops.

However one reaches further into the consciousness of the age when one realises that many pictures function not only at the level of describing the world, but also at the level of commenting upon it. The landscapes can be understood as allegories on the pilgrimage of life, still lifes as elaborate 'vanitas' or 'momento mori' pictures drawing our attention to the ephemerality of things. The underlying themes of much genre painting draw our attention to the moral importance of raising children properly, protecting the virginity of daughters from compromise and (by exploiting the ambiguity of sumptuous interiors) forcing us to detect the clues and recognise right and wrong in apparently blameless gatherings. The paintings are a training ground for the moral eye. Intellectual life in Amsterdam was diverse and rich, despite there being no court to act as a focus. In the early years the rhetoricians' guilds were at the heart of intellectual life. The rhetoricians were groups of amateur poets and performers who had traditionally officiated at public celebrations, composed occasional poems and performed dramas, religious and secular. It is a debased, English form of such groups of citizen rhymsters that Shakespeare satirised in *A Midsummer Night's Dream* with his rude mechanical poets. Poets of great talent emerged from this background—Brederode, Visscher (Roemer and his daughter Tesselschade) and Vondel. It is hardly their fault that they are little known in the world outside—when they wrote, they wrote in one of the main world languages.

In 1581 Leiden became the home of the Netherlands' first University (then called the Academy); Amsterdam also had its own Athenaeum Illustre. The first Professor of Theology there was Jacob Arminius the liberal interpreter of the writings of John Calvin. During the 17C many scholars were attracted to the city not only on account of its famed toleration but also by the prospect of meeting some of the most celebrated thinkers of the age. Baruch Spinoza was born here, John Locke was a visitor late in the 17C.

But intellectual life is not only about famous names, the Golden Age Amsterdammers were curious and energetic amateurs of history, philology, anatomy (Rembrandt's Anatomy of Dr Tulp in the Mauritshuis is only one of many anatomy paintings recording public dissections attended by the élite), botany, geography, the physical sciences, technology and much else and many learned societies were founded then which survive to the present day. The world turned to Amsterdam for its illustrated books; maps and scientific texts poured forth on every topic.

For the ordinary Amsterdammer, the shipwright in Zaandam or the textile-worker in the Jordaan, life centred upon a few important associations: family, work and church. Something has already been said about the church, but in all church communities the family was at the heart of any philosophy of good order and morality. We can read in the writings of Jacob Cats, the Puritan poet and moralist, how the network of duties of spouse and parent shaped the world of good Christians. It would be foolish to think that such writings were actually *descriptive*, they are of course *prescriptive*—we would not have the continuous record of dispute and censure in the parish council records if all Amsterdammers had led blameless lives. However, Cats' many works sold in tens of thousands and in editions from the cheapest to the most expensive—they must represent the aspirations and concerns of a broad range of 17C Amsterdammers, whatever their particular church.

Materially there were such a range of kinds of trade and employments that one can only gesture toward a description. The organisation of workers within quasi-religious guilds remained normal for artisans born into, or who had bought into, the city. Young males would follow their fathers or uncles into trades, independence was assured when they gained master status in a guild. Increasingly during the 17C and 18C craftsmen were employed by capitalists and might never progress beyond being a journeyman.

The guilds themselves were becoming organisations mainly concerned with defending the interests of local manufacturers rather than workers and it seems that there was a free for all approach to employing skilled workers which circumvented the more regularised practice of previous centuries. Despite this wages were higher in Amsterdam during the Golden Age than in comparable cities, but they were pitifully low elsewhere—and prices could be lower in the free market of Amsterdam. We should remember also that workers' incomes were tied very closely to the seasons. The shorter days of winter meant lower wages and in summer workers might put in a 12 or 13 hour day.

Amsterdam's wealth meant that there was work for thousands of domestic servants; the position of servant was a position within a family. The employer became responsible for the moral and spiritual welfare of servants, even to providing dowries for servant girls. Women in the Netherlands retained more control over their dowry than in other countries. But for thousands of working-class women left at home by seafaring husbands their only dowry was their body, which many seem to have put to good commercial use in the city's world famous sex market.

The general prosperity of the city 'trickled down', but very slowly. Fortunes were made and lost in a city which thrived upon speculation. It was in Amsterdam that the shares and futures markets were first invented with, after 1609, a city bank to finance the speculators. Financial speculation was, according to contemporary commentators, practised by all classes of people. Certainly during the great excitement of the earliest East Indian voyages in the 1590s many companies were founded and exploited the good faith of ordinary folk to raise millions, the situation was regularised under the control of the town councillors with the founding in 1602 of the *Vereinigde Oostindische Compagnie* (United East India Company,usually abbreviated to VOC). Over the succeeding two centuries this company grew to become a 'commonwealth within a commonwealth', running an overseas empire larger than those of most European monarchs.

The most famous speculation of the period was the 'tulipomania' of 1634–36 when a general enthusiasm for horticulture exploded into a spiralling market in tulip bulbs which changed hands for extraordinary sums, some for more than f2000 (the price of a substantial family house). The collapse of the market left many ordinary people with expensively purchased and worthless tulip bulbs. The heavy futures trading in bulbs buried growers in paper promises to pay. The authorities prohibited further trading. At all levels in society gambling was a vice—as the admonishments of the genre painters make clear.

The lives of Amsterdam's common people barely changed throughout the lifetime of the United Provinces. Accommodation was cramped with large families crowding into small spaces where sanitation was hardly a feature. The canals were the sewers and, fortunately for all, they were flushed by the flow of the Amstel. Hunger was only rarely a threat to any but the most marginal groups. Water was undrinkable and from infancy beer was the preferred drink of all who could not afford wine. New and dangerous addictions thrived—tobacco was 'drunk' widely by the middle of the century, instant happiness in the form of *jenever* (known as 'Dutch gin) was popular by the beginning of the 18C. The 18C fashion for tea, chocolate (a drink before the mid 19C) and coffee did as much to save urban life from disintegration as the sewers and water supply introduced during the following century. Influenza, typhoid, bubonic plague, syphilis and even leprosy remained a threat until modern times. As the design of the 1649 Town Hall reminds us, social disorder was considered a real threat. Life's nastiness, brutality and brevity were combated with prayer and charity and as rigorous a police force as could be mustered—in times of crisis the police force was the militia companies.

The closure of the religious houses had signalled the end of the medieval concept of poverty and its relief as a means to enter heaven. The emphasis in the puritan Republic was upon self-help, riches were evidence of God's approval of the righteous. The medieval institutions—orphanages, poorhouses, hospitals and the like—were brought within the purlieu of civic life and the idea of service to the community. The boards of governors or regents, there are many 17C and 18C portraits of such groups, administered the charities on the behalf of all the citizens—the charities were principally for natives.

Central Amsterdam (the medieval city that is, not, significantly, the Golden Age city of the encircling canals) is full of buildings which were originally charitable institutions of this kind and as no substantial rebuilding has taken place many remain, albeit with a transformed function. The Amsterdam Historical Museum at Kalverstraat 92 occupies a former orphanage, the present University spreads across a number of charitable foundations. Early tourists were intrigued by the *Rasphuis* (the allegorically ornamented gateway remains in the Voetboogstraat) and the *Spinhuis* (in the University quarter off Oudezijds Achterburgwal), these were houses of correction (*not* mere prisons; this point was made clear in a rhyme over the gateway of the Spinhuis) where men and women were set to work for their own redemption. The men rasped brazil-wood for dye-making, the women worked at spinning. Not that criminals were treated leniently, the commonest punishment for theft or violence was death. There are also many almshouses which are described in the area by area descriptions.

As was said above, the 18C was a period of relative decline for the United Provinces as a whole. The decline was accompanied by a degree of social ossification—the city, in truth, was silting up. Amsterdam's wealth was founded upon sea trade, the families and institutions which had grown from the sea trade now made their way through holding investments. Entrance to the port itself had always been gained through the northern approaches of the present IJsselmeer, but owing to silting the channels became progressively unnavigable and could only be used by the larger ships of the early 19C because of the invention of buoyancy barrels which rolled the ships across the bar making access possible if tiresome.

Trade and the handling of goods, both for import and for re-export, had provided livelihoods for a wide variety of people. Everybody lost out—from the intrepid navigators of the sledge-barrows which were slid across the cobbles of Amsterdam's pathways (with ingenious lubrication systems to get them up and over the humps at the bridges) to the stevedores and the ship-repairmen. Corruption, in both senses of the word, pervaded the city. The Tax Farmer Riots of 1748 were precipitated by a fatal squabble in the Buttermarket (now the Rembrandtsplein) but they brought to a head the discontents of a population sick of seeing their betters share out the dwindling resources of city and nation between themselves. The riots themselves were not mere riot, they were well-organised insurrections which used the Amsterdam mob to terrorise the patricians. Order, however, prevailed and the ring-leaders were publicly executed.

But an opposition was forming. Hardly a political force it was a loose amalgamation of intellectuals, influenced by the liberal philosophy of the French and German Enlightenment, sympathetic patricians like Hendrick Hooft and romantic, usually young, enthusiasts who identified themselves as 'Patriots'. This last group travelled from town to town in growing bands promoting revolutionary ideas derived from Rousseau and the American liberators, ideas such as the brotherhood of mankind, democracy and social freedom. By April 1787 when they staged a coup in Amsterdam, they had become a real political threat—they had already become influential in the government of many smaller towns; they were brutally crushed by the Prince of Orange at the head of a Prussian army.

Eight years later the French Revolutionary armies were welcomed into Amsterdam, they were led by the leaders of the Patriots who had fled to France in time for the French Revolution and had remained actively propagandising during the intervening years. The bizarre natural religion of the Revolution was celebrated on the Dam with the citizenry dancing round a Freedom Tree; the subversiveness of the Anabaptist outrages was born again, as it would be a third time in the late 1960s. This was known as the 'Velvet Revolution' and it stood in striking contrast to the Terrors in France and the chronic cruelties of *ancien régime* purges elsewhere. The United Provinces disappeared peacefully from Europe's map, in its place stood the Batavian Republic the whole of the property-owning class was enfranchised and Amsterdam had its first elected government. The city set itself to surviving another age of European war in time-honoured manner by capitalising upon the trading opportunities.

After seizing the government of France and appointing himself Emperor Napoleon sought to control and manage the satellite republics by appointing members of his family as monarchs—in 1806 his younger brother, Louis, became King of the Netherlands. Louis made Amsterdam his capital and took over the grand Town Hall as his palace. He knocked down the ancient weigh-house, sketched by many artists including Rembrandt, but nevertheless managed to endear himself to his subjects by supporting their breaking the French blockade of English ports, the so-called Continental System. His country retreat was the Château Welgelegde near Haarlem where he brought together a fine art collection which was open to the public. We can date the Rijksmuseum collection back to King Louis. Louis also encouraged the mechanical arts and the sciences; in short, he was an enlightened despot in the manner of Frederick the Great of Prussia, an engaging and attractive man. The monarchical ambitions of the House of Orange had always been a problem for the cities, but the Oranges were a private family, they had never sought to play such a leading role in the life of the country; the House of Orange retained its grip on the public imagination by standing for dogged resistance and the Protestant cause, at least in the minds of their supporters. This is a tradition which endures in their retiring conduct to this day. No Prince, King or Queen from the House of Orange has ever had a fraction of the glamour of King Louis and none of them has even pretended they have.

Other lasting results of French rule are to be found in law and government where the Enlightenment rationalism of the Code Napoleon remained influential in the Netherlands. In free-loving modern Amsterdam the visitor might reflect that it was in 1811, just after King Louis was removed from office by Napoleon and the Netherlands became for a short time part of the French Empire, that homosexuality was decriminalised.

Amsterdam, like the rest of the country, emerged battered from the experience of Empire. The war had been carried into Dutch territory on a number of occasions, as when in 1799 an Orangist/Prussian army landed at Den Helder, but the battering was less directly the result of warfare than that. The British had seized most Dutch colonial possessions, the Continental System had undermined the sea-borne economy, the traditional craft industries were undermined by the increasingly mechanised production methods of neighbouring countries and the harbour, the one-time pride of the city, was incapable of handling the new generations of larger ships. Ingenious solutions such as the one described earlier could not bring Amsterdam into line with its rivals, and one of the first projects of the new King William I was the North Holland Canal.

It was completed in 1824 but was from the start inadequate—there were too many locks, too many bends, it was too shallow and too narrow. More successful were the Keulse Vaart (Cologne Passage) of the same year and the Zederik Canal, both running to the interior. The population of Amsterdam had in fact fallen during the years of the Batavian Republic from 221,000 to 190,000; it was hardly any larger than at the end of the Golden Age and it was still crowded into housing that had not been overhauled during the intervening century. Something had to be done.

The history of 19C Amsterdam is a history of successive attempts to make a medieval trading city work in an Industrial Age. A number of individuals sought to turn the situation around and many of the remaining monuments of the 19C such as the Artis Zoo, the Vondelpark, the Westgasfabriek and the Stadsschouwburg were commissioned by enterprising private citizens. Paul van Vlissingen, for example, who started a steamship company running cargoes and passengers to London and Hamburg in 1825 and who founded an engineering works in the east of the city.

Most important was Dr Samuel Sarphati, an evangelist of modernity, who founded a commercial college, a construction company, a modern bread factory and the Amstel Hotel (1863–67; Professor Tulpplein 1); he also initiated a refuse removal service which took the city's waste to the countryside for use as compost, an idea which had originally been tried out during the 17C. He founded the *Vereniging voor Volksvlijt*, the Industrial Society, which brought new ideas before the city's industrialists and manufacturers. His popularising motto was *Amsterdam Vooruit!*, Forward Amsterdam!

One of his greatest achievements was the extraordinary *Paleis voor Volksvlijt*, Palace of Industry, which occupied the Frederiksplein and was built between 1857 and 1864. This stood at the other end of the Sarphatistraat across the Hogesluis bridge from the Amstelhotel and provided Amsterdam with the kind of modern exhibition space provided by the Crystal Palace (1851) in London, indeed the Crystal Palace was its model; in 1883 Amsterdam held the World Exhibition. The architect of the *Paleis* was C. Outshoorn (1812–75) who, like Paxton, came from a non-architectural background being partly self-taught and part educated as a railway engineer. Amsterdam's recovery, or re-creation, was accompanied by a huge growth in population—to 500,000 before the end of the century and to slightly above the present level of 750,000 by the early 20C. The infrastructure of a modern city arrived—sewage and water provision (cholera was endemic in the mid century), railways and the rest—so that between the time of the opening of the Noordzee Canal in 1876 and the Centraal Station in 1889 one could say that Amsterdam had caught up.

Industries in metals, shipbuilding, clothing, construction, food and alchohol and, famously, diamond cutting were established. This had to be achieved without the usual natural resources of coal and ores and in the teeth of the collapse of the colonial empire which had hit Amsterdam harder than any other city.

The revival of the Indonesian trade after 1828 under the Royal innovation of the *Nederlandse Handelsmaatschappij* (The Netherlands Trading Company) through introduction of the *cultuurstelsel*, the cultivation system, provided immediate profits and contributed to the renovation of Amsterdam. This encouraged the local princes to supervise a system of forced delivery—be it coffee, rubber or whatever. In 1850 Britain 'granted' the Netherlands sole trading rights in the East Indies. It all ultimately led to scandal, most famously that following the publishing in 1860 of Multatuli's novel *Max Havelaar* which exposed the horrors consequent upon the system.

The discovery of oil on the east coast of Sumatra by A.E. Zijlker in the 1880s led to the foundation of the Royal Dutch Company (Shell Oil). Amsterdam's (and the Netherlands') wealth still remains very much dependent on the traditional colonial trades of oil, coffee and tobacco.

In the Jordaan and other parts of Amsterdam's inner city, as in the Indies, the price of recovery was being paid for in misery and exploitation. The reforms initiated under Thorbecke improved opportunities to some extent but before 1860 there was scarcely improvement in the housing stock (indeed, from the aesthetic point of view things got worse as gables were chopped off and replaced with straight cornices). The poor lived in large houses subdivided into miserable apartments and wealthier families moved out. Examples of philanthropic housing commissioned by individuals exist (for example away beyond the Westerdok at Houtmanstraat 1–27/Planciusstraat, built in 1854–56) but they are notably few.

The city's ramparts were pulled down in 1848 and land was made available for middle-class housing along the line they had occupied (for example the Weteringschans) and beyond (in the Plantage and elsewhere) but it was not until 1866 when J.G. van Niftrik, the city architect, produced a city plan that we get any sense of an overview.

The council, free-market Liberal by instinct, did not approve of the compulsory purchases necessary to carry out his vision, but a plan of 1877 by the director of public works, J. Kalff, won enough approval to set an agenda for the expansion of the last quarter of the century though it was hardly followed as a plan. As many houses as possible were built on existing divisions of land along the lines of existing roads and watercourses, speculators had a free hand and the council only gave permissions and helped with infrastructure; a number of these developments actually fell down.

Visitors to the city may notice that as you cross the Leidsebrug out of the Leidseplein the main road takes a sharp turn to the right before continuing along the Overtoom. This is a consequence of the ill-considered planning procedures of the 1870s to 1890s, and is one of the reasons that Amsterdam is such a pain for the motorist; perhaps the pedestrian should be grateful. Both city plans had made provision for parks but late-19C Amsterdam is not green in the working-class areas. The Vondelpark was commissioned by a group of public-spirited citizens and presented as a gift to the city. It sits at the heart of an enclave of upper middle-class streets which set the tone for the genteel developments of the museum area.

A walk through the narrow streets of the Pijp, overshadowed by four- or five-storey tenements, gives a flavour of what speculative building achieved for the rest of Amsterdam. Meanwhile the centre of the city was being renovated piecemeal to form a modern commercial centre with department stores, office accommodation and trams; the Rokin and part of the Dam were filled-in; the Raadhuisstraat was cut through an area of older buildings to form a sort of folksy/Gothic Regent Street.

The Liberals were ousted by the Radical Liberals and the Confessional parties in the 1890s and a new concept of municipal government took hold. The 1901 Housing Act set compulsory regulations and paid subsidies to builders, preference was given to housing corporations. Idealistic architects, like Berlage, were involved in planning (for example, the Plan Zuid of 1917) and aesthetic and environmental considerations played a part; the English idea of Garden Cities was introduced (Tuindorp-Oostzaan and Volenwijk).

Many of the architectural gems of 20C Amsterdam resulted from the work of Amsterdam School architects for housing corporations, such as the Dageraad at P.L. Takstraat. In 1935 the *Algemeen Uitbredingsplan* (AUP: General Development Plan) employed demographic and statistical surveys to prepare for an Amsterdam of 900,000 souls in the year 2000.

The improvement of the city in the period up to the Second World War was not an inevitable and gentle progress, anyone with any knowledge of any comparable Western democracy will know that it was set within a framework of wars and peace, boom and slump, the rise of trades unions and socialism and later on the threat of fascism (the NSB, Nationaal-Socialistische Beweging in Nederland), the gradual emancipation of women, the extension of the franchise and much else.

Primary education became compulsory in 1900 and was followed by legislation for secondary schools in 1909, the Vrije Universiteit Amsterdam (the city's second university set up in 1880 as a nonconformist response to the Gemeentelijke Universiteit of 1877) was allowed to award degrees from 1905; the Labour Contract of 1907 and the employment legislation of 1910 set the foundations of a Welfare State and humane employment law, though they were not entirely implemented until later.

It is said that the Jordaan was the first part of the city to get tarmacadam streets because the rioting locals hurled cobble stones at Queen Wilhemina. Photographs in the Zuidebad on Hobbemastraat show the bathing pools being adapted to accept refugees from the countryside in the early years of the century. In 1902 the first Social Democratic representative was elected to the city government.

If the history of the Netherlands is more gentle than that of many other nations it is because social unrest and human suffering has more often precipitated the search for a humane solution than repression—whatever the particular political slant of the ruling party since the turn of the century, the consensus in Dutch politics seems to have been towards 'social democratic' ideals with a 'conservative' dawdling when it came to action.

The Netherlands remained neutral during the First World War and Amsterdam along with the whole nation suffered from the blockade of the war years—although industrialists profited from selling arms to both sides. The post-war depression and revolution in Germany, Russia and Austria inspired the long-standing revolutionary socialist P.J. Troelstra to strike out against the ruling left-of-centre alliance and declare a Revolution in November 1918. The revolution failed. He had made several demands: votes for women arrived thanks to a conservative government in 1922, his demand for the abolition of the monarchy (his undoing) has not yet arrived.

The twenties saw a tremendous growth in real prosperity as is evidenced by the building boom; it was a confident and self-conscious growth which produced some of the finest 'modernist' architecture to be seen anywhere, theory pushed practice in the design of industrial and domestic buildings. One monument to Amsterdam's status at that time is due soon to be torn down—the Olympic Stadium of 1928.

The thirties hit Amsterdam hard, unemployment was combated by major public works, such as the setting-out of the Amsterdam Bos to the south of the city. By the time of the Berlin Olympics in 1936 the Netherlands were also solving the problems of Depression through re-arming and boasting of 'Fortress Holland' behind the Grebbe Line, a system of flooding the countryside. This only ensured that the Germans made the Netherlands a prime target and Hitler mocked the idea of Dutch neutrality giving his troops specific instructions to capture the Queen.

The German forces invaded on 10 May 1940 (the day Churchill succeeded Chamberlain) using a number of ruses to disorientate the Dutch including the notorious ploy of flying out across the sea as if toward England before doubling back and bombing the unsuspecting Dutch. Four days later, following strong Dutch resistance in Rotterdam, Goering ordered Stuka fighters to destroy the city. When the Germans threatened to do the same to Utrecht the Dutch capitulated, they had no air force to speak of and defence was unthinkable. Their fleet escaped to England, as did the Queen and her ministers.

Amsterdam was not bombed but nearby IJmuiden, the chief port for England, was destroyed. After Japan's entry into the war in 1942 Java and Indonesia were taken despite heroic naval resistance. The Netherlands were occupied and held by the Germans until the bitter end of the war.

Bit by bit the true nature of German cultural, economic and, of course, racial imperialism became apparent, and even the Dutch Nazis were to be disappointed. Arthur Seyss-Inquart, an Austrian, was installed as Reichskommissar of what was called the *Westland* of the 'New Europe'. The NSB leader Anton Mussert was snubbed and only found favour when he set about creating a Dutch regiment for the Waffen-SS; some 10,000 Dutchmen, prized by the Nazi ideologues for their racial purity, died fighting for the Germans.

Resistance was invariably blamed on Jews and every act of defiance was followed by the abduction of Jews who were then sent to death camps. Jews and known enemies of the new order went underground, they were called *onderduikers* (divers) or *fietsers* (cyclists). Life for the onderduikers got more difficult as the grimy bureaucratic reality of German racial policy took control, especially as the German war effort gradually sapped the Dutch economy and stricter rationing was introduced.

Amsterdam, one of the great centres of European Jewry, was the Dutch city most affected by German anti-semitism. The bulk of Amsterdam's Jews (10 per cent of the population before the war) lived to the SE of the city centre, the area was first turned into a ghetto and then evacuated and then flattened. Memorials to this crime can be found all over the city—there is the statue of the *Dockworker* on the Jonas Daniel Meijerplein which commemorates the General Strike of February 1941, the Jewish Historical Museum at the heart of the ghetto and, most famously, the Anne Frank House, a hideout near the Westerkerk.

Towards the end of the war the Germans stripped the Netherlands of everything that they could transport; they removed factories, manpower and even the railway lines as they retreated. The winter of 1944–45 was especially severe. The country had been all but abandoned by the retreating Germans who then held up the advancing Allied forces in the Battle of the Ardennes. Isolated, without supplies and fuel, the population starved. The Allies, who had mastery in the air, refused to drop food parcels for fear of helping the remaining Germans and the long 'Hunger Winter', which is estimated to have killed some 2000, continued until the late spring. When the Canadian troops arrived they were jubilantly welcomed by Amsterdammers, 22 of whom were murdered by German snipers who had remained hidden. The Dutch Nazis were rounded up and put on trial, remarkably few were executed.

After the first few months under Allied military government when the question of whether one had been 'goed' or 'fout'—good or bad—was crucial, the whole issue of complicity was repressed. De-nazification took more practical turns: repairing the thousands of destroyed dams and bridges in the countryside, opening Schiphol airport, re-establishing the guilder and obtaining a fleet of ships.

Trade across the Atlantic and within Benelux set the pattern of the post-war economic development. The growth of the European Community and Rotterdam's phenomenal expansion as Europoort could neither have been anticipated nor imitated by Amsterdammers, though the widening of the North Sea Canal (see above) and the completion of the new Amsterdam-Rhine Canal in 1952 ensured the city was a player in the post-war boom.

The discovery of oil and natural gas, another unexpected bounty, added to the general prosperity of the Netherlands which the city, with its new petroleum industries, could share. Amsterdam was no longer in control of the tropical trades which had sustained it before the East Indies fell to the Japanese but traditional industries based upon tobacco, oil, sugar and coffee continued to expand under the new order.

One result of de-colonialisation, completed during the fifties, was a massive immigration of Caribbean and East Indian peoples, a substantial proportion of whom went directly to Amsterdam. There is a large Chinese community right at the heart of the city in the Wallen, South Mollucan and Surinamese communities are spread throughout many parts of the inner south and east. The expansion of the city, checked during the war, continued apace, the most characteristic expansion being the vast concrete and glass estates of the Bijlmermeer to the SE.

The city centre has also seen much change. Many older buildings have benefited from generous government and municipal investment, prestige office occupancy along the grand canals has ensured that new money is continually ploughed into maintaining appearances. Homes are generally owned by housing corporations and local authorities and these organisations retain a fierce sense of the city's architectural tradition.

The old Jewish quarter has been reshaped over the last two decades by housing projects and the new Town Hall and Opera complex (the Stopera), but the essential features of the city have remained more or less intact. No canals have been filled in, ancient doorways and façades are retained, great thought goes into finding uses for empty structures. Tourism, a major industry all year round, has not turned the old city into a hotel-choked theme park.

The Leidsebrug, one of the many fine Amsterdam School public works erected between the wars

Since the war Amsterdam has acquired a number of reputations. In 1956 it was the setting for Albert Camus' *La Chute*, a seedy proletarian city of shadows, fog and guilt—a mythical city, of course. Ten years later it was the location for a part-successful situationist revolution with the Provos overturning received ideas and setting an agenda for every non-Marxist rebellion since.

In the seventies it was the city of the hippies and the TV detective Van de Valk, a city of drug barons and financial skulduggery. It is presently the green city which has voted to exclude the motorcar.

All these Amsterdams are still to found and lie mere streets apart. The docks have been modernised since Camus walked them, but they retain their gloomy Victorian grandeur on November evenings. The Provos have their successors in the counter-culture capitalists, the squatters, the junkies, and the sexual freedom-fighters. And the Amsterdam police are, as they say, wonderful.

The Provos began as a loose association of bohemian types, Amsterdam's beatniks, they took their name from a critic who had dismissed them as provocateurs. Their protest was initially focused on the evils of tobacco and on Saturday evenings in the Spui at the *Lieverdje* statue, which had been donated in 1960 by a tobacco company, they held gentle and mocking anti-smoking protests. The letter 'K' (for *kanker*, cancer) appeared on cigarette advertising hoardings.

The protests were met with some puzzlement and a degree of violence from the police (who were at that time something less than wonderful) and running battles regularly took place in front of the journalists and university teachers sitting outside the nearby cafés. Coming together as a group the Provos assembled an agenda, the celebrated White Plans—most famously the idea of providing 20,000 free white bicycles for use in the city. In 1966 a Provo was actually elected to the town council though by 1967 the movement was beginning to peter out.

The Provos were followed by the Kabouters, or gnomes, who argued for an ecological programme to save the city and the world. They had inherited the Provo seat on the council and in 1970 they won another four seats with over 10 per cent of the poll.

Meanwhile, and not quite by coincidence, Amsterdam had become a destination for youngsters from all over Europe and North America. Despite confrontations on the Dam (it was hosed down every day to make it less comfortable) the hippies managed to make space for themselves—in and around the red light district, around the Waterlooplein market, in derelict buildings everywhere (initiating the squatter movement) and in the Vondelpark which flowered with tents and happenings. Nightlife centred upon the Melkweg and the Paradiso though events might happen anywhere, publicised by word of mouth. Marijuana and LSD were readily available and widely consumed but there were increasing numbers of junkies too.

It is in the nature of fashion that places should come into and go out of style, but on the streets it was as much the hard drug scene as anything else that spoiled hippy Amsterdam. Sexual freedom was part of the hippy rhetoric but it can hardly be said to have been reflected in the commercial sex available in the red light district which has apparently always been a feature of the Wallen.

That idealism is perhaps more apparent in the city's homosexual life. Not because Amsterdam's clubs and pick-up bars are popular with sexual tourists, which they are, but because of the gay community, male and female, who have achieved real freedoms; for example, gay couples are recognised by municipal departments and take their rightful places in the housing queue.

Since the arrival of AIDS constructive action has been argued for and won from the authorities. In the first decade of AIDS, when it was homosexuals, intravenous drug users and casual prostitutes who contracted the disease, the city authorities were alerted to the dangers. Now that AIDS is everybody's disease Amsterdammers are better educated and more alert than citizens in less tolerant parts of Europe. In 1987 the Homomonument was opened, it commemorates the millions of homosexuals persecuted throughout history.

Amsterdam is not always a pleasant city. It can be bitterly cold and is miserable in the rain; in a power cut it would be hell. Dogs seem to be fed high-fibre diets and they dump liberally all over the pavements which, being uneven and slippery, are hard enough to negotiate at any time. There are no decent parks in the city (nowhere you could fly a kite) and even when you get into the countryside there is not the scope to ramble across land that we take as our right in England (for a start there are ditches every few yards). When they are out for the day the Dutch keep to the paths which they also render hazardous by remarkably anti-social cycling (at top speed, talking to each other and not not looking where they are going). I have never heard a cyclist in Amsterdam apologise.

I'm sorry, but it has to be said: Dutch lavatories do not strike me, after many years of experience, to be an acquirable taste. You deposit onto a little shelf which is then flushed when it is time to go. Perhaps being English I am less inquisitive about the condition of my gut than the Dutch. But why also do the Dutch locate their lavatories in such tiny little cupboards?

And one general complaint, which could serve as a warning though it is often held to be a commendation of the city—everybody speaks English. It is impossible to have a private conversation; everyone seems eager to practise their powers of English comprehension and will stop what they are doing to incline an ear towards your business. If you want to be misunderstood in Amsterdam then learn some Dutch.

Amsterdam, however, rises above these things. One frosty morning with a blue sky will immediately dispel the gloom of a week of dull days—and if there is ice then it is simply the most exciting experience to skate along one of the inner city canals. In spring or summer, in the shelter of a wind-shielded café terrace on a sunny day, you can read the newspaper, drink coffee, beer or spirits throughout the day, eat your way through the snacks menu and stare at the world going by. On a cold, wet November night you can discover the meaning of the word *gezellig* (cosy) in a brown café and stare through the rain-beaded windows at the magic of street lamps reflecting on water and wet cobbles.

Outside the city there may be few wildernesses within reach, but the skies are everywhere magnificent—they can seem to start on either side of you, you feel as though you are looking down at the horizon all around. And if the fields and meadows are not accessible, then they are very neat and clean. The cattle group themselves into elegant compositions, though they appear rather large for the moated little fields.

There are allotments outside the city, you will see them grouped along the railway lines if you travel by train, where flights of fancy, mazes and Tarzan's dens provide weekend retreats for a population who live in flats. And the trains, as is well known, are comfortable, clean and punctual. At the Centraal Station you can pick up a leaflet listing days out for every taste and whim. Or if you do not want to travel then visit a market, wander the streets, step into any bar and carry your *Blue Guide* with you.

DAYS OUT

Blue Guide Holland gives in-depth information on all the towns to visit and sights to see in the Netherlands. Most parts of the country are accessible within a day. The following are all within an hour or so of Amsterdam by public transport, most are in the province of Holland; the emphasis has been placed on older sights and traditional destinations. Ask at the Centraal Station for their list of budget days out. The Amsterdam VVV will provide information on tourist events coming up and VVVs in the towns listed below will have information on local events. You can do any of the following days out using public transport and the roads, motorways and parking places are so well signposted it seems hardly necessary to give directions.

Alkmaar

VVV: Waagebouw, Waagplein. Train from Amsterdam Centraal; 36k N. See also Cheese, below.

Alkmaar is a delightfully well-preserved Renaissance town, with the diamond-shaped spurs of the old defences preserved to the W of the centre. The town itself dates back to a Charter of 1254 and its moment of glory came in 1573 when the town successfully resisted the might of the Spanish army. The town's prosperity is based upon cheese, growing in importance during the 16C and 17C when polderisation created rich pastures for milk production.

The **Grote Kerk**, the church of St Laurence, was built in its present form between 1470 and 1520 and should certainly be seen for the many excellently-preserved furnishings. It contains a fine 17C organ, designed by Jacob van Campen and painted by Cesar van Everdingen; in the apse, the tomb of Count Floris V, murdered by the nobles in 1296; The Last Judgement on the ceiling above was painted in 1519 by Cornelis Buys, the Master of Alkmaar (there is a smaller organ in the N ambulatory which dates back to 1511). As well as having the Friday cheese market (do not miss the Cheese Museum in the Waggebouw, nor the carillon in the tower of the Waagebouw with jousting knights) it has a beer museum in a former brewery.

The **Stedelijk Museum** (Monday–Thursday 10.00–12.00, 14.00–17.00; Friday 10.00-17.00; Sunday and holidays 14.00–17.00) occupies the former militia headquarters of 1520 and is notable for local history, antique toys and medieval sculptures from the Grote Kerk; paintings by Cesar van Everdingen, Maerten van Heemskerck, Willem van der Velde I, Pieter de Grebber and Hendrick Vroom.

Apart from the many interesting features within the town itself there is nearby Kennemerland to the W with many historical sights including Egmond aan Zee (the pleasures of the seaside, also a museum of ship models), Egmond aan der Hoef (remains of the Castle of Egmond), and the great Abbey at Egmond Binnen, founded in 950 and now rebuilt (no admission).

To the NE at Langendijk the ancient, waterborne flower and vegetable auction at the Broeker Veiling takes place on weekdays, 10.00–17.00.

Amsterdamse Bos

Amsterdamse Bos, the Amsterdam woods, is the city's own little piece of countryside. Reached by tram (170, 171 and 172) or, on Sundays in summer, by antique tram from the Harlemmermeer Station where there is an Electric Tram Museum. It is also an easy cycle ride from the centre of town. There are pleasant walks, rides for cyclists and boats for hire on the myriad waterways.

The Bos Museum at Koenenkade 56 (daily 10.00–17.00) tells how the Amsterdamse Bos came to be laid out, as a work-creation project during the Great Depression. Near the museum there is an old farmhouse converted to a restaurant.

Castles

We usually think of the Netherlands as a democratic country, cycling royals and all that. The Dutch, however, think of themselves as an ancient and proud race, and the land is rich and has been fought over for centuries. Walled towns and the remains of walls around towns are commonplace (Breda in Noord Brabant is a good example of the former, the various towers in present-day Amsterdam of the latter). As many castles haunt the landscape paintings of the Golden Age as those of the Romantics.

A few miles E of Amsterdam **Muiderslot** (Monday–Friday 10.00–17.00; Sunday and holidays 13.00–17.00; early closing October–March at 16.00), a fairytale castle with turrets and a moat, has the added distinction of having been inhabited by a great poet, Pieter Cornelisz. Hooft, who was bailiff there. It was built sometime after 1280 by Count Floris V on the Vecht river which it protects. Guided tours are the only way to see the interior and the guides are always kind to Anglophones. The grounds are delightful and the herb garden should be seen.

Brederode Castle (March–October, open daily except Saturday 10.00–17.00) N of Haarlem was a celebrated ruin of the Rebellion; the 15C structure (itself a rebuilding) was demolished by Spanish forces. Some restoration has since taken place. The Brederodes were an ancient family dating back to 1244; their place in Dutch mythology was assured when Hendrik van Brederode joined the League of the Nobility (the 'beggars') dismissed by Margaret of Parma in 1565. But the aficionado of castles ought to travel to Utrecht, Limburg and the northern and eastern provinces.

Cheese

Cheese is one of Holland's most famous exports. A cheese market is held every Friday in Alkmaar between 10.00 and 12.00 on the Waagplein. This is where the porters you see in the promotional literature, dressed in the distinctive white suits, each displaying the colours of one or another of the four cheese porters' guilds on their hats, wheel their barrows to and fro. Cheese is tested for taste, smell and texture by dealers and then wheeled to the Waagebouw (weigh-house) which dates back to a chapel founded in 1341. North Holland cheeses are principally of the Edam type with their distinctively coloured wax coatings.

Gouda's cheese market is held on Thursday mornings at the Waag which dates back to 1668. Traditional costume makes this a colourful tourist event and children are delighted by the deal-making which is carried-out with an exchange of handclaps. Gouda cheese, produced in South Holland and Utrecht, is the most popular cheese in the Netherlands.

Cycling

Hire a bicycle (see Practical Information) and cross the IJ by the free ferry which departs from the De Ruijterkade on the N side of the Centraal Station.

On a pleasant day (i.e. without too strong a wind) you should be able to get as far as Edam and back along the dijk which runs all the way along the IJsselmmer. Or cycle down to the Amsterdamse Bos (see above). The seaside (see below) is also reachable by bike. If it all gets too much then make for the nearest station and train it home, there is no shame in that.

Delft

VVV: Markt 85 (SE corner). Train from Amsterdam Centraal (change at The Hague); 60km S.

Delft is one of the smaller Randstad towns; the historic centre is very compact. It was founded in 1075 and received its charter in 1246. William the Silent was assassinated here in 1584. Delft was the birthplace of the jurist and scholar Grotius (Hugo de Groot, 1583–1645), the microscopist Antonie van Leeuwenhoek (1632–1725) and the painter Jan Vermeer (1632–75). To the world, the town's name is associated with Delftware, the distinctive Dutch pottery. The town's prosperity was established by trade along a medieval canal to Delfshaven (see Rotterdam); long economic decline has preserved the town very well.

Leave the station and cross the West Vest to take the first turn leading to the Oude Delft, a truly delightful stretch of Old Holland. This leads to an open space with on the E side the Oudekerk and on the W the Prinsenhof. The **Oudekerk** (April–October, Monday–Saturday 11.00–16.00) of St Hippolytus was begun c 1250; the last extension (NE side) is early 16C. Note the leaning tower, a testament to the insecurity of the subsoil. The monuments inside are of high quality and celebrate, among others, the Admirals Piet Heyn (1577–1629) who brought home the Spanish silver fleet in 1628, and Maarten Tromp (1598–1653), the Admiral who hung a broom at his masthead to show that he had swept the seas of English ships.

The **Prinsenhof** (Tuesday–Saturday 10.00–17.00; Sunday, holidays and Monday in June–August, 13.00–17.00) was originally the Convent of St Agatha, founded in c 1400 but mostly built during the 16C. It takes its present name from having been appropriated by Prince William I, William the Silent, in 1572. It is now a museum in which the building itself is the principal exhibit; the bullet marks made during the assassination of William the Silent are preserved.

Just to the N at Oude Delft 199 is the **Huis Lambert van Meertenmuseum** (Tuesday–Saturday 10.00–17.00, Sunday, holidays and Monday in June–August 13.00–17.00), a 19C mansion containing a magnificent collection of Delftware in handsome, panelled rooms.

There are many attractive houses and almshouses throughout the town, especially here and to the NE around the Paardenmarkt (horse market). S of the Oudekerk, via the Hippolytus Buurt, is the Markt. Free-standing at the W end is the **Stadhuis** of 1618, by Hendrick de Keyser (1565–1621). The 14C tower is all that remains visible of the medieval town hall destroyed by fire in 1536. To the W of the Stadhuis are the Boterhuis and Waag of 1765 and 1770 respectively.

The second of Delft's two great churches, the **Nieuwekerk** (April–September, Monday–Saturday 09.00–17.00; October–March, Monday–Saturday 10.00–12.00, 13.30–16.00) was founded in 1381 as a wooden church dedicated to the Virgin Mary; between 1384 and 1496 the present Gothic Church of St Ursula was erected. Damaged in the fire of 1536 and again in the great armoury explosion of 1654 (when the glass was lost) the structure survives more or less intact. The spire, familiar from Vermeer's painting (see The Hague), was replaced after lightning struck in 1872. The Niuewekerk is a national monument owing to the **mausoleum of William the Silent** in the choir, designed by Hendrik de Keyser between 1614 and 1622. William is accompanied by his faithful dog who is said to have refused food and drink after his master's death, and died soon after. The tomb is surrounded by allegorical figures and surmounted by a canopy. Beneath are the burial vaults of the Princes of Orange, who are commemorated in memorials about the church.

Returning to the station along the Koornemarkt, which runs from the SW corner of the Markt, you pass the **Museum Tétar van Elven** (May–October, Tuesday–Saturday 11.00–17.00) at Koornemarkt 67, the home of an 19C artist of the same name and filled with furniture and 19C art. Further S at Korte Geer 1 is the **Armamentarium** (Tuesday–Saturday 10.00–17.00, Sunday 13.00–17.00), a much altered building of 1692 housing a military museum.

Dutch Costume

National dress is still worn, admittedly in a rather unconvincing way, in a number of towns. For men it consists of baggy trousers, decorated stockings, waistcoats and clogs. Women's dress includes a full, ankle-length dress, a variety of jackets, the pointy lace caps and, to hold them in place, ear irons in various patterns. You may come across elderly folk in such dress on Scheveningen Harbour (see The Hague, below).

Near Hoorn, at Volendam and Marken (an island until 1957), the locals parade in costume; these places get so crowded with tourists that the sight can only be recommended to sociologists and students of human thick-skinnedness. There are villages in Groningen where isolated religious communities have retained elements of traditional dress, sometimes only on Sundays. Most regional and municipal museums display local dress collections. (For clogs see Walk 3, under 'Klompenboer'.)

Gouda

VVV: Markt 24. Train from Amsterdam Centraal; 29km S. See also Chesse, above.

Most famous for its cheese, but it ought to be more famous for its medieval architecture, its handsome market square (the largest in the Netherlands) and its *Siroopwafels* (syrup waffles). Founded in the 12C, the town received its charter in 1272. It was originally a cloth town, clay-based industries (bricks, pottery, pipes) arrived later, as did cheese. Gouda claims to produce more than three-quarters of Dutch Delftware. Candles are also a local speciality, and in December there is a candle festival when all the lights are turned out and the huge square is illuminated by candlelight. Gouda is one of the contestants as the birthplace of Desiderius Erasmus (1469–1536), the great humanist scholar; it can boast with certainty of being the town where he was educated.

Outside the Waag in the Markt (see Cheese, above) is where the weekly cheese market takes place. The Stadhuis and the Waag stand in the centre of the Markt. The **Stadhuis** (Town Hall, open Monday–Friday 09.00–12.00, 14.00–16.00) is made all the more impressive by standing clear of other buildings. The present building, entirely in stone, dates from 1450, 12 years after a major fire. It is thought to be the oldest Gothic town hall in the Netherlands. Owing to its design, seeming to be wider at the top than at the bottom, it has a giddy, Disney-esque appearance, one which is enhanced by the forest of spires and pinnacles and the bright red window-shutters. This is one of the most popular places in the country for couples to get married, a wedding takes place every few minutes throughout the day. This means that in order to see the interior furnishings (fireplaces, tapestries, glass, sculpture) you will have to sneak in between ceremonies. Superstition has it that the right-hand staircase (dating from 1603) is unlucky, being the one used by condemned criminals, so keep to the left. The façade is decorated with statues of the counts and countesses of Burgundy. The carillon on the E wall is modern, it re-enacts the granting of the charter by Count Floris V every half an hour.

The **Waag** of 1668, to the N of the Stadhuis, was designed by Pieter Post (1608–69). It appears severely classical and dumpy by comparison to the Stadhuis although there are appealing details, such as the sculpted relief on the façade by Bartholomeus Eggers (died before 1692) of cheeses being weighed.

The great church of **St Jan** is renowned for its stained-glass; it is also, at 123m, the longest church in the country. This church was begun in 1552 on the site of another destroyed by fire caused by lightning. Much of the stained-glass for the new building was donated by neighbouring cities, ecclesiastics and others following the disaster. A leaflet in English detailing the various windows is available.

Behind the church, in a street called, appropriately enough, Achter de Kerk, stands the Lazaruspoortje, the entrance to the 17C Lepers' Hospital which was moved here in the 1960s to serve as the rear entrance to the **Stedelijk Museum** (Tuesday–Saturday 10.00–17.00; Sunday 12.00–17.00; entrance fee also lets you into De Moriaan, see below) which now occupies the St Catharina Gasthuis beyond (built in 1665, possibly by Pieter Post though some rooms date back to 1542; the institution was founded in 1310). As well as being a municipal museum with some very good examples of religious art, church silver and reconstructed shops, there are many fine paintings, notably the collection of 19C works (Hague School, Barbizon, Odilon Redon, Isaac Israëls, etc.) donated by the artist Paul Arntzenius. **De Moriaan** (The Blackamoor), a short walk away at Westhaven 29 (same hours as the Stedelijk), is a merchant's house of 1617 presently housing the Stedelijk's ceramics collection; it takes its name from the carving over the door. The ceramics industry is celebrated at **Het Tin en Keramik Huis** (Tuesday–Saturday 10.00–17.00) on Lange Groenendaal 73 where you can see craftsmen at work. Pipes are made at Peperstraat 76 (weekdays 09.00–17.00; Saturday 13.00–17.00). The Netherlands' only occupied working windmill, **De Rode Leeuw**, is at Vest 65 (Tuesday–Saturday 09.00–17.00; admission charge).

Haarlem

VVV: Stationsplein (just to the left as you leave the ticket hall). Train from Amsterdam Centraal; 20k E.

Haarlem is a picturesque water-town on the Spaarne river; it dates back 1000 years and received its charter in 1245 (long before Amsterdam). Haarlem's history is bound up with the history of the Counts of Holland who kept a hunting lodge at the Gravenshal (destroyed in 14C) on the site of the present Stadhuis (Town Hall). What is now the Grote Markt (market-place) was their jousting field. Haarlem was one of the cities that suffered during the Revolt, being beseiged by the Spanish in 1572–73. When it fell the entire militia was put to death; the medieval town was subsequently destroyed by a fire in 1576. Soon afterwards Haarlem provided many of the great painters of the Golden Age.

Make for the Grote Markt at the centre of the town (do not leave the station without seeing the splendid wooden restaurant on platform 2) following the Kruisweg, Kruisstraat and Barteljorisstraat. As you enter the square the view ahead is dominated by St Bavo's Church, the Stadhuis is directly to your right and under the shadow of the church on the far right stands the Vleeshal (meat hall). The statue is of Laurens Coster (1370–1440) to whom is attached a convincing claim to have invented moveable-type printing as early as 1423.

The **Stadhuis** is on the site given to the town by Count William V. The present building is from several periods, the last major rebuilding of 1630 is noted on the façade. When the building is open you can visit the so-called Gravenzaal, a large, wood-beamed room containing some interesting (if ugly) paintings of the Counts of Holland and a narwhale tusk.

The **Vleeshal** (1602), by Lieven de Key (c 1560–1627) is a richly decorated building; the exterior, with its carved cattle heads, is worth a careful perusal. The interior, now an exhibition space, was gutted at the turn of the century.

St Bavo's Church (Monday–Saturday 10.00–16.00 or 15.30 September–March) was under construction during most of the 15C; the buildings attached on the near side are the former Vismarkt (fish market, 1768), now used for exhibitions. Entrance is from the far side, on the Oude Groenmarkt. The bright, spacious interior of St Bavo's is full of interest, especially in the guild chapels which run around the ambulatory (model ships in the Shipbuilders' Chapel, the measured heights of a giant and a dwarf in the Brewers', the picture at the top of the column of the Dogwhippers' Chapel). There are a fine early 16C choir screen and lectern. Frans Hals (see below) is buried under slab 56. The organ, with 5000 pipes, was built by Christiaen Müller in 1735–38. It was the finest in the world when Handel and Mozart came to play on it.

The succession of narrow streets leading S out of the Oude Groenmarkt lead eventually to the Groot Heiligland where, in a group of 17C almshouses, is the **Frans Halsmuseum** (Monday–Saturday 11.00–17.00; Sunday and holidays, 13.00–17.00). The museum occupies the Oudmannenhuis of 1610, and surrounds a delightful courtyard. Frans Hals (c 1580–1666) was an occupant of this hospice in his old age. The most celebrated paintings here are the militia group portraits by Frans Hals; huge and brilliantly-coloured canvases crowded with the higher bourgeoisie of Haarlem and dating from 1616 to 1639 (the last including Hals himself). Paintings from Haarlem painters of all periods including Jan van Scorel, Cornelis Cornelisz., Maerten van Heemskerck, Hendrick Goltzius, Jan de Bray, Jacob van Ruisdael and many more. There is a wing of modern and contemporary painting and sculpture. Hals' portraits of the Regents and Regentesses (1664), two remarkable paintings from a man well into his eighties, are images that will haunt you.

Follow the Singel and Spaarne back to the Dam Straat, just beyond is the **Teylers Museum** (Tuesday–Saturday 10.00–17.00; Sunday 13.00–17.00. October–February closes at 16.00) at Spaarne 16. Founded in 1778 by Pieter Teijler van der Hulst for the encouragement of science and art. The museum has scientific instruments, fossils, paintings and drawings and much more.

The Hague

VVV: Koningin Julianaplein (to the right in the open space in front of the Centraal Station). Train from Amsterdam Centraal; 50km SW.

Getting to The Hague by train can be confusing, there can be either one of two destinations listed on the departure boards at Amsterdam—Den Haag C.S. (which is the more convenient for you) and Den Haag H.S. The two are not far apart and are linked by train, bus and tram services but you might still waste time trying to find out what has gone wrong with your geography were you to end up at the wrong one. Take any train from Amsterdam that passes through Leiden and then change trains at Leiden (same platform, other side), the train should take you to The Hague Centraal.

The Hague shares some of the business of being capital city with Amsterdam; the States General (Dutch Parliament) meets here and many Government departments and Embassies are here too. Yet it has frequently been referred to as a non-city, an overgrown village.

It takes its name from the fact that Count William II of Holland set up his official residence here in 1247; the village which grew up at his gate came to be known as 's-Gravenhage, the Count's Hedge, and this is still the correct form of the town's name (have you noticed how many variations there are in town names in the Netherlands? Dordrecht/Dort, 's-Hertogen-bosch/Den Bosch, etc), Den Haag is the more commonly used form in Dutch.

The centre of the town is still the court at the Binnenhof, a short walk W from the Centraal Station (cross the Bezuidenhoutse in front of the station, walk a little way up the Koningskade past the deer park on your right and then enter the town through the Korte Voorhout for the most spectacular introduction to the Binnenhof, from across the Hof Vijver lake). Across the water you see the whole rambling complex with, on the left, the elegant Palladian box of the Mauritshuis, a house built in 1633–34 for Prince John Maurice of Nassau-Siegen, Governor of the then immense Dutch territories in Brazil. The architect was Jan van Campen (1595–1657) who went on to design the Amsterdam Town Hall. On your left, at Korte Vijverberg 7, is the **Haags Historisch Museum** (Tuesday–Saturday 12.00–16.00) with a well-documented account of the development of the town housed in a former militia headquarters.

The **Mauritshuis** (Tuesday–Saturday 10.00–17.00; Sunday 11.00–17.00) is entered by a door at basement level off the Korte Vijverberg. The collection is laid out on the two main floors with information and café in the basement. The Dutch pictures alone are stunning, they include: Vermeer's View of Delft, Girl in a Turban and Diana Bathing; Rembrandt's Anatomy of Dr Tulp, an early and a late self-portrait, Homer dictating and many more; a number of high-quality Jan Steens, including Girl eating oysters; Paulus Potter's Young Bull (life sized!); several exquisite 'Italianate' and classicist paintings and many fine portraits. Other (northern) schools and periods are well represented with works by Van der Weyden, Holbein, Rubens and Van Dyck. Of particular interest are the pastels by the 18C 'Dutch Hogarth', Cornelis Troost.

Enter the **Binnenhof** (inner court) via the gateway at the E end beyond the Mauritshuis. The large building to the left is the **Ridderzaal**, Knights' Hall (tours when the building is not in use: Monday–Saturday 10.00–16.00; July–August Sunday 12.00–16.00), which is the heart of the complex and dates back to the late 13C. The building gets its name from being the place where the Knights of the Golden Fleece met; the Hall now functions as the meeting place for combined sessions of both chambers of the States General and for the annual ceremonial opening in September. The first chamber meets on the N side, the second on the S.

Leave the Binnenhof by the W gate and you are in the Buitenhof (outer court), a stylish commercial square. At Buitenhof 35 is the **Schildergallerij Prins Willem V** (Tuesday–Sunday 11.00–16.00) with many fine paintings from the Golden Age, most interesting, perhaps, as a reconstruction of an 18C gallery.

The **Rijksmuseum Gevangenpoort** (Monday–Friday 10.00–16.00; April–October, Sunday 13.00–16.00) in the old prison gate has a collection of instruments of torture which emphasis is a pity because the building has an interesting enough history without such crowd-pullers (which do not, anyway, pull crowds).

Be sure to look down the elegant Passage shopping arcade off the SW corner of the Buitenhof before you leave via the passage on the NW corner which leads to the Hoogstraat, turning left to reach the **Oude Stadhuis** which dates, with much alteration, from 1565. Beyond is the **St Jacobskerk**, dating mainly from the mid 15C. On the aisle walls at the W end are the arms of the Knights of the Golden Fleece, some fine windows in the ambulatory and tombs of distinguished Hague figures.

The Oude Molstraat runs N from the Stadhuis to the **Paleis Noordeinde**, the home of the widow of William the Silent and much enlarged since; it is now the home of the Royal Secretariat. The gardens behind are open to the public. The present Queen lives in the **Huis ten Bosch** (the House in the Woods) away to the E, a pleasant walk through the Haagse Bos which lie in front of and to the NE of the Centraal Station; there is no public access.

A walk N up the Noord Einde and Zeestraat will take you to the **Panorama Mesdag** (Monday–Saturday 10.00–17.00; Sunday 12.00–17.00) at Zeestraat 65b, a panorama of the city and environs painted in 1881. At Zeestraat 82 is the **Postmuseum** (Monday–Saturday 10.00–17.00; Sunday and holidays 13.00–17.00) with exhibits of and about all aspects of communications.

At the end of Zeestraat, at Laan van Meerdervoort 7f, is the **Rijksmuseum H.W. Mesdag** (Tuesday–Saturday 10.00–17.00; Sunday and holidays 13.00–17.00) is a collection of paintings donated by H.W. Mesdag (1831–1915) and his wife Sientje Mesdag-van Houten (1834–1909) full of 19C works, notably Hague School and Barbizon paintings.

Behind is the **Vredespaleis** (Monday–Friday 10.00–12.00, 14.00–16.00; guided tours on the hour), the Peace Palace sponsored by the Dutch Government and Andrew Carnegie and opened in 1913. Since 1922 the Palace has housed the Permanent Court of International Justice. The sumptuous furnishings are gifts from the nations of the world.

From Zeestraat you can take Tram 4 to the museums complex on President Kennedylaan and Stadhouderslaan containing the **Omniversum** (shows on the hour: Tuesday–Thursday 11.00–16.00; Friday–Sunday 11.00–21.00, except 18.00), the **Haagse Gemeentemuseum** (Tuesday–Sunday 11.00–17.00) and the **Museon** (Tuesday–Friday 10.00–17.00; weekends and holidays 13.00–17.00). The Omniversum is a domed planetarium with a sophisticated Omnimax 70mm projection system and six-channel sound. The Gemeentemuseum, in a very fine building of 1935 by H.P. Berlage (1856–1934), which houses the town's collections, including the costume museum, a world-famous collection of musical instruments, ceramics, glass and silverware and 19C and 20C art (the place to see Piet Mondriaan's work). The Museon is a lively and innovative museum for education bringing together science, natural history, ecology and anthropology, and will appeal to inquisitive children of all ages.

A walk through the Scheveningse Bosjes (or tram, if you prefer) leads to the miniature town of **Madurodam** (daily March–May 09.00–22.30; June–August 09.00–23.00; September 09.00–21.30; winter 09.00–18.00) which features many recognisable Dutch buildings in one twenty-fifth scale. Madurodam is a memorial to George Maduro, a young Dutch soldier who died in Dachau in 1945, all profits go to charities.

Other attractions in and around The Hague include a handsome 'square', the **Lange Voorhout** (home to the British Embassy, the Royal Library and the Voorhout Palace) to the N of the Hof Vijver, the **Rijksmuseum Meermanno Westreenianum** (Monday–Saturday 13.00–17.00) at Prinsessegracht 30, a museum of the book, well worth a visit, and nearby Scheveningen.

SCHEVENINGEN is the port and seaside resort of The Hague. The original fishing village was drowned by the sea in 1570, the resort dates from 1715. Bathing became fashionable in the early 19C and much capital has been invested over the last 20 years to make it a year-round resort and spa. The Kurhaus in Scheveningen Bad dates from 1887, a flamboyant piece of Victorian seaside architecture. The pier is presently in a state of disrepair but there are indoor and outdoor facilities enough to keep a family happy all day with sea cruises, swimming, sports and the beach.

The harbour at Scheveningen Haven has a pretty 15C church nearby and affords plenty to gaze at; it is worth the 2km walk for the fried fish bars.

Industrial Nostalgia

Industrial nostalgia can be indulged by visiting the **Croquius Expo** at Heemstede (train from Centraal Station. April–November, Monday–Saturday 10.00–17.00; Sunday and holidays, 12.00–17.00; October and November closes 16.00). This is the pumping station which drained the huge inland lake which lay between Leiden, Haarlem and Amsterdam, the Harleemmermeer. There is also a museum telling the history of reclamation from the 15C onwards.

The **Zaanstrijk** across the IJ (free ferry from the De Ruijterkade on the N side of the Centraal Station; take a bike) is worth a visit to see the (now picturesque) tiny houses in this once thriving shipbuilding district. In the centre of **Zaandam** there is a statue of Peter the Great of Russia who visited the town (calling himself Peter Mikhailov) and stayed with a certain Gerrit Kist while he studied Dutch shipbuilding. Kist's house, now the **Czaar Peterhuisje** (Tuesday–Saturday and second and fourth Sundays 10.00–13.00 and 14.00–17.00), just off the main square, is now elaborately preserved. The regional museum is in Zaandijk, just to the N. **Zaanse Scans** is a museum village with working windmills, shops, houses and the rest.

At Utrecht (see below) there is the **Spoorwegmuseum** (Tuesday–Saturday 10.00–17.00, Sunday 13.00–17.00) showing the history of railways in a Victorian Station.

At Schiphol Airport there is the **Aviodome** (daily 10.00–17.00; November–March, closed Monday; see Museums and Galleries above).

Leiden

VVV: Stationsplein 210 (across the road and to the right in the long modern building, behind the wall of bicycles). Train from Amsterdam Centraal; 40km SW.

Although claims have been made to establish Leiden on the map of Roman Europe, its real history goes back to the Middle Ages, and especially to the arrival of Flemish weavers following the Black Death in the mid 14C. Like Haarlem, Leiden suffered during the Revolt and refused to fall, the citizens suffering terrible deprivation during the year-long siege of 1574–75. The University, long petitioned for, was founded in 1575. Rembrandt van Rijn (1606–69) was born here, as was Jan Steen (1625–79) and the great physician, Herman Boerhaave (1666–1738). The Elsevier Press was started here and Carl von Linné (Linnaeus) (1707–78) worked here. Many Scots studied Roman Law at either Leiden or Utrecht (see below), a sympathetically Calvinist city. Leiden lies on the Old Rhine (hence Rembrandt's surname), is criss-crossed with attractive waterways and surrounded by a canal which still follows the course of 17C defensive works.

From the station the Stationsweg leads S past the Volkenkunde (ethnology) and Boerhaave (history of science) museums to the Beestenmarkt which offers attractive views across to the city. The Lakenhal Museum lies 150m directly E on the N of the Oude Vest canal. The Blauwpoortsbrug (bridge) leads, via the Bostelbrug, to the town centre, the Burcht (the medieval citadel), the St Pieterskerk, the Hooglandsekerk, the Rijksmuseum van Oudheden (classical antiquity), the University buildings (which seem to be everywhere in this town) and the Stadhuis.

The **Rijksmuseum voor Volkenkunde** (Tuesday–Friday 10.00–17.00; weekends and holidays 12.00–17.00) has been under re-organisation for so long that one wonders if it will ever be completed. The core collection dates back to the enterprising German Philipp Franz von Siebold (1797–1866) who worked for the Dutch trading post in Nagasaki Bay during the 1820s (Japan was closed to all but the Dutch from 1639–1861) and assembled an enormous collection of Oriental art and artefacts. He put his collection on display in Leiden in 1831 which was bought by the Dutch government in 1837 to found a national Oriental Museum. Subsequently the Rijksmuseum has gathered one of the finest collections of eastern art in existence, notably, of course, Indonesian.

The **Boerhaave Museum** (opening times as for above) has a collection of scientific and surgical instruments and a reconstruction of a teaching operating theatre with rows of seats overlooking the cutting table.

The **Lakenhal Museum** (Tuesday–Saturday 10.00–17.00; Sunday and Holidays 13.00-17.00) at Oude Singel 28–32 takes its name from its premises, the Cloth Guild until 1800, built in 1640 along elegant Palladian lines. The museum combines an art gallery with a local history museum. Entered through a courtyard, you can choose your route with the help of plans available from the information desk. Paintings by artists associated with the town include Lucas van Leyden's Heaven and Hell triptych, an early Rembrandt narrative scene, works by Jan van Goyen, David Bailey, Jan Steen (buried in the St Pieterskerk), Abraham van den Tempel and many more. The Leiden *fijnschilders*, painters who cultivated a learned and painstaking style following Gerrit Dou, are not as well represented as could be wished, but there are good paintings by various Van Mierises, Dou and others. Upstairs there are fascinating displays of local history material, some of it worthy of a place in the art gallery. One strength of the collection is the furniture and porcelain. There are temporary displays of more recent art.

Just north of the Lakenhal at 2e Binnenvestgracht 1a (you won't miss it) is the **Molenmuseum De Valk** (Tuesday–Saturday 10.00–17.00; Sunday and holidays 13.00–17.00), a restored grain windmill of 1743.

The Rapenburg, S of the Bostelbrug, is an elegant, tree-lined canal. Two blocks down on the right is the **Rijksmuseum van Oudheden** (Tuesday–Saturday 10.00–17.00; Sunday and holidays 13.00–17.00), founded in 1818, though greatly enlarged at various times since. Collections include Egyptian and classical sculpture and artefacts, and an entire, if small, Egyptian temple, which adds a certain distinction to the entrance hall. The second floor pays special attention to prehistoric Netherlands. Smaller than the British Museum, well laid-out and lit, this is an excellent introduction to mainstream archaeology and a treasure trove to enthusiasts who come from all over the world.

The heart of Leiden University lies across the Rapenburg from the museum—you can wander through the picturesque streets and the sympathetically designed new complex beyond. The **University Museum** is at Rapenburg 73 (Wednesday–Friday 13.00–17.00). At the same address is the entrance to the **Hortus Botanicus** (Monday–Friday 09.00–17.00; hothouses 09.00–12.30, 13.00–16.30; Sunday 10.00–17.00; hothouses 10.30–12.30, 13.30–15.00) which was laid out in 1587.

Behind the museum, approached through narrow, quiet streets, is the St Pieterskerk with the Latin School (1599) to the N; this is where Rembrandt went to school. The **St Pieterskerk** is in brick, built during the 15C and contains a number of monuments associated with University figures, as well as the grave of Jan Steen and an unexplained mummified figure (not Egyptian).

The Pieterskerkchoorsteeg leads away from the church E to the Breestraat. Across that street is the **Stadhuis**, designed by Lieven de Key (c 1560–1627) and faithfully rebuilt since a fire in 1929. It is an unusual, elongated building of some charm, note the town crier's platform. On the far side of the square, behind the Stadhuis, is the 15C Korenbeursbrug, Corn Exchange Bridge, roofed over in 1825 and where the corn market was held.

Across the bridge and to the left is the massive **Burcht**, a 12C fort on an ancient artificial mound. To the right, down Nieuwstraat, is the **Hooglandsekerk** built in the 15C and 16C, the adjoining tower is on a much older foundation. There are many small museums associated with university departments in the city and a full list is available from the VVV.

Provinces of the Netherlands

The provinces (see map) include, in alphabetical order: DRENTHE: too far for a day trip (and therefore miraculously free of tourists generally) but of especial interest for its prehistoric remains, peat-colony villages and open heathlands; FLEVOLAND: only a province since 1986, only land since c 1950; visit the new town of Alsmere, the bird sanctuary at Oostvaardersplassen, the farm museum at Flevohof, the **Museum of Marine Archaeology** at Ketelhaven; FRIESLAND: with its own language (spoken by 300,000); Sneek for boats, Leeuwaarden for the **Fries (Friesian) Museum**, the Frisian Islands for windswept retreat, there are a number of day trips usually on offer at the Centraal Station, if you have a car be sure to take the crossing over the Afsluitdijk; GELDERLAND has two kinds of countryside, the Veluwe (badlands) and Betuwe (good-lands), both pleasant for walking and cycling; head for the **Hoge Veluwe National Park**, the **Kröller-Müller Museum of Modern Art, Paleis Het Loo**, William III's retreat, and near Arnhem the **Openlucht Museum** (Open-air Folk Museum); GRONINGEN: the ancient city of Groningen itself with the **Groninger Museum**, peat-colony villages and terp villages built around prehistoric mounds are better explored by car or cycle; LIMBURG away to the SE has mountains! Maastricht dates back to Roman times and has a cosmopolitan, European feel; the countryside is dotted with attractive castles, farmhouses and small towns; NOORD BRABANT: the Netherlands' vigorously Catholic deep south with a 19C replica of St Peter's in Rome at Oudenbosch; 's-Hertogenbosch's Gothic cathedral is worth a long drive/train journey; for families **De Efteling**, a fairyland theme park, is a do-able if wearisomely distant day out from Amsterdam; Breda and Bergen op Zoom are fortified towns worth seeing; OVERIJSSEL: visited by Hollanders for its Lake District, beautiful towns such as Zwolle, Kampen and Deventer, the province stretches all the way to the German border; UTRECHT is well within reach of Amsterdam as the many prosperous commuters know; the city of Utrecht (see below) is a cathedral city of great interest, rivers and lakes provide opportunities for boating; Wijk-bij-Duurstede, Rhenen, Amerongen and Culemborg are all fine and ancient towns; ZEELAND is composed in part of the archipelago of the Rhine-Maas Delta (visit the **Delta Expo** on the Oosterscheldedam for the history of the heroic war against the sea); interesting towns include Vlissingen (Flushing), Middelburg and Veere and all are within day return range. Visit the Amsterdam VVV and Centraal Station information for travel information, maps and directions to any of the above.

Rotterdam

VVV: (Main Office) Coolsingel 67, also at Rotterdam's Centraal Station. Train from Amsterdam Centraal; 73km SW.

The centre of the city was so badly bombed during the last war that little of the architectural diversity familiar in other cities is to be found here; only the shell of the great St Laurenskerk remained, the few odd houses that survived or have been restored sit oddly with the modern architecture. With a population of a little over half a million, Rotterdam is the Netherlands' second city and is the world's greatest port serving much of Europe via the Rhine and the Maas rivers. Erasmus (see Gouda, above) was born here, as were the painter Pieter de Hooch and Charles II's bastard son, the Duke of Monmouth. There are numerous attractions, including three local history museums, the Museum Boymans-Van Beuningen, the Maritime Museum Prins Hendrik, the Museum voor Land en Volkenkunde (Ethnological Museum), the Belasting (Prof. Dr van der Poel) Museum of taxation and the Toy-Toy Museum (out of the city in the eastern suburbs at Groene Wetering 41; open Sunday–Thursday 11.00–16.00; closed July and August). The VVV will give you details of the **Waterstad (water city) Walk** which will take you past many of the sites listed below, as well as showing you the city Rotterdammers want you to see, including the bizarre and beautiful Paalwoningen houses in the old harbour designed by Piet Blom and built in 1978–84.

Emerging from the Centraal Station you are confronted with an aggressive and modern motor car city. The busy Wester Singel stretches S towards the Museum Boymans-Van Beuningen and relative peace and quiet; follow the right-hand side for about 10 minutes as far as the Mathenesserlaan and the museum stands across the way. The **Museum Boymans-Van Beuningen** (Tuesday–Saturday 10.00–17.00; Sunday and holidays 11.00–17.00) is one of the world's great art galleries. The original collection, which opened in 1849, was destroyed by fire in 1864; the present holdings are subsequent purchases and include Hieronymus Bosch's Prodigal Son, Rembrandt's

Titus and an excellent collection of Golden Age paintings as well as one of the finest small collections of graphic art in existence. The modern collection is also first-class covering Impressionism to Pop. Sculpture (especially Renaissance bronzes and 20C works), ceramics and glass make this museum an important visit on any itinerary. There is a garden with sculptures on display.

Leave the Boymans-Van Beuningen and turn right down the Wester Singel, following the road to its end which brings you to the West Plein; a right turn takes you to Parklaan 14, the **Belasting Museum Prof. Dr van der Poel** (weekdays 09.00–17.00), a fascinating collection of materials, instruments and papers telling the history of taxation (and, concomitantly, smuggling)—this is one of the most unusual and interesting museums you are likely to find anywhere: birth, death and taxation are the lot of all humanity.

Heading S out of the West Plein takes you to the Willemskade and the **Museum voor Land en Volkenkunde** (Tuesday–Saturday 10.00–17.00; Sunday and holidays 11.00–17.00). This is a recently renovated Victorian building with up-to-date audio-visual presentations on a range of ethnographical themes.

A 10 minute walk up Willemskade to the NE, crossing to the Schiedamse Dijk and along the Leuvehaven docks, brings you to the new white building housing the **Maritime Museum Prins Hendrik** founded as long ago as 1863 though recently much revamped. Children will be delighted by the ships moored alongside in the docks which date back to the Middle Ages, and the interior is full of fascinating exhibits on the history of shipping, especially shipping in Dutch history; if you try to look at everything you will never get home.

Not far to the N in the Korte Hoogstraat is the **Schielandshuis** (Tuesday–Saturday 10.00–17.00; Sunday and holidays 11.00–17.00) a handsome building of 1665 which houses the city's historical museum. Of particular interest are the prints and drawings relating to Dutch history generally. There are two other branches of this museum (see below).

N of the Schielandshuis is the city's thriving business and shopping centre, walking through the Churchill Plein and up the Coolsingel to the Hof Plein brings you back to the Weena and the station once more.

A visit to **Delfshaven** is also a good day out; take the metro or tram directly there or follow the route to the Belasting Museum and follow Parklaan to Het Park. On the far side of the park is the **Euromast** (daily March to mid October 09.00–22.00; mid October to March 09.00–18.00; Space Tower 11.00–16.00 only). The Euromast (minus the Space Tower which was added later) was put up in 23 days in 1960. It is topped with restaurants at 100m, the Space Tower soars to a revolving cabin at 185m. Delfshaven lies beyond. Built originally as a port for the city of Delft, though now part of Rotterdam, from here the Pilgrim Fathers started their journey to New England in 1620 (transshipping to the *Mayflower* at Plymouth). On the far side of the docks' complex, at Voorhaven 12, is the **Dubbelde Palmboom** (Tuesday–Saturday 10.00–17.00; Sunday and holidays, 11.00–17.00), a warehouse of 1825 which has also served as a distillery, factory and coal store. It now serves as part of the Rotterdam Museum and contains a thematically organised history of the region (best followed by starting on the top floor, you might find the café inviting if you have walked here).

At Voorhaven 13 the **Zakkendragershuisje** (Tuesday–Saturday 10.00–17.00; Sunday and holidays, 11.00–17.00) is the third part of the Rotterdam Museum. Sited in the Guild House of the Grain Sack Carriers it is now a pewterer's workshop and museum of pewter, selling pewter goods.

The Oude Kerk nearby has a plaque commemorating the Pilgrim Fathers who held their last service here.

The Seaside

The sea is not far away, though it is a raw version of the sea which graces these shores, more like Northumberland than Brighton. Zandvoort is Amsterdam-on-Sea and the beach seems to be sorted into neat sections. Vulgarity and chips dominate around the town; to the N there are walks in the dunes above Bloemendal and nudist beaches (gay and straight ... keep walking N until you find what you want). If you visit The Hague you should not miss Scheveningen beach, a tram ride away.

Tulips

Tulip bulbs were introduced into the Netherlands around the end of the 16C. Johan van Hooghelande of Leiden discovered how to vary the shape and colour of the flowers and by 1630 there was a rapidly growing fashion among all sections of society for collecting and growing these exotic plants. The fashion became a mania and by the summer of 1636 bulbs were changing hands for ridiculous prices; more than f2000 was frequently demanded and paid—f2000 would buy a substantial family house; it was the annual income of a wealthy man and it would have bought numerous Rembrandt portraits. From the start of this mania, dealers traded in tulip bulb futures. When the market collapsed in early 1637 thousands were left with worthless bulbs on their hands. Tulips, along with crocus, daffodils, gladioli and hyacinths, are still big business in Holland and increasingly in North Holland, Zeeland and Friesland, too.

The main bulb fields are to be found between Haarlem and Leiden in the Bloemenbollenstreek (the flower bulb district). The **National Bulb Centre** is at Hillegom, which with Lisse is at the heart of the Bloemenbollenstreek; in Lisse at Heereweg 219 there is the Museum voor de Bloembollenstreek (April and May 10.00–17.00; June–March, Tuesday–Sunday 13.00–17.00). Obviously spring and early summer are the times to visit the bulb fields; you may wish to time your visit to see one of the great parades and the NBT publishes a guide to these events annually. When the season is on, tours are organised and the VVV is the best source of information on what is happening if you are in Amsterdam at the right time. If you want to do it yourself, take the train and bus (usually offered at a discount at Centraal Station) to Lisse and visit the **Keukenhof**, some 30ha. of flowers plus more under glass. The Keukenhof is open every day from late March–late May 08.00–18.30. If you go by car you can follow the signposted bulb routes but be prepared for huge traffic jams at the height of the season.

Bulb auctions (Bloemveiling) are held at Aalsmeer, just south of Schiphol, on weekdays from 07.30–11.00. Despite computerisation and automation (perhaps because of it, for the modern magic adds to the spectacle) this is a magnificent daily event which takes place in one of the largest buildings I have ever seen.

Utrecht

VVV: Vredenburg 90 (at the NE corner of the aggressively modern Hoog Catharijne/Station complex). Train from Amsterdam Centraal; 40km SE.

Utrecht is the capital of Utrecht province and the seat of what was throughout the Middle Ages the Netherlands' sole bishopric. The history of the city is bound up with the ambitions of the bishops. Utrecht is now a busy, modern city with about a quarter of a million inhabitants, and home to the Netherlands' largest university, founded in 1636. Adrian VI (Adriaen Florisz., 1459–1523), the only Dutch pope, was born here. Not surprisingly, the focus for tourists is upon the ecclesiastical. Running N–S through the centre of the city is the Oudegracht which is well below street level; unlike in Amsterdam, goods were not winched upstairs for storage but rolled across the quays to basements. Architecture in Utrecht is therefore distinct from that of Holland's water-towns. The quays are now crowded with cafés and shops.

Leave the Hooge Catharijne/Station from the Vredenburgkwartier and follow Lange Viestraat to the Viebrug which gives a splendidly characteristic view S of Utrecht. On the right-hand side at Oude Gracht 99 is the 14C Huis Oudean, at various times a French Embassy and a hospice, and opposite, at the corner of Drakenborchstraat, the Huis Drakenborgh. Boat trips start from this part of the canal. Follow the canal, at which ever level pleases you, as far as the Maartensbrug, to the E of which stands the Dom, or cathedral. On the W side of the Maartensbrug stands the **Buurkerk**, Utrecht's oldest parish church, founded in the 10C. The Buurkerk shows evidence of various building episodes from the 13–15C. The church presently houses the **Rijksmuseum van Speelklok tot Pierement** (Tuesday–Saturday 10.00–17.00; Sunday 13.00–17.00), mechanical musical instruments from the 18C to the present.

Utrecht has many fine churches: the Jacobikerk, to the N, which lost its tower during the French Empire so that the Paris–Amsterdam telegraph could function (the tower has since been replaced), the Janskerk, the Pieterskerk and many more, each of which has stories enough for a book. The **Domkerk** (daily May–September 10.00–17.00; October to April 11.00–16.00) is the episcopal seat (the interrupted history of Christianity dates back to c 500, St Willibrord was consecrated as the first Bishop in c 700). The present structure dates from between c 1254 to 1517; the nave was destroyed in a fire in 1674 leaving only the choir and transepts. There are tombs and monuments dating back to the 14C; two Emperors have their hearts buried here. The original lines of the nave are marked out on the pavement in front of the church.

The 112m tall **Domtoren** (weekends 12.00–17.00; April–mid October, weekdays 10.00–1700; holidays, 12.00–17.00) is the highest church tower in the country. It was built between 1321 and 1383 and has been separated from the church for all but 150 years of its existence; it contains two chapels. The ascent involves 465 steps taking you to 102m. Former church buildings off Achter het Dom behind the Dom are now part of Utrecht University.

Opposite the Dom, at Achter het Dom 14, is the **Museum voor Hedendaagse Kunst** (Tuesday–Saturday 10.00–17.00; Sunday, 13.00-17.00), the Museum of Contemporary Art which has a small collection and mounts exhibitions. At the S end of Achter het Dom is the Pausdam, the Pope's Dam, with the Paushuize (1517) built for Pope Adrian who never actually saw it himself. From here the Nieuwe Gracht runs S, lined by handsome houses. Take the right-hand side so as to pass the **Rijksmuseum het Catharijne Convent** (Tuesday–Friday 10.00–17.00; weekends and holidays 11.00–17.00) behind the St Catharijnekerk, the Dutch national Catholic Cathedral, at Nieuwe Gracht 63. As the name suggests, the museum (opened in 1979) is situated in a converted convent, a Carmelite foundation of 1468, finished by the Order of St John in 1550. The museum traces the history of religion in the Netherlands and gives a level-headed and fascinating account, using modern display techniques, of what has often been a depressing and violent story. Of special interest are the vestments, religious art (sculpture and paintings) and displays on disputes within the history of the church in the Netherlands.

Schalwijkstraat, opposite and to the right of the museum entrance, leads towards the Malibaan Station across the Malibrug where you will find the **Nederlands Spoorwegmuseum** (Tuesday–Saturday 10.00–17.00; Sunday 13.00–17.00). The station buildings, which date from 1874, have exhibitions covering the history of railways, and in the sheds and on the platforms there are trains and trams.

Follow the line of the Stadsbuitengracht S and W along the Malie and Tolsteeg Singel to cross the Abstederbrug and follow the Agnietenstraat to the **Centraalmuseum** (Tuesday–Saturday 10.00–17.00; Sunday and holidays 13.00–17.00) at Agnietenstraat 1. The museum is housed principally in the former convent of St Agnes (founded 1420). This is a local history museum and covers archaeology, social and ecclesiasticl history and art history in the town and province. One of the most extraordinary exhibits is the Utrecht Ship, a wooden boat from the 9C dug up in 1930 from the Vecht riverbed. The art collection focuses upon Utrecht painters and painters with a special relationship with the city, such as Jan van Scorel and the Utrecht Caravaggisti whose distinctive chiaroscuro and illusionism, often on Catholic themes, is very appealing to modern eyes.

Windmills

Windmills have served two basic purposes, powering heavy industrial tasks and removing water in drainage schemes. Industrial mills came first and may well have been in use by the 11C although the first record is one of the 13C; the first polder mill was recorded in 1414. Windmills powered many industries: seed grinding for oil or other products; grinding wheat; wood sawing; mulching rags for paper; grinding tobacco for snuff; fulling cloth, a whole range of activities which contributed to Dutch industrial and mercantile ascendancy during the early modern period. Drainage windmills at first operated under the disadvantage that a scoop-wheel could not raise water more than about two metres, but improvement came with the invention of the screw-pump carrying water some three times higher. But even with this the differences in level were too great and a system evolved by which mills were used in rows and in series, as many as 60 mills sometimes being required for a large reclamation.

Windmills are now used as private houses, museums, tourist attractions, and some even for industrial purposes. Windmills are be seen throughout the Netherlands, especially in the west and the north. Four places at which there are good groups are Kinderdijk near Ablasserdam between Rotterdam and Dordrecht, Zaanse Schans (see Industrial Nostalgia, above), Schermerhorn (near Alkmaar), and the town of Schiedam (near Rotterdam). There are also several mills in the Openlucht Museum at Arnhem (see Provinces, above), and there are windmill museums at Koog aan de Zaan (see Industrial Nostalgia, above), Leiden and Gouda (see above).

INDEX

The following index lists Amsterdam streets, rivers, etc, under TOPOGRAPHICAL; museums, art galleries and other places of interest under MUSEUMS and monuments and buildings under MONUMENTS.

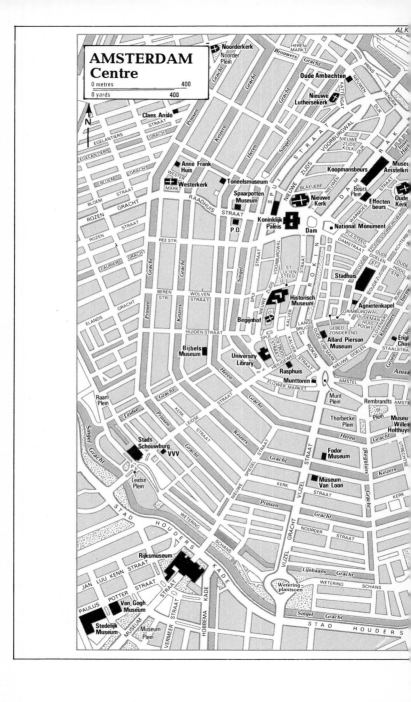

AMSTERDAM
Centre

| 0 metres | 400 |
| 0 yards | 400 |

N

Noorderkerk
Noorder
Plein

HEREN
MARKT

Brouwers Gracht

Oude Ambachten

Nieuwe
Luthersekerk

KATENGAT

Claes Anslo

PRINS

NIEUWE

HENDRIK

STRAAT

Prinsen

EGELANTIERS
STRAAT

Keizers

Heren

Singel

STRAAT

VOORBURGWAL

NIEUWE
ZIJDS
KOLK

R A K

DIJK

Inner
Hart

EGELANTIERS

EGELANTIERS
GRACHT

Anne Frank
Huis

WESTER
MARKT

Westerkerk

Toneelsmuseum

Spaarpotten
Museum

NIEUWE
ZIJDS

BLAEUERE

NIEUWE

Nieuwe
Kerk

Koopmansbeurs

Muse
Amstelkri

BLOEM
EGRACHT

BLOEM
STRAAT

RAADHUIS

STRAAT

SPUI

Beurs
Plein

Effecten
beurs

D A M

Oude
Kerk

WARMOES

ROZEN
GRACHT

Koninklijk
Paleis

P.O.

VOORBURGWAL

Dam

National Monument

ROZEN
STRAAT

REE STR.

SPUI

PIJLSTEEG

DAMSTRAAT

OUDE

ACHTERBI

LAURIER
GRACHT

Prinsen

Keizers

Singel

BEREN
STR

WOLVEN
STRAAT

NIEUWE
ZIJDS

VOORBURGWAL

ST
LUCIEN
STEEG

Stadhuis

OUDE
DOELEN
ST

HOOG
STR.

BURG

ELANDS
GRACHT

Historisch
Museum

Agnietenkapel

GRIMBURGWAL

OUDEMANES
HUIS
POORT

LOVENIERS

KLOVENIERS

HUIDEN STRAAT

Begijnhof

KALVER

LANGE
BRUG
ST.

OUDE

GEBED
ZONDER END

Engl
Chu

STAALSTRA

Bijbels
Museum

University
Library

SPUI

Heren

HEILIGEWEG

KALVER
STRAAT

OUDE
TURF MARK

Allard Pierson
Museum

NIEUWE DOELEN

ROKIN

Ams

Rasphuis

Munttoren

FLOWER MARKET

Munt
Plein

AMSTEL

Raam
Plein

Leidse

Prinsen

KERK

Singel
Gracht

Gracht

STRAAT

Gracht

Rembrandts
Plein

AMSTE

Thorbecke
Plein

Museu
Willel
Holthuys

Stads
Schouwburg

VVV

LEIDSE

STRAAT

SPIEGEL

NIEUWE

Keizers

Heren

VIJZEL

Gracht

REgulie

Keizers

Leidse
Plein

Fodor
Museum

STRAAT

KERK

STAD

HOUDERS

WETERING

Prinsen

Gracht

Museum
Van Loon

STRAAT

NOORDER

STRAAT

VIJZEL

KERK

Gracht

SCHANS
KADE

Lijnbaans Gracht

WETERING

SCHANS

Rijksmuseum

STRAAT

Wetering
plantsoen

JAN
LUU KENN STRAAT

POTTER STRAAT

Singel

Gracht

STAD

HOUDERS

PAULUS

Van Gogh
Museum

MUSEUM

HOBBEMA

VERMEER

Stedelijk
Museum

Museum
Plein

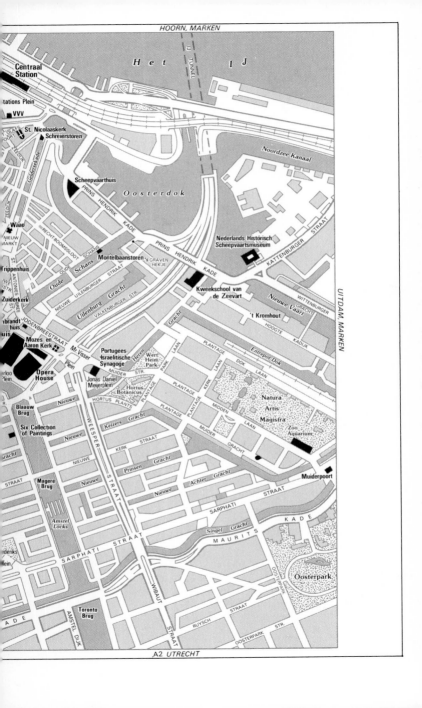

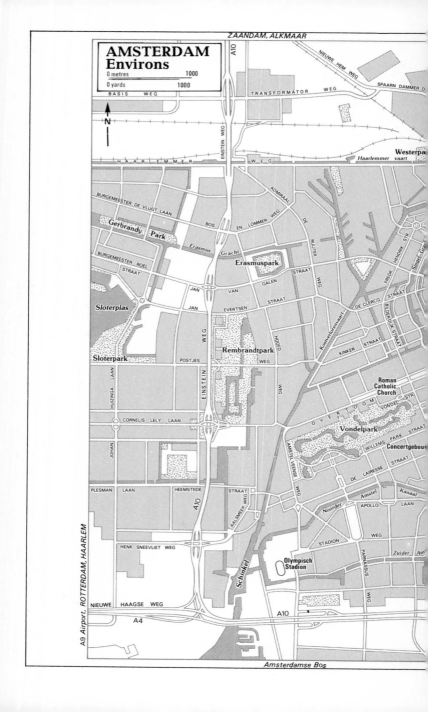

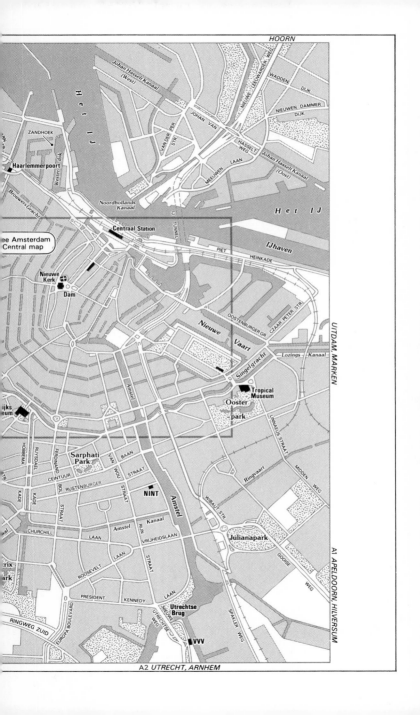

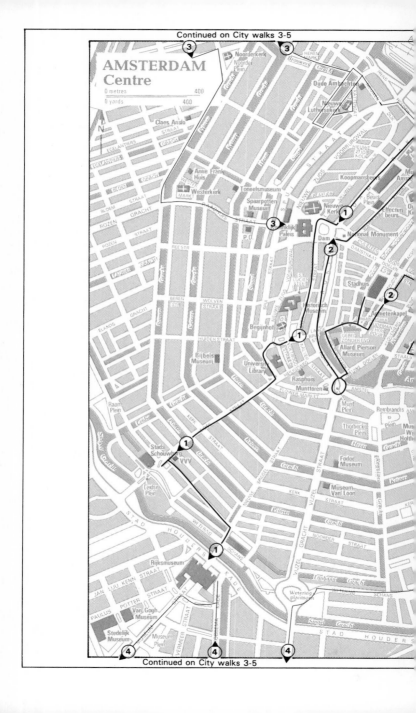

AMSTERDAM
Centre

0 metres   400
0 yards   400

Noorderkerk
Noorder
Plein
HEREN
Brouwers Gracht

Oude Ambachten

Nieuwe
Lutherse kerk

Claes Anslo

EGLANTIERS STRAAT

EGLANTIERS GRACHT

Koopmansbeurs

Anne Frank
Huis

Westerkerk

Toneelmuseum

Spaarpotten
Museum

Nieuwe
Kerk

Effecten
beurs

Beurs
Plein

Koninklijk
Paleis

National Monument

Dam

Stadhuis

ROZEN GRACHT

ROZEN STRAAT

BLOEM GRACHT

ST LUCIEN STEEG

BEREN STR

WOLVEN STRAAT

Historisch
Museum

Agnietenkapel

LAURIER GRACHT

ELANDS GRACHT

Begijnhof

Allard Pierson
Museum

HUIDEN STRAAT

Bijbels
Museum

Rasphuis

University
Library

Munttoren

AMSTEL

Raam
Plein

Munt
Plein

Rembrandts
Plein

Stads
Schouwburg

VVV

Thorbecke
Plein

Fodor
Museum

Leidse
Plein

Museum
Van Loon

Rijksmuseum

Van Gogh
Museum

Wetering
plantsoen

Stedelijk
Museum

Museum
Plein

STAD HOUDER

Centraal
Station

ations Plein

VVV

St. Nicolaaskerk
Schreierstoren

②

Noordzee Kanaal

Scheepvaarthuis

Oosterdok

PRINS HENDRIK KADE

②

Schaus   Montelbaanstoren

penhuis

Oude   Graci

NIEUWE UILENBURGER STR.

iderk

Uilenburg   Gracht

apdt
huis

Nederlands Historisch
Scheepvaartsmuseum

KATTENBURGER STRAAT

④

Kweekschool van
de Zeevart

Nieuwe   Vaart   WITTENBURGER

't Kromhout

HOOGTE   KADIJK

Mozes en
Aaron Kerk

Portugees
Israelitische
Synagoge

②

Opera
House

Jonas Daniel
Meijenplein

Werf
Heini
Padt

Hortus
Botanicus

PLANTAGE

MIDDEN   LAAN

Entrepot Dok

Blaauw
Brug

Nieuwe

Keizers   Gracht

HORTUS PLTSN.

PLANTAGE

Natura

Artis

Magistra

Zoo
Aquarium

Six Collection
of Paintings

Nieuwe

Prinsen   Gracht

KERK   STRAAT

MUIDER   GRACHT

④

ch

RAAT

Mager
Brug

Nieuwe

Nieuwe   STRAAT

Achter   Gracht

Muiderpoort

Amstel
Locks

④

SARPHATI   STRAAT

Singel   Gracht

KADE

MAURITS

rks

Oosterpark

DE

Toronto
Brug

WIBAUT   STRAAT

AMSTEL   DIJK

KAST.   STR.

WINTERPARK   CYP.

City Walks 1 to 4

0 metres   500

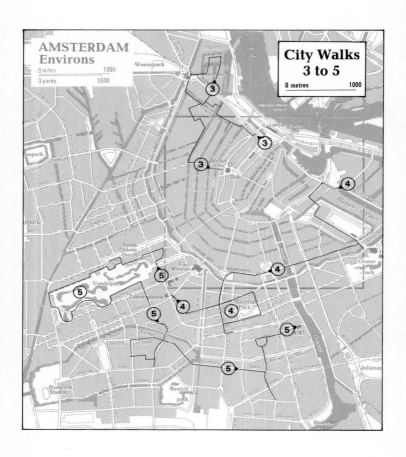

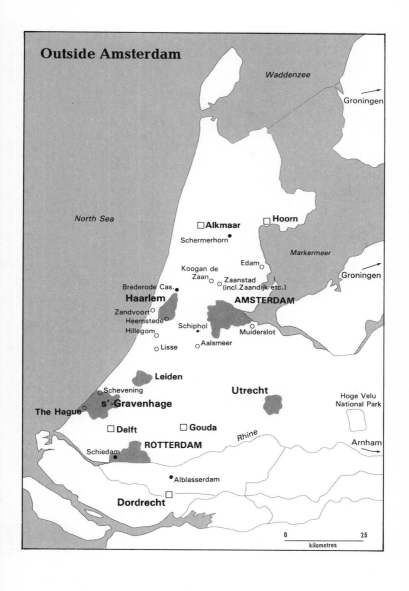

Outside Amsterdam

Waddenzee

Groningen

North Sea

☐ Alkmaar   ☐ Hoorn

Schermerhorn

Markermeer

Edam

Koogan de
Zaan   Zaanstad
            (incl. Zaandijk etc.)   Groningen

Brederode Cas.   AMSTERDAM
Haarlem

Zandvoort
Heemstede
            Schiphol   Muiderslot
Hillegom
        Aalsmeer
    Lisse

    Leiden

Scheveningen
s'-Gravenhage   Utrecht
The Hague   Hoge Velu
                                     National Park
☐ Delft   ☐ Gouda
                    Rhine
    ROTTERDAM   Arnham

Schiedam

    •Alblasserdam

Dordrecht ☐

0   25

kilometres

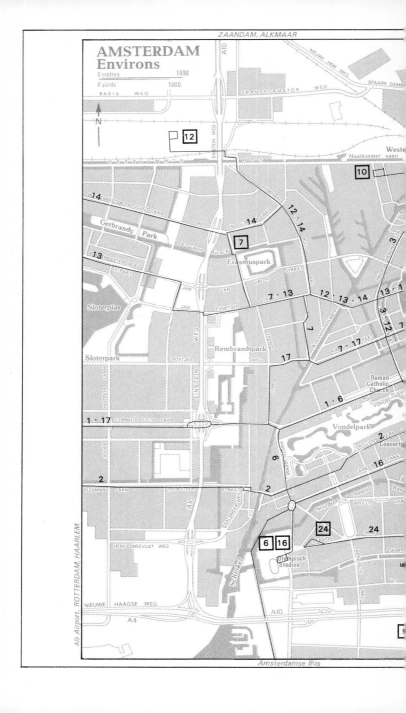

AMSTERDAM
Environs

0 metres   1000
0 yards   1000

BASIS   WEG

N

A10

NIEUWE HEM WEG

SPAARN DAMM

TRANSFORMATOR   WEG

EINSTEIN WEG

12

West
Haarlemmer vaart

10

BG MEESTER DE VLUGT LAAN

14

Gerbrandy Park

Erasmus Grac

BOS   EN   LOMM

WEG

KIMPRA W

SPUISTR

12 · 14

14

7

BURGEMEESTER ROEL
STRAAT

13

Erasmuspark

GALEN

STRAAT

12 · 14

13 · 14

13 · 1

Sloterplas

JAN

VAN

JAN

EVERTSEN

7 · 13

STR

12 · 13

KOSTVERLOREN

3 · 12

Sloterpark

WEG

Rembrandtpark

EINSTEIN

POSTJES

WEG

17

7

7 · 17

KIN STRAAT

7 · 17

Roman
Catholic
Church

VONDEL

ST

1 · 17 CORNELIS LELY LAAN

1 · 6

OV

Vondelpark

2

Concert

HUIZINGA LAAN

JOHAN

WILLEMS PARK

STRAAT

PLESMAN LAAN

HEEMSTEDE

STRAAT

6

AMSTELVEENSE

DE LAIRESSE

16

2

WEG

2

Nieuw

Amstel

APOLLO

LAA

Rai

A10

HENK SNEEVLIET WEG

KAREMKE WEG

Schinkel

24

24

PARNASSUS

Zuider

6

16

Olympisch
Stadion

STADION

NIEUWE HAAGSE WEG

A10

A4

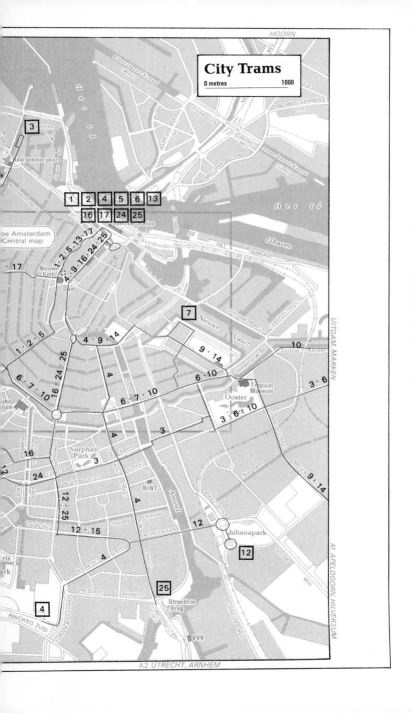